Workers' Co-operatives
Jobs and Dreams

Workers' Co-operatives

Jobs and Dreams

Jenny Thornley

 HEINEMANN EDUCATIONAL BOOKS

Heinemann Educational Books Ltd
22 Bedford Square, London WC1B 3HH

LONDON   EDINBURGH   MELBOURNE   AUCKLAND
HONG KONG   SINGAPORE   KUALA LUMPUR   NEW DELHI
IBADAN   NAIROBI   JOHANNESBURG
EXETER (NH)   KINGSTON   PORT OF SPAIN

First published 1981

British Library Cataloguing in Publication Data

Thornley, Jenny
  Workers' co-operatives.
  1. Employee ownership – Great Britain
  2. Employees' representation in management
  – Great Britain
  I. Title
  334'.6'0941   HD5660.G7

  ISBN 0–435–83890–3

Printed in Great Britain by
Biddles Ltd, Guildford, Surrey

Contents

Foreword

Workers' co-operatives are suddenly being hailed as panaceas for unemployment, alienation, inner city decay and industrial strife. After years of neglect or contempt the long-established co-operative movement is bemused to find that its old ideals have become politically fashionable. But while the ideals have flowered in various rhetorical hot-houses, they have had very mixed success in the stony ground of economic reality. Small co-operatives have sprung up but many have withered and died. Two of the big co-operative ventures funded by the last Labour Government – the *Scottish Daily News* and KME – have failed. Elsewhere in Western Europe, however, workers' co-operatives have flourished almost unnoticed. This book explains this paradox.

As well as giving a detailed account of the success of workers' co-operatives in France and Italy Jenny Thornley examines the history of the co-operative movement in Britain, which began with the producer co-operatives even though it has been dominated for a century by consumer retail co-operatives. She also looks critically at the wide range of organisations, ideologies and attitudes that cluster now under the umbrella of the new workers' co-operative movement.

The co-operative principles have always received lip-service from the labour movement even though they conflict with the objective of centralising economic power in a strong state machine. This second paradox has to be resolved if Labour ministers and local councillors are to give more than ineffective gestures of solidarity to those struggling to make their co-operatives succeed. They have to be clear about whether they regard co-operatives as islands of socialism, or just inconsequential flotsam in the capitalist ocean.

By sorting the reality from the rhetoric, without in any way dismissing the idealism, the author provides guidelines for a consolidation of the workers' co-operative movement which will ensure that, when political fashion changes, the jobs – and dreams – will live on.

John Tilley
MP for Lambeth Central

Acknowledgements

I would like to thank those inside and outside the co-operatives who have helped in my research. Some I have already mentioned. I cannot list all those who helped me but those to whom I must give special thanks are Pauline Benington who typed my manuscript, Dilys Matthias who also helped with the typing, Gray Standen who translated into English a large number of documents published by the Italian federations, Richard Anderson who was employed at the Centre for Environmental Studies (CES) for a temporary period in 1979 to extract and make sense of statistical material on co-operatives from Companies House and the Registrar of Friendly Societies, and Jane Hustwit who supplied me with many newspaper and journal cuttings throughout the research period.

I am also very grateful to Tom Cunliffe of the Co-operative Development Agency, John Tilley MP, John Morley (CCAHC), Peter Willmott of CES and Antoine Antoni of the Confédération Générale des Sociétés Co-opératives Ouvrières de Production, who all commented extensively on my manuscript, and to Tom Black of the Manpower Services Commission, Ian Brierley of the Co-operative Bank, David Ralley of Scott Bader, and Michael Angerson of Trylon, who all corrected sections of the work. Thanks also to Dave Smith of the South Wales Anti-Poverty Action Centre, Simon Watt, Cairns Campbell of the Scottish Co-operatives Development Committee, Anna Whyatt and Geoff Hill of the Leeds Council for Voluntary Service, Monsieur J. Fleury of SCOP, and Franco degli Esposti and Cesaro Bassoli of the LEGA in Bologna who helped arrange interviews with co-operatives. Finally, thanks to Richard Minns, Richard Meegan and Bert Nicholson of CES, Oonagh MacDonald MP and Jack Winkler of the Cranfield Institute of Technology, who advised me in the early stages of the research.

Introduction

This book is the result of two and a half years' research, from September 1977 to April 1980. The research was funded by the Joseph Rowntree Memorial Trust, and was carried out at the Centre for Environmental Studies. Towards the end of the project CES was the victim of the Thatcher Government's 'quango-axing' campaign and all its government funds were withdrawn. The Rowntree funds enabled me to finish the work in an orderly way, for which I am grateful. Even more important, this funding body encouraged me to explore the subject of workers' co-operatives in an independent way, and set up an advisory committee to which I turned regularly for advice. The committee was composed of the following: Larry Tindale, chairperson – Industrial and Commercial Finance Corporation, John Morley – Central Council for Agricultural and Horticultural Co-operation (CCAHC), John Tilley – Labour and Co-operative MP, Reg Poole and Robin Guthrie – Rowntree. Peter Willmott, Director of CES, also attended. I am grateful to all these people for their help.

A co-operative is a particular kind of firm which has grown up around a set of ideological beliefs in response to external economic and social circumstances. There are a number of different types of co-operative, such as consumers', housing, fishing and workers' co-operatives. This book is about workers' co-operatives. The basic features of a workers' co-operative are that it manufactures goods or provides services, and that it is owned and controlled by those working in it. Workers' co-operatives (called co-operatives in most of the book) have to compete alongside other firms in the capitalist market and at a superficial glance appear to suffer many of the same problems that face most small firms. However, no direct comparison can easily be made between co-operatives and other firms. Any analysis of how co-operatives function in the market must contain an examination of the ideology of their supporters, and the political and economic background to their formation.

The starting point of this research – which made it appropriate for CES – was the growing interest of the state in workers' co-operatives by central and local government. I wanted to explore the reasons why the state, for the first time, was involved in setting up and assisting co-operatives. I was particularly keen to discover how far the current economic crisis had provoked this interest and whether, by 1980, the strength of the movement could be attributed mainly to the actions of the state or to other factors.

The research has shown that British co-operatives had always arisen out of conditions of hardship or disillusion caused by capitalist development. They have a fundamentally weak capital structure since only the workers (and in some cases a few sympathetic outsiders) can contribute to the share capital, and the number of shares each co-operative member can hold is limited. This may be compensated for by the high level of commitment among the work-force. The workers are often as determined to practise co-operative principles as to make profits. Much confusion has surrounded these ventures, which have so many apparently contradictory objectives. They have attracted supporters from all the main political parties, whether as experiments in industrial democracy, as firms which can reduce industrial conflict, as a way of creating jobs, or simply as small firms. Their promoters have frequently distorted the evidence about co-operatives, and made exaggerated claims about the number existing and their speed of growth, and have made wild suggestions about their potential in the economy.

I set out to study this complicated field, examining the motives of the people and organisations supporting co-operatives, the practical difficulties co-operatives face in the market, and their place in the economy. They have developed within a capitalist mode of production, receiving state assistance mainly because of the contribution they make to the economy, while at the same time attempting to develop a radical alternative to the way production is organised. The research concludes that co-operatives can develop into a significant movement only if their promoters follow a common strategy along with other sectors of co-operation. It is also essential that co-operatives appeal to the broad mass of the working class. And it is crucial that the promoters of co-operation recognise that these enterprises are dependent on a close relationship with the market. By isolating themselves from the world around them, co-operatives can only turn inwards on their utopian dreams and fail, as history has demonstrated.

A comparison with co-operatives in France and Italy was made to bring out this conclusion more clearly. Workers' co-operatives are more numerous in these countries and have a history of close association with the state. For many years the state has provided contracts and other help to co-operatives because of their efficiency and value to economic development. In all three countries co-operatives have offered the labour movement experiences in industrial democracy and the production of socially useful goods and services. This book never loses sight of these important aspects, but they were not central subjects and therefore they have been mentioned only where they affect the ability of co-operatives to compete in the market. The well-known co-operatives of Mondragon in Spain have been excluded deliberately from the analysis because they developed independently of the state as a voluntary movement under the repressive Franco regime. There is, of course, much that the British movement can learn from the Mondragon co-operatives. Several studies have already been made of them which will be referred to later. But I selected for comparison only those countries where co-operatives have been recognised at a political level to benefit national economic development and have been affected by state interventionist policies.

The research was conducted through case studies of co-operatives in Britain, France and Italy (see Appendix I). The Confédération Générale des Sociétés Co-opératives Ouvrières de Production introduced me to seven co-operatives in different parts of France. In Italy, the Lega in Bologna assisted me with interviews in six co-operatives. In Britain, I visited, or spoke to members of, some 40 co-operatives. Five were in Scotland, four in Wales, and the rest in England – six in London, four on Tyneside, three in Leeds and the others in small to medium sized towns and rural areas.

For the purpose of this study I accepted a loose definition of workers' co-operatives. Any venture which seriously tried to practise co-operative principles was included – irrespective of how or whether it was registered. In fact, most were registered under the Industrial and Provident Societies Acts (I & PS Acts). It is widely accepted that workers' co-operatives follow six broad principles:

(1) the establishment is autonomous;
(2) employees are able to become members of the enterprise by nominal holdings of share capital, usually £5 or less;

(3) the principle of 'one person one vote' prevails;
(4) formal provision exists for direct employee participation in decision-making at all levels within the enterprise;
(5) employees share in profits;
(6) return on capital is limited.[1]

Within these principles workers' co-operatives can vary widely in form because they were set up for a variety of purposes and at different periods. However, most fall into two categories defined in the Industrial Common Ownership Act, 1976 as common owner-ship and co-operative enterprises. (For the exact definitions of these types and interpretations of their meaning see Appendix II.) Under the 1976 Act a common ownership enterprise is defined precisely, whereas the definition of a co-operative has been left vague. Never-theless, for both types of enterprise, to be accepted by the Registrar and Secretary of State respectively as eligible for government assistance under the Act, they would have to adopt the six principles outlined as a minimum requirement. Co-operatives cover a broad range of forms, including companies registered under the I & PS Acts and firms registered under the Companies Act as companies limited by guarantee with no share capital. Also included are co-operatives with a two-tier structure, such as Scott Bader. This is a company limited by guarantee without share capital where all shares are held by a holding company and where membership is limited to the employees of the trading company. This structure was developed to overcome difficulties connected with changing a private company to a co-operative enterprise.[2]

The British co-operatives studied were chosen to exhibit a wide range of features, and to demonstrate the different ways they can survive in a capitalist economy. They include one which was formed after an occupation – the famous Meriden Motorcycles. However, less attention was paid to this co-operative as it had already been researched extensively by others. Five were created out of the ruins of collapsed firms like Courtaulds in Skelmersdale and Philips Medical in Balham; three were set up after a dispute in the work-place of private firms; 14 were funded by the Manpower Services Commission; three were formed by skilled workers who saw the prospect of better wages and conditions from forming a co-operative; at least three were converted from private firms by their owners, such as Scott Bader, the chemicals company; and 13 were founded by workers or promotional bodies for other reasons.

Most were formed after 1970, with over half appearing after 1975.

Six have been included which were set up between 1873 and 1900. These are referred to as Co-operative Productive Federation (CPF) co-operatives, though not all of them are now affiliated to this promotional body. Of all the co-operatives studied, only four employed over 200 workers; 23 employed less than 30, and 15 less than 20. Turnover was low in most of the examples, as is typical of co-operatives in general. There are, of course, exceptions, such as Scott Bader whose turnover in 1977 was over £3 million, or Equity Shoes with a turnover of nearly £2 million in the same year, or Walsall Locks at around £800,000. Compared with private firms, the co-operatives in the sample employ a high proportion of female labour, sometimes on jobs like building, woodwork and printing which have been considered as men's work, and at other times employed in work traditionally dominated by women because of its low pay, like cleaning and machining.

Many co-operatives are labour intensive and make small profits. 21 in the sample were engaged in some kind of manufacturing work, while 16 were providing services of different kinds and three were in the building industry. This does not accurately reflect the split between manufacturing and service co-operatives. No precise record exists yet of the different types of co-operative. While compiling an index, the Co-operative Development Agency reported in March 1980 that, out of a total of 365 co-operatives, 175 were 'industrial' and 151 were in 'services'. 85 of the service co-operatives were shops or distributors – mostly wholefoods. It is thought that the index under-represents the service co-operatives. According to the Industrial Common Ownership Movement, the growth rate among these is higher than among industrial co-operatives.

Chapter 1 traces the growth of workers' co-operatives within the labour movement struggles for better wages and working conditions. It shows how the impetus for co-operative experiments came both from the working class and from liberal-minded members of the bourgeoisie. The latter group of pioneers was aware that life for the majority of working class people was degrading and demoralising, and saw the chance of a more humane and democratic society through the development of co-operatives. Alliances were, at times, forged between radical middle-class philanthropists and working class leaders and organisations. But a strong co-operatives sector failed to develop.

This raises a number of questions. Was the failure caused by the difficulties co-operatives faced in the market? Were the co-operators themselves – mostly skilled workers – unable or unwilling to gather political support for their movement? Did the promoters – with their dreams and impractical ideas – alienate the trade unions by causing dramatic collapses among the co-operatives? And did the religious fervour which permeated the movement make it difficult for co-operatives to form political alliances with working class organisations?

The historical analysis of Chapter 1 provides a background for examining the recent growth of interest in co-operatives. Chapter 2 looks at the numerous agencies which are now promoting co-operatives and the people joining these enterprises. It points out that, as in the 19th century, many of the new promoters of the co-operative philosophy are middle class philanthropists whose beliefs arise more from religion than from socialist vision. Many of the co-operators too are middle class and young. Few have close links with organised party politics or trade unions. More often their allegiances are with the ecology movement, the peace movement, the women's move-ment and the 'alternative life-style'. Alongside this strand of co-operation are groups closely aligned to the Liberal Party who see more limited benefits in co-operation. The professed political neutrality of all agencies (apart from the local authorities and the Co-operative Union) has enabled them to work together to some extent. But at the same time it has prevented any common strategy from emerging and contributed to the failure to gain acceptance among wide sections of the labour movement.

Chapter 3 attempts to show how the structure and practices of co-operatives make them less able than other firms to raise finance both internally and from outside. This is because they have an entirely different relation to capital. Making matters worse, the ideology of co-operation tends to make co-operatives hostile to the market in which they must survive. Often they have uncompromis-ingly shunned opportunities available for raising funds. All sorts of devices are practised to overcome financial difficulties. Some co-operatives encourage loans and shares from their own members; some buy second-hand machinery; some pay very low wages. An important factor in their survival has been the finance made available by the state. Since the mid-1970s the state has recognised the benefits of co-operatives, particularly in creating jobs. Since they have also proved attractive to all the main political parties, limited finance on favourable terms has been made available at local, regional and national levels and has considerably strengthened the sector.

In Chapter 4 factors other than finance are examined which also contribute to co-operatives' vulnerability in the market. The question of who manages a co-operative is explored. It is emphasised that the workers collectively decide how their firms are managed. But co-operatives have regarded management, like finance, as being tinged with 'capitalist' qualities. Some of the smallest co-operatives have been able to side-step the issue by sharing management tasks between them, preferring to build up their efficiency slowly rather than appoint managers. In other co-operatives, where the workforce has been less capable of taking up this challenge or where the size of the enterprise demanded a high level of leadership, the right management skills have often been absent for long periods.

Commitment to the co-operative ideal has in many cases offset the problem of skill shortages. But when workers only want jobs from a co-operative the survival of the venture can be put in jeopardy. With some important exceptions (as at Meriden Motorcycles), middle class workers have shown the strongest commitment to co-operative principles. But these people have not always had a commercial outlook. Working class co-operators have been more likely to compromise their principles in the face of market pressures. Others have barely understood the co-operative philosophy and have behaved in conventional, defensive ways towards those in management positions. This has deprived these co-operatives of the creative and flexible attitudes necessary for their survival. The chapter finishes by describing several ways in which organisation structures have protected co-operatives from the full rigours of the market and suggests that the labour and co-operative movement could do more to strengthen the co-operative sector in these ways.

Limitations on the goods and services co-operatives can produce are explained in Chapter 5. As in the last century, co-operatives tend to be in areas of industry where technological change is slow and which rely heavily on hand skills. Often these are the low wage industries, with high female employment. Sometimes co-operatives have been prey to large firms which have grasped the opportunity to hive off their least profitable parts. Fear of over-dependence on 'capitalist' customers has led many co-operatives to shun the open market altogether and to seek out buyers from among organisations sympathetic to their aims. It is argued that the use of the labour and co-operative movement for this purpose is vital but should not form the exclusive outlet for co-operatives.

An examination of the growing role of the state in assisting co-operatives is the subject of Chapter 6. Although the scale of this

help is still small, local authorities are increasingly seeing benefits to
the local economy in these ventures. However, their main attraction
has been for job creation. It is reasonable to suggest that Meriden is
the sole survivor of the Benn co-operatives partly because of its value
in retaining motorcycle manufacture in Britain. But few other co-
operatives could claim to be assisted for their specific importance to
the national or local economy.

Assistance is coming more from local councils than from other
levels of the state. It has been given in a variety of forms, from direct
loans to co-operatives to grants for promotional work by voluntary
organisations. While the value of all this to a new and struggling
sector should not be underestimated, there is a danger that the
resources made available may be wasted. Too often co-operatives
are regarded as just another type of firm and an answer to unemployment. Experience is showing that co-operatives cannot be handed to
workers who have no enthusiasm for the principles of co-operation.

Chapters 7 and 8 deal with the co-operative movements in France
and Italy. As already explained, these countries demonstrate how
strong co-operative sectors can be developed when the state gives
them support primarily for the value co-operatives have to economic
development. They have rarely been assisted in mainline manufacturing industry, but state contracts have often been given to
co-operatives to provide essential services to industry and for infrastructure.

Chapter 9 looks critically at the trends in Britain against the
experiences in France and Italy. It suggests that co-operative growth
in Britain will depend on continued state support. But if the sector is
to contribute substantially to the labour movement's struggles for
radical changes which go beyond campaigns for industrial democracy,
it will need to gain greater acceptance by government, the Labour
Party and trade unions. Co-operation as a concept can be used for
many purposes. Its supporters in Britain have often been radical
liberals. The new movement, however, has also attracted a section of
young middle class enthusiasts who are more fundamentally critical
of capitalism. This book argues that, if these people are to contribute
towards achieving a socialist society, they will need a platform in the
labour movement to voice their beliefs and to describe their
experiences. The Labour Party and trade unions will have to make
room for the energy of these co-operators in their own organisations.
Equally, the co-operative promotional bodies will have to discard
their political neutrality and draw up common policies to win

support from government, local councils, regional authorities and trade unions.

However, there is evidence to indicate that it is not enough for the co-operative promoters to recognise that commitment arises from a positive action of protest against unemployment and the dehumanising effects of capitalist production. They must accept and alleviate the capital weakness and skill shortages that often characterise these enterprises. Also, they can expect substantial assistance from the state only if co-operatives are capable of creating jobs *and* assisting capital accumulation. Experience in France and Italy shows that co-operatives are tolerated by the private sector and supported by the state in industries and services usually associated with public enterprise. To get the help they need – especially in the early stages of the movement's development – it appears that co-operatives must provide some of the basic infrastructure needed to support both the manufacturing process and the labour force itself.

1 Right Turn at Toad Lane

Co-operatives and the Labour Movement

Workers' co-operatives are rooted in the struggles of working people to emancipate themselves from wretched conditions. Widespread suffering among the poor – powerless, and barely conscious of their oppression as a class – led them to form numerous associations to help one another. Workers' co-operatives are a sophisticated type of association which developed around particular conditions and beliefs. They re-emerged again and again throughout the 19th century, a protest against hardship, a practical solution and a vision of a new social order.

At times workers' co-operatives sprang up spontaneously, in isolation from any other labour struggles. At other times they were promoted by leaders and developed into a movement with similar objectives but also conflicts of principle. By downgrading the relentless push for profits they were a challenge to capitalist methods of production. Co-operators had social objectives. They wanted to make decisions democratically and to have job security, a decent wage, welfare benefits and a humanitarian respect for the potential capabilities of all working people.

However, co-operatives in Britain have never existed in large numbers. They have rarely exceeded 200 at any one time. There are several reasons for this. To begin with, their socialist aims make it very hard for them to survive in the market. In the 19th century money was raised from people and organisations ideologically committed to the co-operative but the funds were inadequate. Without major shareholders who were risking their capital for profit it was difficult to convince banks of a co-operative's creditworthiness. Co-operatives were generally undercapitalised and highly vulnerable to fluctuations in market conditions. Also, they usually comprised groups of skilled workers without any management skills between them. Attempts to develop democratic practices within a hostile economic environment, and with a largely undisciplined labour force, frequently led to quarrels, inefficient methods and failures. Invariably, the energy needed to run a co-operative turned workers' minds inwards to their experiment, their personalities and their dreams.

Organised labour has rarely found co-operatives appealing as a means of achieving a more socialist society, and has maintained a sympathetic but broadly sceptical attitude towards them. This seems inevitable because of the practical difficulties of raising enough capital to start co-operatives in anything other than craft-based industries. Dominated by skilled workers, the early co-operatives failed to attract the working class in general. Their cause was not helped in this respect by the people who emerged as their leaders. These were largely philanthropic members of the bourgeoisie who were anxious to alleviate the extreme poverty created by the industrial revolution. Usually they were non-radical and religious, preferring practical solutions to political agitation. Fired by utopian visions of a new moral world, they believed governments and industrialists would eventually be convinced by their propaganda and gradually a commonwealth of co-operatives would be achieved.

Attempts to impose co-operative ideals on working people were a recurring feature of the 19th century and were responsible for many dramatic failures. Co-operatives were developed outside the political arena. Politics were thought to be irrelevant unless there was a practical reason (like the need for limited liability status), to win political support for them. The trade union movement was treated with the same detached opportunism. While criticising trade union practices, co-operators always saw potential in trade unions as a means of furthering co-operative aims. The unions were cajoled and persuaded to donate funds, undertake co-operative production themselves and supply co-operators.

Without a radical theory of social change, workers' co-operatives were easy targets for criticism. Some social reformers saw them as impractical and idealistic. Others denounced their individualism and said they were divisive of the working class. However, their persistence in their own right and alongside the retail co-operatives helped to give working class people confidence that they could run businesses, and generated a widespread belief in the value of social ownership of the means of production. Ultimately, co-operatives played an important part in paving the way for the welfare state.

The socialist aims of co-operatives rarely led to any intense hostility from those ideologically opposed to them in government or industry. In fact, they were ignored for the most part by governments and tolerated in the market place. This was despite the persistent articulations by the leaders of the co-operative movement of the virtues of co-operation and of its salvation in state support. But as demonstrations of political protest, co-operatives were regarded as trivial and irrelevant. Far from being seen as a threat to the established capitalist system, co-operatives became acknowledged as a way of encouraging working class thrift and protecting workers' savings. They had the additional attraction of generating worker commitment and increased productivity. For many people they were hardly distinguishable from capitalist experiments in profit-sharing and worker participation.

Early Co-operatives and Industry
In 1760 cornmills were built and run co-operatively in Woolwich by the dockyard workers. At the same time, mills and a bakery were built in Chatham. The private mill owners had a monopoly and charged high prices, often adulterating the flour with chalk. Worsening economic conditions stimulated workers elsewhere to embark on similar ventures. A flour mill was built in Hull in 1795, and a number of others appeared in the same area. It seems there was, for a time, a rudimentary movement developing there among working people. Co-operative store-keeping emerged at about the same time, the first recorded store being that of the Weavers' Society at Fenwick, in Ayrshire, in 1769. These were largely isolated experiments.

By the early 1900s industry had become vastly more productive through new mechanical inventions, steam power and improved care of machinery. But the degree of mechanisation varied between industries, and by no means covered all the processes of production in one industry. Sometimes machinery was only used in the preparatory or finishing stages, with the main body of the production process left unaffected. A very large proportion of the British workforce earned a living by their hand skills until the end of the 19th century.[1]

Mechanisation in industry was a slow, discontinuous process involving many failures.[2] Its introduction was retarded because of the plentiful supply of skilled as well as unskilled labour, and often profits were increased by cutting capital costs. For instance, child and female labour was used widely. Women and children's pay was so low that it was hardly worth introducing machines to replace them.[3] Also, the irregular nature of demand in a volatile, *laissez-faire* economy until the mid-19th century meant product runs were often limited and better suited to workshop conditions. Industrialisation created a proliferation of small firms as well as large factories. In metal and engineering most production was carried out in workshops until the 1880s. Similarly, boot and shoe manufacture and building were small workshop operations.[4]

Throughout the 19th century many people worked for low wages in cramped conditions at home. The factory workers were hardly better off. Factory buildings were often unhealthy places where little attention was paid to workers' safety and where hard, repetitive jobs were done for long hours for subsistence pay. The labour process was more dependent on the strength, skill, speed, and sureness of touch of the individual worker than on the machinery introduced. The conditions of the working class were deteriorating, not improving, with industrialisation.

The workforce became more and more unruly and difficult to control. Absenteeism in factories was high and ill-health meant a continual turnover of labour. 'The poor were unsightly, a source of guilt, a heavy charge on the country, and a danger.'[5]

Owen and the Philanthropists
Robert Owen (1771–1858) was one of the first industrialists to realise that healthier and happier workers would improve productivity. If they were better educated, worked shorter hours and had better living conditions, he claimed, they would provide a more stable and energetic workforce. Owen was one of many philanthropic employers of the 19th century who built factories and townships with better conditions of work and better housing. Following him, there were the Lever brothers who built Port Sunlight (1887), Sir Titus Salt of Saltaire (1851), and Ebenezer Howard who founded the Garden City Association (1899).[6] The patrons of these and other experiments were interested primarily in increasing profits and reducing the financial risk. Only as a secondary aim were they keen to improve the conditions of factory workers. Owen was exceptional in realising the potential of caring for labour in his factories as well as the machinery. He was a manufacturer at a time when extensive exploitation of labour was commonplace. By the second half of the 19th century industrialists had become richer and more confident,

without the constant threat of bankruptcy characteristic of the days before limited liability was widely available.[7]

Pauperism was usually ascribed to individual weakness, but Owen and other philanthropists claimed it was caused by the social conditions in which people worked. The philanthropists believed it could be reduced if the working class would acquire the virtues of thrift, temperance, industry and family responsibility.[8] They accepted the existing social order, rejecting the class hatred found among working people. Their solution to the country's social and economic problems was to develop people's character within a philosophy of universal love and to provide practical means of alleviating poverty and hardship.

The work of the philanthropists had two important effects. In the late 18th and early 19th centuries it influenced the development of town planning as a technical solution to the physical problems caused by the industrial revolution. Robert Owen, subsequently named the Father of English Socialism, was important in defining the problems he saw as social ones for which a social solution was required. In doing this he founded a tradition and school of thought which ran right through to the Fabians and the Labour Party. But, more importantly, he inspired a newly emerging working class to challenge capitalist methods of production. He believed that all wealth was the result of human effort; the sole object of wealth was the satisfaction of human desires; human desires should be gratified with a view to improving the quality or increasing the quantity of human effort. The keystone to his system was the elimination of profit and the extinction of the profit-maker. But his was a system of state socialism; he did not think workers could take control of their destiny. The ruling class and the state, argued Owen, should improve their lives and opportunities, so improving 'man' himself, who would then become a more useful tool of society. Despite his own belief that working people needed leadership from among the establishment, his experiments led them to have faith in their ability to control their own future. Owen took no account of class in his analysis, neither was he religious. His system was based on abstract ideas of right and justice. In fact, he was one of the last adherents of 18th century Rationalism. Since there was no coherent theoretical basis to his ideas they easily developed into idealism.[9]

Owen began his experimental work in the cotton mills at New Lanark. As a successful businessman he bought the mills in 1800, probably as an investment.[10] New Lanark itself was not a co-operative but a benevolent autocracy. Owen introduced humanitarian practices to encourage more discipline among the labour force.[11] From observing the results, he developed his models of co-operative villages. He prohibited corporal punishment, reduced the working hours to 10½ per day, introduced freedom from summary dismissal (except for drunkenness), and the right of appeal to himself against disciplinary decisions. He provided better houses, good quality food and drink in the factory shop, social facilities, and education for children and started a contributory sickness benefit scheme and a savings bank.[12]

In 1813–14 he published *A New View of Society*, which expressed his principles of how society should be run, and in 1819 he helped to start or stimulate a succession of Owenite communities in Britain, Ireland and America, such as New Harmony (1824), Orbiston Community (1825), the Rahaline Community in Ireland (1831–33) and Queenwood (1839–45). These community experiments were based on the concept of social equality among people. Each tackled the problem of reconciling individual incentive and participation with efficient decision-making in the democratic process.[13] Economically they were disastrous, attempting to by-pass capitalist markets by substituting for private property a communal possession of land and the accumulation of wealth. All failed, often accompanied by large, outstanding debts.

Owen's influence on the establishment was minimal. He argued vigorously for the acceptance of his ideas and campaigned for new laws to be passed which were in sympathy with these, such as Factory Acts and Education Acts. But like many other patrons of social reform he paid little attention to political power, thinking he could win support by argument and example alone. Also, for much of his life he made little contact with labour movement leaders. In his appeals he achieved some success in the field of education, but his co-operative ideas were ignored. As a form of co-operation his models did not stem from the articulated needs of the working class. Nevertheless, they had more lasting appeal than any other millennial experiment of the early 19th century, and he inspired a new move-ment – Owenism.

Owenism and Trade Unionism

Owenism developed out of Robert Owen's experiments but was entirely different from them.[14] From the 1820s, Owenism, or socialism as it became called, developed alongside Chartism among the skilled workers. The Owenites were the first to develop an awareness of their worsening position as their skills were being replaced by unskilled factory processes. They recognised that the new forms of industrial production and exchange were debased and corrupt, and turned towards methods of mutual aid. Capitalism was no longer regarded as the natural order, and ways were sought of controlling capital for social goals. The Owenites groped their way forward, experimenting with many different forms of alternative organisation, among them co-operative workshops.

By the mid-1820s the new working class enterprises had become inspired by wider considerations than immediate economic benefits, in particular by the ideals of some of the early social thinkers. A co-operative movement had started which grew rapidly with the legal restrictions on association lifted by the Repeal of the Combination Laws in 1824. But without a political movement to take up their ideas and apply them more widely, the Owenite experiments were not rooted in reality; their plans were, according to Lenin, 'fantastic'.[15]

In each experiment the workers tried to short circuit the capitalist system. For instance, they eliminated the profits of the middle man in co-operative systems by buying wholesale. More typical were the Labour Exchanges. These attempted to price goods on the labour time that produced them, and they sprang up in Leeds, Liverpool, Birmingham, London and other major cities. Without a clear relation to the market and access to adequate finance, most of the workers' co-operatives and the Labour Exchanges failed. But while they were alive they attacked every principle of capitalist society and helped to educate the working class in the causes of their oppression. They taught people that they could by themselves run commercial and productive enterprises.

The repeal of the Combination Acts also gave rise to a growth in trade unionism alongside co-operation. The same people were often involved in both movements. But it was still a common law offence to enforce the long term determinants of better wages, such as the closed shop, apprenticeship, higher ratios of skilled to unskilled, shorter hours. As mere organisations trade unions could do little. They needed the backing of the community at large, which they achieved only in isolated localities, like the radical cotton towns of Lancashire.

Early trade unionism was usually organised among people in skilled trades. In 1830 John Doherty made the first attempt at organising workers on a national basis by forming the National Association for the Protection of Labour. Disillusion following the Reform Bill of 1832 encouraged further organisation, and in 1834 the union was transformed into the Grand National Consolidated Trade Union. Its form and aims were heavily influenced by Robert Owen, then at the height of his fame and interested in helping the working class to become more widely organised to work for social change. For a time he saw the union movement as a way of introducing his own social reforms.

In the first few weeks of its life the GNCTU gained a quarter of a million members. But it collapsed the same year through internal disputes and brought down many co-operatives in its wake. Owen's presence had introduced moral values as well as more radical objectives, and the two were incompatible. Local and sectional trade unions continued to exist into the 1840s but there was no further move towards national organisation until the 1850s.

The Chartists

It is not surprising that Owenism was, until 1834, the main influence on working class thought. Afterwards it turned in on itself, becoming no more than a religious sect, overtaken by Chartism. This new movement began in the London Workingmen's Association, formed in 1836 as an educational and political body. It was radical and Owenite, and its members, mainly artisans, were more used to political discussion than action. The body drew up a People's Charter in 1838, demanding the vote.

The idea quickly took hold in the North of England in the major industrial areas where there was a growing proletariat. Journals preaching its aims were on sale everywhere, helped by the existence of a cheap press. A radical intellectual culture developed, with its tone set by Cobbett in his writings about the conditions of the working class. Cobbett nourished a class culture of individualism.[16] This was developed in painstaking detail by Samuel Smiles, a doctor and journalist, who wrote many tracts on its virtues. *Self Help*, published in 1859, was widely read among the middle and working classes. By 1905 a quarter of a million copies had been sold.

Samuel Smiles was radical but not a believer in physical violence. His values and sympathies were with the working class. He showed in his writing how working people could, by their own efforts, become capable of social usefulness to their fellow men and women. Like Cobbett he had no great faith in grand social or economic theories. Individual savings, he thought, could form the basis of national accumulation of capital. In other words, the sum of individual effort was enough to create a major social change. This was not, of course, socialism, which had come to mean the emancipation of workers in a political sense. But the spirit behind this philosophy often appeared the same in many people's eyes.

In this atmosphere the Chartists were divided in their strategies for achieving the vote and winning support. There was a London-based group led by Lovett which was essentially peaceful and compromising and represented the right wing of the movement. In the North the movement was led by Feargus O'Connor, representing the centre, and had the majority of Chartist supporters. O'Connor was an individualist of the 19th century kind, and an opponent of socialism. A less popular strand was led by Bronterre O'Brien, George Julian Harney and Ernest Jones. O'Brien had been influenced by socialist ideas and the co-operative ideas of Robert Owen, and had a greater understanding of the nature of class struggle than the social pioneers before him. Harney and Jones were both influenced by Marx.[17]

The first of the Chartists' petitions gained 1,280,000 signatures. Rejection by Parliament led to widespread violence and bloodshed, and to prison sentences for the Chartist leaders. When they were freed, in 1840, the movement regained its momentum and a National Chartist Association was formed. Although illegal and lasting only until 1853, this was the first political party representing the working class. A second petition was signed by 3,315,000 people, which was equivalent to half the adult working population. Again it was rejected by Parliament, in 1842. An economic crisis followed with widespread strikes and the frequent use of troops to suppress the masses. Chartism declined abruptly, unable to keep up its momentum against this state oppression without a better organised working class.

The Rochdale Pioneers

The 1840s were bleak years. The working class was defeated and demoralised. Chartism, Owenism and trade unionism had all taken a severe hammering. 1842 was a bitter year of depression, accompanied by unemployment and wage reductions, and by large strikes among textile workers and coal miners. Factory innovations were frequent but continued to have little impact on improving life at work. Intense competition among the numerous small firms also contributed to their suffering. Firms were often undercapitalised and, with limited liability still a decade away, their owners scraped every penny they could from the working class. The economy was unplanned and business actions were extremely individualistic. Rapid fluctuations occurred, bringing frequent depressions, more suffering and more poverty.

Reactions among the workers varied. Some accepted their fate, drifting miserably to the poor house or starvation. Some joined the middle class in the Anti-Corn Law League. In the cotton and woollen industries strikes were commonplace but largely unsuccessful. Other workers put their hopes in millennial dreams. The Chartists founded their Land Settlement scheme; the Owenites retreated into their ideal communities.

Against this background the Rochdale Pioneers emerged, in 1844, with their own utopian solution. They developed a system of co-operation which was moulded directly to their own conditions and needs and, unlike its predecessors, did not derive from middle class philanthropy. The Pioneers consisted of weavers, wool sorters, a clogger, a cabinet maker, a tailor, a joiner, a hatter and a shoe maker – all skilled workers. Their model spread rapidly throughout the North of England and Scotland.[18]

Rochdale itself had experienced many serious strikes in the first half of the 19th century against wage reductions, with the handloom weavers at the centre of the discontent. The energies of these and other skilled workers, still the most radical section of the working class, were now channelled into an industrial context. Political struggle was abandoned for an alternative system of production and exchange.

The Pioneers aimed to create a series of home colonies, beginning with a co-operative store in Toad Lane, Rochdale. This was the easiest and cheapest starting point. Their scheme comprised a package of individual ideas, all tried separately before, but unique as a whole:

democratic control, so that each member had one vote;
open membership;
a fixed or limited interest on capital;
distribution of the surplus, after payment of interest and collective charges, in dividends to members in proportion to their purchases;
trading strictly on a cash basis, with no credit;
selling only pure and unadulterated goods;
providing for the education of members in co-operative principles;
political and religious neutrality.[19]

Crucial to the success of this scheme was its sense of commercial and social reality. The Rochdale Society had a business structure which incorporated co-operative principles and at the same time was competitive. Also, it recognised the individualism of the times and the need to give immediate benefits to members. The utopian element in the Pioneers' belief was that enough capital could be made to start productive societies and eventually to create a co-operatively run society. The co-operative store was successful, helped by the better trading conditions of 1844–47, but the Co-operative Manufacturing Society, set up in 1854 to make calico, had degenerated into a joint stock company by 1862.[20]

Growth of Consumer Co-operatives

Consumer co-operation grew quickly and, as in the period 1828–34, came to dominate the co-operative movement. It was more able to survive periods of deep economic crisis than producer co-operation, always a small, struggling section of the movement. Undoubtedly, the consumer movement helped workers' co-operatives to survive by providing markets for their goods, capital, and a national organisation. Also, its sheer size gave it political strength.

Workers' co-operatives continued to be formed through the 1840s but were always highly vulnerable within the market to changes in demand and competition. The greatest problem they faced was a shortage of capital. They depended on capital from workers and from outsiders willing to take a high risk because of sympathy with the ideal. Consumer co-operatives, on the other hand, had access to the savings of many more people in the community, lured by the cash benefits and the low risk involved. Both had to compromise their principles to survive in a capitalist economy. However, consumer co-operatives could trade successfully even though their members might be more interested in cheaper goods and the opportunity to save than in co-operative principles. Workers' co-operatives which developed an overwhelming interest in profits either wound up during periods of depression or brought in outside shareholders and became joint stock companies. While the 'divi'[21] could become an end in itself for consumer societies, a similar concern for financial reward in a workers' co-operative would almost certainly lead to its collapse as a co-operative. Few co-operative enterprises were very successful and unless they valued other aims, co-operators would not have continued to struggle to keep them alive in hard times.

Christian Socialism

In the 1850s interest in workers' co-operatives was revived by the Christian Socialists. These were a group of middle class lawyers and clergymen concerned at the neglect of Christian obligations of people to each other, and especially in their economic relations. Inspired by the revolutionary struggles of 1848 in France, and after the abrupt decline of Chartism, they found a receptive audience for their propaganda on the virtues of mutual love and friendship.[22]

One of the group, John Malcolm Ludlow, had studied the *associations ouvrières* encouraged by Louis Blanc and Charles Fourier in France. He successfully persuaded Frederick Denison Maurice, Charles Kingsley, Thomas Hughes and other Christian Socialists that similar co-operative workshops could be developed in Britain. With little knowledge of the co-operative experiments by Robert Owen and the Rochdale Pioneers, together they went ahead with their plans, often ploughing large personal fortunes into co-operatives, using their influence in Parliament to get laws passed benefiting co-operative formation and publicising their ideas widely.[23]

The movement survived only seven years but had a lasting impact on co-operative development. The greatest benefits were the achievement of a proper legal standing and limited liability for co-operatives under the Industrial and Provident Societies Acts of 1852 and 1862. Also of importance was the devoted bank of supporters that they left behind, such as E. V. Neale and Thomas Hughes, who continued to fight for workers' co-operatives for many years after confidence had dwindled in their capacity to succeed and while the consumer movement was galloping forward.

But the Christian Socialists failed dismally in their attempts to stimulate viable co-operatives. In 1850 they started the Society for Promoting Working Men's Associations, which was intended to spawn self-governing workshops for artisans. Some 12 workshops were formed between 1850 and 1852, including one in engineering supported by the Amalgamated Society of Engineers. Others were formed by tailors, shoemakers, builders, piano-makers, printers, smiths and bakers. All collapsed quickly. They were launched in boom conditions in the early 1850s and could not survive subsequent downturns in the economy. At that time there was no centralised, practical body of advice to help them resolve their many problems of management, marketing, finance and, in particular, their internal discipline.

Another factor may have contributed substantially to their failure.

The co-operatives were not formed by working class people themselves, out of distress; the co-operative idea was imposed on skilled
craftsmen who were far less determined to make their experiment
work than their predecessors, the Owenites and the Rochdale
Pioneers. While most co-operatives were formed in hand-craft
industries suited to the co-operative form of enterprise, they were
not set up with enough incentive to succeed in a capitalist market.

The movement collapsed with the failure of the co-operatives and
after disagreements had developed among the Christian Socialists
over whether or not co-operatives should be converted more deter-
minedly to the morals and religious beliefs of the movement's
leaders. Neale, the least devout of the group, disagreed with Ludlow,
Maurice and Kingsley, who quickly lost interest in the whole idea,
leaving Neale and a few other followers of the movement to carry on
in their individual capacities.[24]

Co-operatives from the Mid-1850s

After the mid-1850s co-operatives continued to be formed and some
were successful for a short time. But despite Neale's tireless
enthusiasm for encouraging them – often with over-generous
personal loans – and despite the boom conditions between 1865 and
1879, there was no rapid increase in their numbers. Between 1862
and 1880 only 200 or so were formed. The growth centres were
Glasgow, Newcastle, Lancashire and the West Riding, with co-
operatives being formed in coal mining, heavy engineering and
textiles. All these were capital intensive but ways round the problem
of raising finance could often be found. In the cotton industry, for
instance, machinery could be hired to reduce costs, and the co-
operatives could take work as sub-contractors to avoid having to pay
for their yarn.[25] Financial difficulties in the start-up stage were
sometimes reduced by workers doing administrative and other jobs
without payment.[26]

The co-operatives in coal mining were mostly non-starters, and
the most dramatic failure occurred in 1875, causing considerable
damage to the image of co-operation as a genuine possibility. This
was the Ouseburn Engineering Works on Tyneside. A large loan
from the Co-operative Wholesale Society and the Halifax Co-operative
Society had supplemented the capital put in hand by the workers
themselves, the co-operative retail societies and trade unions. But
Dr Rutherford who set up and ran the co-operatives was an inept
manager, and the lenders of capital had calculated their risk badly.

On its collapse, the co-operative incurred £12,000 of liabilities, of which about 90 per cent was never repaid.

Co-operatives also continued to be formed in industries dominated by hand-craft work such as boots and shoes, hosiery, iron trades, wool, building and printing, and were scattered throughout the central belt of Scotland, the North of England and the Midlands. They survived by having retail outlets in the co-operative movement and by getting loans from sympathetic people and organisations. Their production methods, it seems, were rarely different from those of similar private firms. These were the labour intensive and most exploited industries which developed alongside, and were necessary to, the introduction of new technology. They employed outworkers, required their workers to compete with machines in other factories by working extremely hard, introduced wage cuts when times were bad and paid low wages at others.[27] Sometimes they were able to provide better terms and conditions for their workers than other firms, as in the nail industry, which, until 1890, was plagued by low wages and the truck system. Certainly, the quality of work produced by co-operatives was consistently high.[28]

Changing Attitudes
During the latter part of the 19th century attitudes towards co-operatives changed. The middle class regarded them as a useful means of encouraging working class thrift and enterprise, dissociating them from their previously close links with the trade union movement. The 1867 Reform Act had given many more people the vote, and led to better legal foundations for trade unionism to build upon. Co-operation became respectable while trade unionism did not, and the two movements drifted apart. Working class attitudes towards co-operatives were less favourable. While co-operatives continued to be formed out of strikes and other rebellious actions, they were beginning to serve another purpose besides that of radicalising the working class. It was argued that capitalists were creating a labour aristocracy which was helping to discipline their workforces[29] by rewarding certain jobs better than others. The consumers' and workers' co-operatives, with their moral codes and their adult education institutes and Sunday schools, assisted in developing the authority systems among the working class. It is probable that the proletariat increasingly saw co-operatives in a less radical light.

After 1855 there were opportunities for working class people to form companies much more easily and without the enormous risk they had faced before. Gradually the co-operative ideal was drowned in the more modest ambitions among the working class to have a stake in their firms. The boom of the early 1870s temporarily put more money in workers' pockets, and new forms of enterprise were started which gave workers a share in the profits, such as working class limiteds, and profit-sharing schemes. Co-operatives lost popularity to those forms which did not restrict shareholding and were run on conventional lines in industries such as cotton, which needed a lot of capital, good management and highly skilled workers.

Meanwhile the consumer co-operative movement continued to flourish. In 1862 the Co-operative Wholesale Society (CWS) was formed as the first national organisation. Not long afterwards it was agreed the CWS would benefit from having factories of its own. The retail movement needed more control over the goods sold in the co-operative shops and had to reduce the price of goods in order to remain competitive. This proposition began a major debate within the co-operative movement which has continued to the present day. It raised the question of whether or not the CWS factories should be owned and controlled by the workers in them. Edward Owen Greening, Rutherford and Neale argued passionately for the factories to be run as workers' co-operatives, while other leaders of the co-operative movement disagreed, claiming the retail movement would not be able to keep any control over their production in their factories.

From 1870 the retail societies began to form a central organisation which became known as the Co-operative Union. In 1889 it was registered under the Industrial and Provident Societies Act, becoming a federation of co-operative societies.[30] In 1873 the first factories were built and run as ordinary joint stock companies, but in 1874 J. T. W. Mitchell, then president of the CWS, agreed to a limited experiment in workers' participation, profit-sharing and bonuses on wages. This was quickly abandoned, though it was kept going in Scotland until 1914.

Principle and Practice within the Movement

The call for consistency in co-operative principles between the consumer and producer sectors was putting the whole movement in jeopardy of collapse. To run an integrated system of production and retailing, as Neale proposed, would inevitably have weakened the position of the retail sector in a capitalist market. Compromises had to be made. It was extremely idealistic to expect the CWS factories to be run as co-operatives when benefits to the workers might have led to problems, not improvements, for the retail movement.

However, there is a more fundamental reason why the debate was never resolved. Consumers' and workers' co-operatives each have a different relation to the market. Both were formed as a response to capitalist retailing and production respectively, but this does not mean they can be run together as part of a cohesive alternative system. The link between them is largely philosophical. The essence of both is their autonomy from outside control. Once that is relinquished their relation to the market is changed and they are no longer truly co-operative. In practice, the interests of consumers and industrial workers were often in conflict, and that conflict was too great to be resolved within alternative forms of enterprise that were already highly vulnerable in the market. In addition, these conflicts were intensified in Britain by the different class interests involved in consumers' and workers' co-operatives. The retail societies invited into membership any consumers, regardless of their political beliefs and objectives. But the conflicts of interest between politically opposed groups in society could not be resolved. And the vision held by many supporters of co-operation within a co-operative common-wealth was as utopian as Owen's villages of co-operation.

The dominance of the CWS in the co-operative movement and its growing band of lower middle class supporters enabled commercial interests to win over pure co-operative idealism. CWS factories produced sweets, boots and shoes, soap, blankets, bread and other goods in high demand. In some cases the factories were in direct competition with workers' co-operatives. Competition was often healthy, however. The CWS factories were the main rivals of the producer societies as both had their outlets wholly or mainly in the retail stores. The CWS factories introduced the latest equipment and techniques and were able to produce goods competitively with private firms. The producer co-operatives were forced to bring their own prices somewhere near the CWS prices. Often they were higher but the percentage share of profits, e.g. 20 per cent bonus given to the stores, lowered the actual price.

The depression of 1878—80 caused the widespread collapse of many firms. Co-operatives went down with them in large numbers, and by 1882 there were only some 20 left.[31] Many had degenerated

into joint stock companies because of their need for capital. Others
had become federal societies mainly owned by retail societies, for the
same reason.[32] From 1880 to 1910 a more realistic approach to
forming co-operatives developed. The stronghold of the new movement was now the East Midlands, particularly in the boot and shoe
industry, which did not easily lend itself to large-scale factory
production and was late in passing through a technical revolution.
There was still room for the small workshops. Also late in transferring
to a factory process were the printing industry, clothing trades, and
other branches of small-scale manufacturing where co-operatives -
were formed. Even at this stage it was cheaper to use hand labour
rather than machines to make certain goods or, at least, by
enormous physical effort and by using inferior machinery, competitive prices could be achieved. Pressure from foreign competitors
finally forced firms to convert to the more widespread use of
machinery.

Socialists and Fabians

At this time the co-operative movement was injected with renewed
vigour from socialists like William Morris, and supporters of the
Social Democratic Federation formed in 1881. Continued interest in
co-operation, particularly by Neale, led to the setting up of the
Co-operative Productive Federation in 1882. The CPF was intended
to promote unity of action among its members, secure capital for
their use and find markets for their products.

In 1884 the Labour Association was formed for education and
propaganda purposes, while the CPF was left to concentrate on
co-operative business affairs. In the same year the Co-operative Aid
Association was set up to encourage co-operatives by giving loans,
but this was quickly wound up as losses accumulated. The Labour
Association drifted towards encouraging conversions rather than
forming new co-operatives, and moved away from the movement.[33]
The increased productivity achieved through profit-sharing and
worker participation became an end in itself. However, the formation
of these new national organisations disguised the fact that this sector
of co-operation was at a low ebb. Although the new co-operatives
paid more attention to conditions in the market and were often
successful, their number was not growing and the idealism behind
them had diminished. The same was true of consumer co-operation
where the 'divi' had become its most attractive feature.

With the formation of the Fabian Society workers' co-operatives were to receive sterner criticism. These social reformers of the late 19th century no longer believed in blueprints but in a gradual emergence, through reforms, into a socialist world. Through legislative change, through scientific inquiry and the wide publication of its results they looked forward to a socialist society.

Beatrice Webb, an active social reformer among the Fabians, publicised the popular views on workers' co-operatives in numerous pamphlets and books. Consumer sovereignty, she claimed, was consistent with the Fabians' beliefs, while workers' co-operatives were divisive of the labour movement and the community. They benefited only those who worked in them and could in no way be seen as a strategy for achieving democracy in the wider community. To strengthen her argument, Beatrice Webb examined the co-operatives existing around 1890 and said that, in her view, only about 20 were genuine. She maintained that such a small number could hardly constitute the kernel of social change. Also, she pointed to the many weaknesses of co-operatives, such as lack of capital, markets, adequate skills, and administration and management techniques.[31] All this was indisputable.

Political attitudes towards co-operatives did not change radically after that. Shortly afterwards, in 1900, the Labour Party was formed and was dominated by the views of the social democrats. Public intervention in the economy, always accepted as necessary by earlier supporters of workers' co-operatives, was preferred in a different form by the Labour Party. Municipal enterprise was favoured as a means of bringing public services and other activities under social ownership in the most democratic way. Co-operatives were never considered as an alternative.

While co-operatives continued to be formed in small numbers, the movement declined from this period in political history. The consumer movement continued to grow. With a large proportion of the working class in the trade union movement and with the establishment of the Labour Party as the main opponent of the Conservative Party, the stage was set for workers' co-operatives to play a different part in a socialist strategy. This does not mean there was a change in their role in the economy. In fact, co-operatives continued as before to manufacture mainly specialist goods in craft industries for limited markets when the bulk of goods were being produced in large quantities in factories. However, the changes occurring in this period meant that when co-operatives again appeared in response to structural changes in the economy, they would not be seized upon by the labour movement as a way of creating an alternative method of production which could lead to fundamental changes in society.

The Movement in Decline
Enthusiasm for co-operatives among middle-class social reformers evaporated with the death of Neale in 1892. The pioneering spirit had gone and the CPF declined steadily. This decline was attributed to a number of causes, according to an Independent Committee of Inquiry, set up in 1958 to look at marketing and production of co-operatives between the CPF, the CWS and the Scottish CWS. The Committee said that it was mainly due to the smaller number of co-operatives, the rising costs of inflation, the falling off of subscriptions and the honouring of a guarantee of one society that went into liquidation.[35] However, this is jumping ahead.

From the turn of the century until 1958 there was only one short period, between 1920 and 1921, when the idea of workers' co-operatives rekindled the imagination of the labour movement. Following the First World War, there was a sudden growth in building co-operatives. In 1920, a National Building Guild was set up as the outcome of the Guild Socialist Movement.[36] Guild Socialism was in essence a plan for transferring industries and services to public ownership, and delegating their management to guilds, including all workers. Industry was to be run as a service to the community, not for profit. The idea was popular. However, the state had no desire to nationalise industry, and another way had to be found to realise this ideal. Co-operatives were formed, closely tied to trade unions, but without profit-sharing.

These co-operatives built housing for local authorities on contract. The demand for houses was high. Homes fit for heroes had been promised. The costs were high if the private sector built because of the particular method of subsidy used by central government: all residual costs were paid, regardless of the amounts claimed.[37] The Building Guilds built on a non-profit basis, and so quickly attracted local authority support. They spread rapidly, but collapsed dramatically when a new system of subsidy of maximum sum contracts instead of costs plus was introduced in 1921. The Building Guilds were wound up in 1922, followed the next year by the entire Guild Socialist Movement. The co-operatives had relied heavily on borrowing from the CWS which was ideologically in favour of the development. But when the market was returned to a normal competitive one, no more money was forthcoming. Many co-operatives collapsed with large debts, partly on account of capital shortages and partly because of their social objectives; they often employed too much labour in an attempt to soak up some of the unemployment in the building industry.

Like the co-operatives of the 19th century, those of the Guild Socialists were set up with a challenging spirit, and achieved both better quality housing than the private sector could produce and more democratic conditions of work for those employed in them. But once again they were unrealistic in their aims. They were an attempt at changing the capitalist economy by forming companies with social objectives, and without a corresponding political struggle. They were not competitive in any lasting sense because the market was distorted by a subsidy system which encouraged extremely high prices to be charged by the private sector. Once the subsidies were reduced the co-operatives could no longer compete.

Conclusion

This chapter has described the waves of enthusiasm and the practical experiments among workers' co-operatives which continued through-out the 19th century. This was an important period in their history because it established their place in the labour movement. Their constant struggle for co-operative ideals within a capitalist economy brought them respect from fellow workers, but more faith was put in trade unionism and in the ability of the state to democratise industry through public ownership. Chapter 2 will show that the attitude of the labour movement to the new batch of co-operatives has hardly changed. This time the opportunities are much greater for co-operatives to gain strength as a sector. But they need to be more aware of the benefits to be gained from an alliance with the Labour Party and trade unions.

2 New People, Old Ideals

New Enthusiasm

Workers' co-operatives in the 1970s have evoked a sympathetic response across political boundaries. Among their supporters are Tories, Liberals, Labour Party members, trade unionists, and more frequently, people who regard themselves as politically non-aligned. In most cases those involved in co-operative formation do not represent the mainstream ideas of their organisations or movements, but hover on the fringes, regarded variously as cranks, Utopians, fanatics, or as progressive pioneers of alternative life-styles.

New leaders have emerged with enthusiasm not seen since the days of Owen, Maurice, Ludlow and Neale. But the widely diverse ideology among the new co-operatives they promote throws some doubt on whether or not they constitute a movement. Organisations advancing co-operatives have multiplied over the last decade, publicising different nuances of co-operative philosophy, offering advice to potential enterprises, and sometimes actually setting up co-operatives. Before 1958 the Co-operative Productive Federation (CPF) alone existed for this purpose. But Democratic Integration in Industry (Demintry) was formed in that year, and its successor, Industrial Common Ownership Movement (ICOM), has attracted many new co-operatives under its wing. Between 1975 and 1980 Job Ownership Ltd (JOL), Commonwork, the Mutual Aid Centre, local co-operative development groups, the Centre for Alternative Industrial and Technological Systems, and the Socialist Environment and Resources Association (SERA) started to rival ICOM with separate campaigns.

Promotion has not been confined to voluntary bodies. Local councils have also shown a keen interest in supporting co-operatives in their areas, and at the national level the Co-operative Development Agency (CDA) was set up by Act of Parliament in 1978 as a non-governmental organisation, or so-called 'quango'. Finally, the consumer co-operative movement has played its part. The Co-operative Union has cautiously welcomed the revival of a tradi-tionally troubled and struggling sector, feeling a duty to support the new ventures as a branch of the wider co-operative movement, wanting to be associated with any successes achieved and grateful for any political strength the new co-operatives might lend to the movement. Publicity has flowed steadily from all these bodies, picked up by the media which has been dazzled into making its own contri-bution. Considering the small number of people involved as co-operators or promoters, the exposure co-operatives have received has been disproportionately large.

It is important to look carefully at the various developments within this plethora of efforts and to examine the ideology behind the agencies supporting co-operatives. While it is hard to pin-point the contribution co-operatives have made to the advancement of the British labour movement in the 19th century, it is even harder today to make claims about their position in working class struggles for socialism. This chapter outlines the different philosophies of each promotional body in the voluntary and non-governmental sectors. It looks at the leaders and those whom they claim to represent, and the antagonisms between the different organisations. It aims to show how much more complex the relationship between co-operatives and capitalist development has become since the last century.

Followers of Tradition
Many of the new promotional bodies grew out of the philosophies which underlay co-operative experiments in the 19th century. Industrial growth and class struggle have affected the structure of industry and the working class and have generated new political campaigns like the peace movement, the ecology movement, the 'alternative life-styles' movements and the women's movement. The pattern of support is not a mirror image of the 19th century but there are enough similarities to make a comparison useful and to raise the question of why this repetition has occurred.

The same mixture of self-help and utopianism that characterised Owenite experiments has re-emerged among some local enterprise trusts, JOL, the Mutual Aid Centre and Commonwork. Members of all these organisations believe that work can be more satisfying if it is carried out on a smaller scale. By removing the conflicts between workers and management they believe more enthusiasm and personal commitment can be generated. This will, they think, increase productivity and the competitiveness of British industry. With these objectives, it is no surprise that they see co-operatives in the same light as share ownership by workers and participation in company decision making. Co-operatives are not seen as a special form of enterprise created under conditions of distress and industrial conflict. Rather, they are thought to be formed by enlightened leaders.

No radical theory of economic development or social change lies behind these beliefs. They come from the liberal tradition of support, for co-operatives. The working class is assumed to have developed a 'them and us' mentality towards their employers, thus reducing their own creativity and driving them into defensive actions. The division of labour and its effects on the workforce are not mentioned in this liberal thinking. Nor is the increasing insecurity of labour as the economic crisis deepens, causing many redundancies as large firms rationalise and restructure themselves in their effort to remain competitive in international markets.

The spirit of self-help is radical in that it generates criticism of capitalist society among people facing a daily routine of drudgery and boredom. But the sum of co-operative efforts is thought by liberals to add up to a vast improvement in standards of living, personal happiness and economic advancement. Ownership of the means of production will not, it is believed, be snatched forcibly from the ruling class, but will be given away sensibly when the rational arguments of the co-operative protagonists are accepted. No success is guaranteed, but technical structures for the operation of co-operative systems are carefully studied and presented by the leaders to their friends in the establishment for consideration.

Each organisation harangues groups of people with ideas which they believe could transform society, if only their listeners could see the light. None of these organisations has grown organically out of the labour movement. They have emerged as personal ideas in the philanthropic tradition. Their schemes appeal more to banks, governments, nationalised industries and other bodies with resources to fund and assist co-operatives, than to potential co-operators. They are likely to attract people keen to start a small co-operative business as an experiment which they are willing to try because they can obtain a package of technical assistance and finance.

For a co-operative to succeed in the last century its members needed a deep commitment. With a few exceptions co-operatives were formed out of desperation and need whereas today the growing interest in alternative life-styles has produced a spate of co-operative experiments among the middle class. But apart from this, little has changed. Trade unionists prefer to fight job loss and deteriorating conditions at a political level, focusing attention on bad management, poor investment strategies and solidarity among their members. Proposals to form tiny co-operatives for a handful of redundant workers have received ridicule in some areas. The principle of co-operation may be acceptable, but trade unionists know it is useless as a means of solving the enormous problems Britain is facing.

Job Ownership Ltd

JOL was formed in 1978 as a company limited by guarantee, with no share capital. It was given a grant from the Rowntree Social Services Trust for two years, after which it intended to become self-financing. JOL maintains that it is not aligned to any political party, as do most of the umbrella organisations. Nevertheless, a number of its founder members are closely associated with the Liberal Party. The chairman is Jo Grimond MP. Political neutrality is explained in JOL's claim that it has members 'who vote for each of the three main political parties and people who normally choose not to vote'.[1]

JOL believes that co-operatives are formed out of 'enlightened self-interest' and comprise groups of individuals who, by working together co-operatively, can be more efficient than a private firm. The term 'granulated capitalism' has been used to describe this form of co-operation, meaning each member is maximising his or her personal financial gain within the constraints of the co-operative organisation. A personal capital commitment of a substantial kind is regarded as essential both to the viability of the enterprise and to give an incentive to the members. Since the Industrial and Provident Societies Act forbids ownership of over £5,000 shares per member, JOL expects that most co-operatives it generates will be incorporated under the Companies Act, though it is admitted that registration as a co-operative will be useful for the small ventures which would then have access to government funds under the Industrial Common Ownership Act of 1976.

The system of co-operatives developed since 1956 in Modragon, in the Basque area of Spain, was adopted as a model by JOL. The Mondragon co-operatives grew up as a particular political and economic expedient in cultural conditions conducive to co-operation. The movement began among the Basques in the aftermath of the Spanish Civil War when 'trade union and independent working class action became illegal and Basque Separatism was brutally stamped on'.[2] It was started and strongly supported by the Catholic church. JOL members believe that the structural form in which the movement developed as a viable and successful operation can be transplanted into Britain and will take root. Among the main features of the Spanish system, duplicated in JOL's scheme, are capital investment by all members (contributed out of earnings over a period or subscribed in other ways), a personal share in asset growth for all members and the formation of secondary servicing co-operatives at an early stage.[3] Like other support agencies, JOL believes that direction and control of the enterprises should be by members' meetings, and management should be separated and directed through an elected control committee which appoints the management team, and members should have one vote each. However, the co-operative nature of JOL firms has not been immediately apparent to the Registrar of Friendly Societies who must be satisfied that the benefits enjoyed by co-operators depend on their participation in their organisation, and not on the amount of their investments. To gain recognition as a co-operative, JOL is presenting its enterprises case by case for examination by the Registrar and Department of Industry.

When JOL first started its promotional work, attention was focused on the owners of small businesses and managers of large firms. It was hoped they could be persuaded to convert their firms into co-operatives. Six different ways of converting were identified:

(a) A small or medium sized family business where the existing owners are reaching retirement and the next generation of the family is either non-existent or unwilling to take over the business: the classic 'succession' problem.

(b) A large company or conglomerate wishing to divest itself of a more or less peripheral subdivision of its business: the classic 'de-merging' problem.

(c) A large company working in an industry where, whether for reasons of changing tastes and markets or on other grounds, the comparative advantage is switching back from larger to smaller units: the baking and, arguably, the brewing industries, say, provide examples.

(d) A small or medium sized enterprise with a sound product

range and market but which is in difficulties for some reason that could be corrected, perhaps, by the conversion to co-operative structures. Where the main problems were those of industrial relations the successor co-op might, for example, have a fair chance of success. And the same could well be true where the problem was one of bad management.

(e) Small and medium sized businesses, perhaps mainly 'white collar' or 'service' businesses, where a genuine wish to convert into a workers' co-op develops from the bottom upwards.

(f) A small or medium sized company which fears take-over and which could make itself invulnerable by conversion into a workers' co-op.

It goes without saying that with the exception of (a) and (f) all the situations referred to above could involve enterprises in public as well as private ownership.[4]

After two years of work there has been a small response to JOL's efforts. One or two firms are said to be interested in converting to a co-operative form. However, the British Steel Corporation, looking sympathetically towards new schemes for job creation to dampen down the harsh reality of its massive redundancy programmes, has found the JOL ideas attractive. In 1979 Corby Development Corporation gave JOL a grant to research into the skills and machinery available in the area and to generate ideas to offer potential co-operators among the unemployed. In addition, a grant of £17,500 was given to JOL by BSC (Industry) Ltd to open an office in the town for six months from February 1980 to put the ideas into practice. At the time of moving into this office, JOL had developed some 12 schemes based on feasibility studies for co-operatives in, for instance, printing, machinery maintenance, woodwork, road haulage, light engineering and drawing and design work.

It was envisaged that each co-operative would be small, employing between eight and twenty workers. The range of co-operatives available off the JOL shelf was strongly reminiscent of the ICOM list of co-operatives and of those funded by the Manpower Services Commission (MSC) – each requiring small start-up capital, most being in service industries or specialised manufacturing, and all being in lower paid sectors than the steel industry. Each member was expected to put around £2,000 of redundancy pay into their venture, depending on its capital needs.

About 1 per cent of the redundant workers have shown interest in the scheme so far. No co-operative has been formed, but two or three are said to be 'in the pipeline'. Enthusiasm has been most marked among men in the 45–55 age group who consider their chances of finding another job are slim. The disappointing responses to both JOL's conversion scheme and the Corby scheme have moderated their aims. The plan for a central resource agency has been abandoned for the time being.

JOL has been looked on with some suspicion by the consumer movement and by ICOM, but has been accepted as a legitimate organisation by the CDA, which has two JOL members on its board. Its path was eased by the consumer movement's need for all-party support in getting co-operative legislation passed during a period when the Labour Party was weak or in opposition. Co-operation had to be presented as a way of encouraging self-help in the community, and gave a platform to bodies like JOL which were atttracted to the idea for managerial reasons. The consumer movement is still unclear about its attitude to JOL, as exemplified by its employee from the Co-operative Bank on JOL's board. He was the spokesperson who explained JOL's aims to the shop stewards at Corby, and may have blurred the aims of JOL in their eyes.

Commonwork

Another organisation recently established is Commonwork, set up by Neil and Jennifer Wates in 1976 with £2 million. The philosophy behind this venture again was mutual aid and self-help (and the desire to reduce the scale of industry to make work more meaningful), to reduce the conflicts between labour and management and to explore new ways of working together which would release creative energy. Another of its aims is to identify new products or processes and develop them so that small co-operatives can be set up for their production.[5]

Commonwork consists of commercial projects, organised through Commonwork Enterprises Ltd, and charitable activities which are the concern of the Commonwork Trusts. At the moment all its work, with one exception, is based in Kent. A large dairy herd of 300 cows is tended on a teamwork basis, and there are also stock rearing, sheep and arable farming. Organic farming methods are being evolved. Also, there is a brickmaking project, with sun heating systems manufactured for the workers' houses, and there is a fish-farming experiment. By mid-1980 there were 28 workers involved in these activities, drawn from the local community and elsewhere.

Projects are intended to be test beds at first, requiring subsidies from Commonwork, but it is hoped they will gradually develop into viable common-ownerships. Commonwork differs from JOL in being less concerned with improving the economy by creating better industrial structures and more concerned with ecological issues and with human development. For instance, aware of the limited supply of raw materials in the world, Commonwork aims not only to find replacements but 'to develop awareness of our relationship to the natural world'.[6] The Wates are concerned to interest working class people in their ideas. There are many young school-leavers, for instance, who have had little chance to develop an awareness of wider social goals.

To achieve its aims Commonwork has, through its Trusts, embarked on an educational programme. Between 1978 and 1980 a full-time worker was employed to explore the educational needs of co-operatives, working at Commonwork's residential education centre, at the Open University, and in the wider co-operative movement. In the long term it is hoped that the centre will become a resource for community groups in London and the South East who want to promote co-operative-type ventures, providing advice on all kinds of training and legal matters. With apparently no political axe to grind and no favoured set of co-operative principles, this agency expects to complement the work of others in the field. Again echoing the beliefs of Robert Owen, Commonwork holds co-operative structures in esteem because they are felt to be just and humane and can help to bring about the peaceful development of society without conflict. The increased efficiency that might result is only a by-product. While its supporters make no claim to know how society could evolve towards Commonwork's ideals, they are critically aware of the tragedy of capitalist exploitation of human and natural resources, and recognise the need for a radical approach to achieving a better society.

Mutual Aid Centre
The Mutual Aid Centre, formed by Michael Young (Lord Young) in 1979, also encourages workers' co-operatives, but is more concerned to stimulate consumer awareness and consumer rights. Its founders believe consumers should have a greater say in defining what they want, in the quality and price of goods and services and in bringing decision-making down to a grass roots level.[7] Like the Fabian Society and Social Democratic Federation in the late 19th

century, they see consumer co-operation as democratic, involving all the community instead of a single workforce. But they believe new vigour should be injected into consumer co-operation, and are keen also to promote worker democracy, seeing no contradiction between the two. So far the organisation has helped to form a number of consumer co-operatives. For instance, there is a parent-teacher co-operative which runs a small village school that had been closed down by the local education authority; a motorists' co-operative in Milton Keynes where people can do their own repairs and servicing under skilled supervision, which has over a thousand members; and some 17 study clubs on British Rail trains which have become known as 'the Brain Train'. In parallel with these self-help initiatives workers' co-operatives are being encouraged. For both types of co-operative the choice of goods produced or services offered are a vital concern to the Mutual Aid Centre. Social usefulness is preferred to the profit motive.

Co-operative Production Federation

There are two other strands of co-operation which have even stronger links with the last century – the Co-operative Productive Federation and the Industrial Common Ownership Movement. The former started in 1882, promoted by E. V. Neale, one of the early recruits to the Christian Socialist movement, and some close associates. A brief return to the 19th century is necessary to describe the nature of this organisation and to explain its present predicament. By the 1880s co-operative formation was based on sounder, more practical principles than in the 1850s, but the underlying philosophy was still imbued with the morality of working for aims other than profit. E. O. Greening's manifesto[8] used at that time as propaganda included clauses such as: 'pride of craft, largely destroyed by machine production, might be restored in a workshop which engendered collective pride in product and organisation,' and 'consciousness of personal responsibility might be developed through worker direction and finance of undertaking'.

In the context of a more advanced industrial technology these are worthy aims, but Greening had in mind the reabsorption of factory workers into self-supporting agricultural communities where model factories and schools set up by the reformers would produce ideal men.[9] For the Christian Socialists, poverty and the sweated trades were more important than the conflict between labour and capital. These problems should, they argued, be tackled by getting Parliament to enact legislation and by setting up workshops run as co-operatives.

After an active period between 1894 and 1899, when over 100 co-operatives were in operation, the importance of the CPF declined. Then for some 60 years producer co-operatives rarely featured in labour movement strategies as a serious philosophy or an alternative way of gaining socialist followers and improving working conditions. As J. H. Plumb (now Master of Christ's College, Cambridge) commented in his history of Equity Shoes, a member of the CPF:

> There has been a decline in co-partnership ideals because a more modern generation has realised that the forces of capitalism are so deeply entrenched as to be irremovable by coalitions of workers in production.[10]

By 1944 there were only 41 productive societies left affiliated to the CPF and 89 affiliated to the Co-operative Union. By 1958 only one-third of the productive societies were CPF members. In 1976 the CPF suspended the rule on subscriptions, at that time 75p per £1,000 of trade – since so little was being provided by this central advisory and propaganda agency. By 1978 eight co-operatives remained in the CPF and in 1979 the majority of those remaining wanted to wind it up. In May 1980 a sub-committee of the Co-operative Union recommended that the CPF be absorbed within its own organisation. Soon afterwards arrangements began to be made for the transfer to take place.

Until then, the secretary, Paul Derrick, had struggled alone to perpetuate the organisation. He attempted to draw up a new set of model rules which were in line with the Industrial Common Ownership Act of 1976, so achieving recognition for the CPF as a 'relevant body' under the Act. But the CPF was refused a grant under the provisions of the Act. The reason given was that the CPF would not accept a trade union member onto its council, even though this was not a requirement of the Act. This demand was later dropped but Derrick got no further in his application for funds. Possibly the Department of Industry was aware of the internal dissent in the CPF and its dwindling membership. Certainly the lack of enthusiasm among members became more obvious by early 1980 when the CPF declined to pay for the proper establishment and publication of the new rules, so preventing their recognition by the Registrar of Friendly Societies and their use by new co-operatives.

The remaining CPF societies differ in many ways from the new co-operatives. Usually they are larger and more capital intensive.

Often a sizeable section of the workforce has little enthusiasm for co-operative principles and does not readily join in the democratic decision-making processes. For the workers, mostly recruited in the last ten years, there are few benefits to be gained from co-operation. Facilities like canteens, sickness benefit schemes, holidays and so on, were often introduced in advance of private firms, but are no longer unique features. The co-operatives offer little more than other factory jobs for school leavers looking for work. In most cases, only their boards and management include long-standing members of the co-operative movement, with a strong sense of the struggles waged in the co-operatives' early years and holding on to their ideals.

The CPF's old model rules have received severe criticism from the new co-operatives on the grounds that they allow workers to have an unequal stake in the firm. It is often forgotten that many CPF co-operatives were formed out of strikes and lock-outs in very adverse conditions. The incentive to survive was often greater than for co-operatives today. Members' share and loan capital was a vital source of finance, particularly during the start-up period and during crises. Without it they could not have survived; no assistance was forth-coming from the state. In practice, members were encouraged to put their bonuses and dividends back into the co-operative as share or loan capital, and gained little from either in the short term.

The rules have also been criticised for allowing individuals and organisations from outside the firms to be members which, it is alleged, sometimes led to outsiders dominating the membership and voting to wind up the business and distribute the assets between them. But it is forgotten that these outside members were co-operative retail societies, trade union branches and individuals sympathetic to the co-operative ideal. By allowing them to join, the workforce was more closely tied to the local labour movement than are the new co-operatives. In most cases the membership as a whole was keen that the co-operatives survived. There were benefits to both sides. The co-operatives' major sales outlet was the retail store, and the capital provided by this and other outside members was vital to the co-operatives' asset base. The retail societies and trade unions, for their part, supported the co-operatives for the jobs they provided for their members. The retail societies also benefited some-times from receiving a proportion of the co-operatives' profits as customers.

Industrial Common Ownership Movement

Christian Socialism is also the founding principle of ICOM. On the face of it the ICOM co-operatives are a very different breed from the old co-operatives. ICOM was begun in 1958 by a Quaker and Christian Socialist, Ernest Bader, after he had handed over his successful chemical firm to the workforce in 1951. ICOM's objective is to promote common ownerships, a specific form of co-operative with very pure principles based on equality and the furtherance of the co-operative movement.

ICOM's aims are expressed in the objects of its Memorandum of Association, Clause 3. This talks of 'the achievement of democratic control and ownership by people at work of the enterprises in which they work' and states that the Movement 'shall have regard to promoting the physical, mental and spiritual well-being of society in general and, in particular, of those persons who participate in the activities of the aforesaid enterprises or the Movement'.

Ernest Bader gathered a number of other Christian Socialists around him. Like their predecessors, Manuela Sykes, David Spreckley, Michael Campbell and others see the expansion of co-operatives coming through legal changes and promotional efforts. They have consistently and successfully fought for the introduction of new Acts of Parliament and changes to existing Acts to benefit co-operatives. All possible sources of funding from the state and elsewhere have been tapped to finance ICOM's work, and friends have been cultivated in all political parties to achieve its aims.

Unlike JOL, ICOM does not lay emphasis on improving the economy, but is more concerned to create a better society which is based on personal fulfilment and satisfying human needs. Its members are opposed to the profit motive of capitalism, in the spirit of 19th century co-operation, and believe 'labour should hire capital' rather than the other way round. They would like to see co-operatives growing in all sectors of industry – and also in housing, agriculture, retailing, fishing and credit unions – ultimately forming a co-operative commonwealth.

They are conscious of the difficulty of starting co-operatives in capital-intensive industries, but do not see this as a permanent barrier. A number of factors are contributing to the rise of co-operatives today, they say. Government agencies are keen to find new ways of creating employment; there is a greater demand by people for direct democratic control over their working lives; there are pressures to develop alternative sources of energy using wind

and solar heat which can be developed in small enterprises like
co-operatives. More than anything else, 'conventional businesses'
are failing in large numbers, and people are looking for alternative
ways of running industry. The time is right for a major growth of
co-operatives.

Many more factors have been involved in stimulating the formation
of ICOM co-operatives than was the case in the 1880s. But the same
belief exists in the encapsulation of socialist objectives within an
organisational form. ICOM does not consider there is a need for a
political movement to bring about a socialist society. Most of its
leaders and members are pacifists and abhor revolutionary strategies,
believing that if co-operative formation can be made easy and
attractive, people will be drawn towards it. They regard strands of
the labour movement, like the trade unions, as a source of organised
people to be captured by the co-operative idea. Emphasising the
political neutrality of the Movement, David Spreckley of Landsmans
Co-ownership, and chairman of ICOM from 1979, said in his election
statement:

> Our aim is to achieve the ownership and control of an enterprise
> by those who work in it . . . I am opposed to tying this movement
> to the Labour Party, the Liberal Party, Pacifism, Vegetarianism,
> conservation, Women's Lib, or Gay Rights, although personally I
> am in favour of all of them.[11]

The limited support for co-operatives, concentrated among the
skilled workers in the 19th century, and largely among middle-class
intellectuals today, has not deterred the Christian Socialists from
their visions.

ICOM's rules make no concessions to the financial problems of
co-operatives. Profits are encouraged only to the extent that they
enable viability and social benefits for members, and the capital of
each ICOM enterprise is considered to be collectively owned. While
the need for external capital has increased for firms generally,
ICOM members cannot own more than one £1 share each, to
prevent them from benefiting differentially from dividends on share
capital.

Loans from co-operators are not frowned on but most enterprises
prefer to avoid obtaining capital this way, again for fear of giving
some co-operators a greater incentive to make profits. Where it has
occurred, co-operators have put in equal amounts. The only
inequality in capital ownership among ICOM firms is in the start-

up capital put in by the founder members which has often varied between them.

The common-ownership objective is reinforced by two further rules. First, no outside members are permitted in case they have a financial interest in the enterprise which would conflict with worker interests. Secondly, on winding up, the profits of a co-operative must be used for the benefit of another common-ownership firm, or for charitable purposes. In other words, the rules ensure that each co-operative operates to achieve democratic and other social objectives and does not work in the members' own financial interests or against the expansion of the movement.

The rules reflect an elitist view of co-operation which ICOM's founders wanted to spread by teaching and practice. They did not emerge out of necessity in harsh circumstances, like the CPF rules. ICOM's first co-operatives were conversions from private firms in which finance was not a major problem and where social objectives could receive priority. The looser rules of the CPF have allowed compromises to be made in the face of market realities, though in most cases the spirit behind co-operative formation prevented any abuse for short-term gains. While ICOM's rules are strict about ensuring equality, they are lacking in safeguards against financial collapse.

ICOM's Idealism

Little collaboration has occurred between ICOM and the CPF. ICOM has ignored the older co-operatives. From the other side, only Paul Derrick has made contact with ICOM. For some years, until 1978 he was co-opted onto the ICOM council as a representative of the CPF, and was also a member of Industrial Common Ownership Finance (ICOF). Derrick wanted to see a merging of the two organisations to save the CPF from extinction, and to enable all co-operatives to acquire shares up to the legal maximum, or to encourage workers' loans.

Derrick has criticised ICOM repeatedly for its lack of pragmatism in putting equality before practicality. However, the ICOM leaders have been adamant about retaining their ideals. Among ICOM's members and affiliated members there are many co-operatives which support this view, including those in the large, wholefood sector and others involved in alternative life-styles, such as in printing, bookselling, publishing and distribution, and co-operatives in the arts and professions like architecture and computing.

Many ICOM members join a co-operative out of choice more than necessity because the idea fits their philosophy of life. they want to provide a genuine alternative service or product, one which is not produced primarily for profit but in a democratic environment. While some have built up successful businesses, a heavy reliance has often been placed on state support, particularly from the MSC and local authorities. It is commonly held among ICOM co-operatives that the consumer co-operative movement and the state should help workers' co-operatives because of their underdeveloped condition and their benefits to society.

In 1979 the London ICOM co-operators began a campaign demanding loan capital from the Co-operative Bank to be given at a high risk and against few assets. They claimed that their personal commitment and past investments were proof of their intention to succeed, and accused the Bank of conservatism in its approach to funding them. Similarly, they have asked local councils for high risk loans, and in some cases received them. Councils have been keen to create jobs and found co-operatives an attractive prospect. But in a number of cases co-operatives have been funded on criteria which are far from commercially sound, and based more on political objectives.

ICOM's stance on share capital has been criticised by many bodies outside their organisation as well as by the CPF, such as joint stock banks, the Co-operative Union, the Co-operative Party and the CDA. Nevertheless, ICOM has attracted the largest following among new co-operatives. The lack of alternative model rules and business advice, and the reduced costs of registration under the Industrial and Provident Societies (I & PS) Act and Industrial Common Ownership (ICO) Act may undoubtedly have encouraged a number of them. But another important factor is the type of people attracted to co-operatives in the 1970s.

A great many are from middle-class, educated backgrounds and are under 35. They are repelled by work in hierarchical large-scale industry, and want more control over their working lives. Most use the term 'collective' to describe their type of co-operative to distinguish it from those formed by conversion. The collectives have many features in common. Often their members are disillusioned by party politics or trade unionism, and few have links with these organisations or with the consumer co-operative movement. Co-operation for them is an alternative way of running a firm which is insulated from the normal processes of capital accumulation and provides a forum for the practical application of their beliefs. Often they trade with sympathetic firms and customers and turn down contracts from businesses of whose aims they disapprove. They compromise their principles only to survive. Normally there is strong cohesion among the workforce which has jointly set up the co-operative, and work is thought to be an integral part of their total lives. They have invested immense resources of energy into thinking out more democratic ways of making decisions and improving the quality of decisions. A pool of experience exists among them which is not widely known.

As the collectives grew in number during the 1970s, conflicts emerged between them and the earlier ICOM co-operatives. But these were contained within the organisation. Possibly the ideological differences between the two groups were insufficient to generate a split, or a take-over of leadership by the collectives. By 1980 the ICOM council was evenly balanced with representatives from each side. The collectives' reluctance to take a more active part in the movement may also result from the relentless struggle they have to face to break even in a market hostile to their aims. And like the founders of ICOM, they rarely regard their work as political.

In 1977 ICOM began to develop regional branches. A better use of local resources was in line with its democratic principles. Also, with over 100 co-operatives, the meagre central resources were overstretched. Regional branches, it was believed, would provide voluntary and full-time help to local co-operatives from among the co-operators and sympathisers and would publicise ICOM more widely. Much of the enthusiasm behind the move came from the collectives. It was envisaged that future representation on ICOM council would be through elections held in the regions, many of which were dominated by collectives. By the end of 1979 branches had been successfully set up in London, Oxford, Cambridge, Northamptonshire, Milton Keynes, Derbyshire, the West Midlands and South Wales, and there were plans for more in Southern England, Bristol, North Wales and Scotland.

In practice, the branches did not function as power blocks for the collectives. Their main use has been to bring co-operators together to discuss common problems. As far as setting up new co-operatives was concerned, they have been largely ineffective, even on Tyneside where there were full-time workers funded by the MSC from 1978–80. By the end of 1979 ICOM's role as the guardian of co-operative philosophy was emerging clearly as interest grew in co-operative development groups.[12]

A Co-operative Commonwealth

For the consumer movement, 19th century attitudes towards co-operation have remained unchanged, but a more positive approach to workers' co-operatives has developed. Democratic socialism reduced the popularity of workers' co-operatives in the 19th century. Sidney and Beatrice Webb and J. T. W. Mitchell had insisted that use was the basis of all values, and argued that this meant the consumer's interests were more important than the producer's. They envisaged a system of exchange dominated by consumers which was run on co-operative principles.[13] Harold Campbell, now a board member of the CDA and director of the Greater London Secondary Housing Association, writing in *Wanting and Working* in 1947,[14] supported this view, saying:

> . . . consumer control is the only classless control. The consumer interest is all embracing: any other is a limited interest. We are all consumers. Whatever other interest we may have, however we get our living, whatever function we may serve, we all have this, at least, in common. Moreover, the end of all production is, quite obviously, consumption.

The democratic socialists of the 19th century, like the Christian Socialists, believed in the concept of a co-operative commonwealth. They looked to a society composed of interrelating associative groups which were free and voluntary and run on democratic lines, and which existed alongside the key industries and services run by the state. The consumer co-operative movement eagerly grasped this philosophy and it still endures today as a hardy perennial in the Co-operative Union, the Co-operative Party and the CWS. However, while holding onto a belief in consumer sovereignty, they no longer feel threatened by workers' co-operatives. In fact, since 1976 the Co-operative Union has been active in trying to co-ordinate their development.

In the North of England and Scotland where the Co-operative Union has been strongest, it has attempted to lead the recent growth in local co-operative development groups. These it regards as local organisations which could form the basis for democratising life in this country and lay the foundation for a co-operative commonwealth. After a long interlude of indifference towards workers' co-operatives it is not a coincidence that a kinder attitude has developed as retail co-operation comes under increasing threat from the highly competitive private supermarkets. Against these difficulties, any advances in co-operation, whatever the sector, give the retail movement greater political strength.

The Co-operative Union could not afford to let other interests like ICOM, local authorities or SERA take the initiative in reviving this sector. But so far its success has been limited because the new protagonists of workers' co-operatives are suspicious of the Co-operative Union's intentions and resentful that this powerful and relatively wealthy body at the centre of the co-operative movement has done so little in the past 100 years to assist the weaker strand of co-operation.

Role of Co-operative Development Groups

The co-operative development groups drew in many new supporters for co-operative enterprises. The ideology of the first batch of promotional bodies had clearly restricted their growth. By insisting on particular models of co-operation they caused potential backers to mistrust the idea. Once a method of organising co-operative development emerged that could encompass different ideologies and political objectives, larger sections of the labour movement were attracted in. The first co-operative development groups (CDGs) were formed in Scotland and West Glamorgan in 1976 and 1978, providing a forum for a range of interested bodies and individuals enthusiastic to develop co-operatives in their area. By 1980 there were some 30 CDGs scattered throughout Britain. Each one was set up with a central executive of representatives from trade unions, retail societies, councils for voluntary service, local councils, workers' co-operatives, housing co-operatives, and the like. MPs were also invited to join.

Some CDGs act as resource centres to give practical advice to new or existing co-operatives; others concentrate on publicising the idea. A growing number of them have obtained funds to employ full-time staff. Information about each CDG quickly spread from area to area, assisted by enthusiasts like Alan Taylor of the Co-operative Party and SERA, and by the national CDA, the Co-operative Union and voluntary action workers. The constitutions for the first ones were used as models for subsequent groups. Speed was vital because the idea had arisen when money was available for local employment-creation projects under the Inner Urban Areas Act, 1978 and in the temporary Urban Aid Programme for funding employment schemes.[15]

The CDGs in Scotland, West Glamorgan and Brent received Urban Aid money, and the Hackney CDG was formed with funds from the Hackney/Islington Partnership budget, in each case enabling co-operative development workers to be employed for a period. The Northern Region Co-operative Development Association received funds from the Tyne and Wear Council and the Co-operative Union, but these were only enough to cover promotional expenses.

Council representatives are on the executive bodies of each group, but all the CDGs except two are autonomous, only tapping the local council's resources when they need to. This arm's length approach is attractive to most local councils because their own resources are limited and more can be gained by supplementing the efforts of a voluntary movement than by taking control of it. The co-operatives themselves usually favour this relationship with the state as it gives them more freedom to pursue their social goals with the minimum of interference, and to develop a democratic structure which better suits their needs.

Some Inner-London CDGs

The approaches to co-operative formation taken by the CDGs vary widely. Since 1977 Wandsworth Council's officers have tried to set up a CDG as part of the local authority. A change of council in 1978 watered down political enthusiasm for the venture, but with great perseverance by Manuela Sykes (one of the founders of ICOM) in February 1980 money from the Urban Aid budget was allocated to the Wandsworth Enterprise Development Agency for five years and a loan fund established specifically for financing co-operatives. In this case the CDG will be uniquely accountable to the Council and will have to take on board Council policies.

Camden does not have a CDG in a formal sense, with aims and a constitution. However, a *de facto* group has existed there since October 1977, with the Council playing a central co-ordinating role. This consists of an advisory group of about ten experts invited by the Employment Opportunities Officer of the Council. The group (the Co-operatives Working Group) is represented by the Council, the Co-operative Bank, Industrial Common Ownership Finance, ICOM, Calverts (a Camden printing co-operative), local business and interested individuals. It meets regularly to discuss co-operative promotion and to examine and make recommendations on applications to the Council for loans and grants from new or existing co-operatives. All the development and promotional work is carried out in the local authority, where final decisions on funding are taken.

Camden concentrated on publicising the idea of co-operation through a poster campaign which offered financial and other support from the Council. But the take-up was largely from people more interested in forming partnerships, who saw this as a way of getting public money to start up in business. The unemployed, whom the Council envisaged would benefit from their co-operatives policy, were scarcely visible.

Lambeth's CDG is autonomous of the state, backing a belief that 'local authority enthusiasm for co-operatives can smother the movement while trying to nurture it'.[16] However, in practice the CDG is heavily serviced by the local Council along with the Lady Margaret Hall Settlement. It was instigated by John Tilley MP, the trades council, local co-operative retail societies and local co-operatives, though the latter were only drawn in after much persuasion by the trades council.

Money from the Urban Programme enabled the CDG in the summer of 1980 to appoint a full-time co-operative worker. Before this, local voluntary organisations provided the resources to assist co-operatives. For instance, the Lady Margaret Hall Settlement played a large part in establishing Kennington Office Cleaners, a co-operative of women cleaners formed in June 1978, and has since given it continuous assistance. The Council gave loans and other help to Kennington Office Cleaners, Arkwrights (crafts), and 50 Products (timber goods). Also, it has paid the national CDA to do feasibility studies for Arkwrights, Flypress and Badger (screen process printers), Metropolitan Motor Cab Co-operative, and the House of Lambeth (wood workshop), and to examine the potential for setting up co-operative laundries on council estates.

Lambeth Council set up a Co-operative Enterprise Panel in 1979 to ensure co-operatives received the necessary advice and assistance and to consider applications for financial help from the Council. In this way it ensured that each project was adequately capitalised, that the risk was realistically assessed and that other sources of funds were taken fully into account. The panel is a sub-committee of the Council's Economic Activity and Employment Committee. Its members include representatives from the Council, the trades council, the local CDG, local consumer co-operative societies and employers.

Scottish Co-operatives Development Committee

The Co-operative Union was dominant in setting up the Scottish

Co-operatives Development Committee (SCDC), the Northern Region Co-operative Development Association and the Bristol CDG. In Scotland co-operative sympathisers felt that ICOM, the only active agent promoting co-operatives in 1976, was heavily under-staffed and could afford little time to help the Scots. An organisation was needed in Scotland itself. This sentiment was a useful lever for the Co-operative Union. A CDG was formed by the Co-operative Union, the Scottish Council for Social Service and the Workers' Educational Association, and was in time to gain recognition under the ICO Act 1976 as a 'relevant body' and to claim a portion of the funds available under the Act for development and advisory work.

This group, like those in the Northern Region and Bristol, has emphasised in its publicity the satisfaction people would get from owning their job and controlling their lives. No special appeal was made to trade unionists under threat of redundancy, or to young, disadvantaged groups with poor job prospects. Instead, the SCDC cast its net widely across Scotland using the press and local radio. It was hoping to find people with skills and a business flair who liked the idea of joining a co-operative venture, and owners of private firms who might be persuaded to convert. The SCDC recognised that these were not the only methods of starting co-operatives, but thought they would produce viable enterprises faster than any other way. The immediate aim was not job creation or job saving, but to build an image of success which would attract future co-operators. However, this strategy did not address itself to the question of whether co-operation with an image of paternalism and middle-class professionalism would attract the labour movement. The SCDC measured its own success between 1976 and 1979. The attempts to create quick successes had failed, they said, but of the 16 co-operatives existing, four or five might have collapsed without the help of the SCDC's development officer, Cairns Campbell.

Different Aims, Different Approaches
The East Midlands CDG (the East Midlands Association of Common Ownerships and Co-operatives) is different again, dominated by representatives from five ICOM co-operatives, four of which were formed by conversion from private firms or as a spin-off from a con-version. It has taken the least aggressive approach of any CDG. Only members of existing co-operatives attend meetings, which serve the purpose of sharing experiences rather than promoting new co-operatives. The largest body represented, the common ownership

firm, Scott Bader, has since 1958 continuously helped new and existing ventures with loan capital and acted as a godfather in line with ICOM's beliefs. But it has had no time for broader-based approaches to co-operative formation which involve the labour movement.

The CDGs in Hackney, West Yorkshire, Islington and Brent have all approached their work in the radical community development tradition. They have acted as a stimulus in the community so that co-operatives grow up from grass roots identification of local needs. Nothing is imposed on people, but the CDGs are there to offer opportunities, guide discussion towards co-operatives where they may be appropriate and provide the full range of resources for setting them up. Sometimes the CDGs will set up new co-operatives themselves.

The sponsors and full-time staff, where they exist, believe most resources can be found locally. They are suspicious of centralised organisations like government departments, the Co-operative Union and the national CDA, believing these bodies have little sensitivity towards local needs. They also maintain that much of the expertise claimed by these bodies can be made accessible to local groups by demystifying the professional jargon they use. Where staff are employed they are low-paid and identify more closely with the workers in small co-operatives than with the staff of the Co-operative Union or the national CDA. To those involved in the politics of co-operation they often appear as anarchists, wilfully denying themselves the chance to grow through contact with more powerful sections of the movement.

Only in Skelmersdale and West Glamorgan were political motives clearly behind the CDGs. In Skelmersdale the initiative was taken by Louise Ellman, leader of the opposition on Lancashire County Council, and James Mason, her predecessor and board member of the CWS. Stimulated by requests from shop stewards at Courtaulds to form a co-operative there after closure was announced, they set up a broadly-based CDG to look at the possibility of creating a large network of co-operatives in the area to combat unemployment. The aims of the West Glamorgan CDG were more modest. Again it was not interested in forming co-operatives directly out of closing firms, but put its faith in small enterprises. With the help of the South Wales Anti-Poverty Action Centre it has tried to form co-operatives out of government-assisted projects for creating work, like training workshops and enterprise workshops. By 1980 two had started in this way, Drym Fabricators and Dowlais Knitwear, employing about 33 workers between them.

So far the achievement of the local CDGs has been tiny, but it may be too early to judge them. In May 1980, only the SCDC had existed for more than two and a half years. However, the notable exception of Skelmersdale highlights an important point. While the CDGs are broadly based and willing to take a more flexible approach to co-operative formation than the CPF, ICOM or JOL, there is rarely a political strategy behind their efforts, and the relationship of the CDGs to the labour movement is far from clear. Sympathetic individuals from different organisations are exploited as a way of drawing in more resources for co-operative development, and to attract attention to the idea. Not surprisingly, the TUC and Labour Party have not yet given their wholehearted support to co-operation. The CDGs are mostly autonomous and have not yet attempted to federate or to assume a status in direct relation to the Co-operative Union or national CDA. Many have remained aloof from these bodies and criticise their efforts to assist local developments. This has prevented any common political strategy from developing. With cohesion also lacking among the national co-operative organisations a wide variation exists in the aims and activities of promotional bodies at all levels, with no clear policies which the labour movement can take on board.

SERA Support for CDGs
The Socialist Environment and Resources Association (SERA) has played a major behind-the-scenes role in whipping up enthusiasm among local organisations for CDGs, and in creating some consistency between their aims and functions. Alan Taylor, in particular, has been central to SERA's policies and campaigns. Concerned with achieving a socialist society, SERA's members believe 'co-operatives should not remain isolated, but should join together to develop an awareness of their potential for transforming the economy'.[17] Their effort to form a network of local CDGs is one of several SERA campaigns. They include:

criticism of the existing control of capital through the financial institutions;
working out ways of assembling capital from the community for co-operative development; and
examining ways in which employees of private firms can be enabled to take them over if they wish, to be run on a co-operative basis.

SERA believes working class support for socialism can be rebuilt in practical ways such as through forming co-operatives of all kinds. CDGs, it maintains, will help to prevent alienation from the trade union movement by assisting co-operatives to become more successful, to pay competitive wages and to provide good working conditions.

Its philosophy has similarities with that of the early Fabian Society. Both have emphasised the. need to democratise local communities as the bedrock of socialist support, and both have looked for a 'peaceful path to reform'. SERA's apparent obsession with CDG constitutions and federation arises from these ideological underpinnings. For instance, SERA believes that if the CDGs are not controlled ultimately by the co-operatives themselves, they cannot be at the centre of a new socialist movement. Any support for them from trade unions, local councils and other sympathetic organisations would be subsidiary to broader objectives. By 1980 the majority of CDGs had accepted the aim of giving more places on their executive committees to co-operatives. SERA also encouraged CDGs to build up local sources of capital for lending to co-operatives, through charging levies on local co-operatives and supplementing these with grants and loans from local authorities and elsewhere. This ties in with its belief that communities should invest their money locally in socially worthwhile projects, by-passing the profit-oriented financial institutions. Again it has been successful in persuading most CDGs to insert this aim into their constitutions.

The recommendations promoted vigorously by SERA have appealed to the ICOM co-operatives; majority control on CDG executive committees is compatible with ICOM's own goal of a co-operative commonwealth, and ways of finding capital for new starts and expansion are always welcomed. Many ICOM co-operators have also identified with SERA's old-fashioned concept of 'community', with its connotations of small-scale collective unity in work and living arrangements.

There is some overlap and duplication of activity between ICOM's regional branches and local CDGs. This is particularly marked in the North East where ICOM North and the NRCDA have co-existed with almost identical aims. ICOM North has clearly been hostile to the NRCDA, refusing to support a Co-operative Union-backed organisation.

The CDGs have looked to ICOM for their model rules and for advice on management in a co-operative, but otherwise they have found little need for close contact with this pioneering body of the

1960s and early 1970s. For its part ICOM has been reluctant to join these new bodies. In 1979 at ICOM's Annual General Meeting a motion was debated on CDGs, calling on ICOM to ask to join such groups as long as their constitutions gave co-operatives a majority on the executive committees. It was defeated, with some people arguing that CDGs were peripheral to ICOM's activities and others feeling that ICOM could not make a firm stand on the form of CDGs.

Setting up the Co-operative Development Agency

The call for a national organisation for promoting and assisting workers' co-operatives was first made by Neale and in 1884 the Labour Association was formed. It was repeated in 1969 when Ian Wrigglesworth, Labour and Co-operative MP, and Terry Pitt, Research Officer of the Labour Party, suggested a CDA should fund the rationalisation programme of the consumer movement. They argued that state funds should be sought to help regionalise the consumer societies, which were suffering badly from competition with the growing number of giant retail stores in the private sector. With large government grants going to private firms from the Industrial Reorganisation Corporation to help mergers and takeovers as part of the government's developing interventionist role in the economy, they thought it only right that co-operatives should benefit in the same way. And a boost for co-operatives would also help to build an alternative sector to private industry in a more progressive way than nationalisation.

The proposal for a CDA appeared in Labour's Economic Strategy 1969. However, the CWS opposed the move, fearing any heavy degree of state involvement in an essentially voluntary movement. The Parliamentary Group of Co-operative MPs kept the CDA idea on the Labour Party's agenda with the assistance of ICOM, the Society for Co-operative Dwellings, the Credit Union League of Great Britain, and other lobbying bodies which envisaged a CDA helping the less developed areas of co-operation.[18] The proposal was repeated in a joint Labour/Co-operative Party statement in February 1970 and in Labour's 1970 election manifesto, and in the same year it was debated at the Co-operative Congress where new arguments in its favour emerged. It was proposed that instead of limiting its scope to the retail sector, the CDA should perform a wider role promoting all sectors of co-operation.

In 1973 and 1974 the new-style CDA was presented again in Labour's election manifestoes, and by 1977 there was broad agreement in the co-operative movement, across a broader political spectrum, that a CDA was needed. In that year, both the Labour Party Conference and Co-operative Party Congress called for a CDA, and in October the Prime Minister, James Callaghan, speaking at a Co-operative Party rally, promised to legislate for a CDA. Callaghan's personal support for co-operatives is thought to have helped the CDA's passage to the statute book. For the left wing of the Labour Party, co-operatives had also become attractive after the experiments at Meriden, Kirkby Manufacturing and Engineering and the *Scottish Daily News*, and also because the Co-operative Party had moved nearer to it in one sense by taking an anti-Common Market stance.

But in the run-up to the Act a bitter struggle developed within the co-operative movement over the form and aims of the CDA. In March 1977 a working party was set up under the direction of the Department of Industry's Small Firms Division, which included representatives from all the major co-operative organisations[19] and the TUC. The working party agreed that the co-operative movement already had a democratic form with the Co-operative Congress, but that it was dominated by the retail societies while industrial, housing and agricultural co-operatives were only weakly represented. A CDA could provide a forum for the whole movement. This was important since new strands of co-operation were developing which needed a national voice and assistance. It was thought that a range of commercially linked co-operative activities could be a key to the movement's future success.

But beyond this, disagreements emerged between ICOM and the consumer movement, who were backed by the Department. ICOM was afraid the CDA would promote the interests of the retail sector at the expense of workers' co-operatives because of its sheer size and economic strength. ICOM demanded that the CDA be a funding body, that it concentrate its efforts on helping underdeveloped sectors and that its board comprise representatives from the co-operative organisations.

While the retail movement recognised the need to assist new areas, it was disturbed by the crusading spirit of ICOM and wanted the CDA, as a non-party political organisation, to represent co-operative interests. In October 1977 a majority and a minority report[20] appeared together, signed by nine and four organisations respectively. The majority report recommended initial government funding for the CDA and an appointed board, but did not state that the CDA should have funds to lend to co-operatives.

The day after these reports were published the Prime Minister announced support for the majority report and indicated clearly that he considered co-operatives had a useful role to play in alleviating society's current problems, echoing the majority report's statement that co-operative enterprises could make a contribution to reducing unemployment and halting the collapse of small firms.

Despite Callaghan's positive response to the working party's recommendations, there were growing fears that the issue had been killed by the internal conflict within the co-operative movement. A campaign to lobby MPs to get a bill drafted was hurriedly started by the Parliamentary Group and by the Liberal Party-dominated Outer Circle Policy Unit. The Liberals had now emerged as major supporters of workers' co-operatives, fired by the enthusiasm of people who had studied the Mondragon co-operative system in Spain, including Jo Grimond, Peter Jay and Robert Oakeshott.

In March 1978 a bill was drafted and received Royal assent in June of that year. The CDA was set up with a broad remit to promote all sectors of co-operation and a budget of £900,000 which it was estimated would be spent at a rate of £300,000 a year. A further sum of £600,000 could be made available by statutory order. Of the eight directors appointed to the board one was a Liberal Party nominee, but ICOM's own nominee was not selected. When workers' co-operatives were chosen by the board as the CDA's first priority, ICOM's lack of representation and the absence of funds for on-lending were a huge blow to the supporters of these ventures, creating tensions between ICOM and the CDA for a long time to come.

The CDA Act was passed with all-party support. The Tories, Liberals and Labour Party all believed co-operatives could contribute usefully to industrial development and wanted the CDA to concentrate its attention on promoting producer and service co-operatives. But beyond this they parted company. The Labour Party saw workers' co-operatives as a third sector of the economy, with potential to introduce greater democratic control in industry and to redistribute wealth. The Liberals and Tories saw them as reducing worker militancy, increasing productivity and encouraging self-help among individuals in a crisis.

Role of the CDA

In practice, the work of the CDA was heavily influenced by its board and its directors, all appointed by Alan Williams, Secretary of State for Industry. The director was Dennis Lawrence OBE, a civil servant who had reached retirement age after being an Undersecretary at the Department of Industry, and among other things head of the Small Firms Division. He became director after being chairperson of the CDA working party. He saw the CDA's role as a catalyst for co-operative development along the same lines as other state interventionist agencies like the National Enterprise Board, Scottish and Welsh Development Agencies, and the Northern Ireland Development Agency. As the Act required, he was expected to publicise the existence and advantages of workers' co-operatives and other forms of co-operation, giving advice on legal, financial and other matters. But within this remit he considered co-operatives should only be encouraged if they had a chance of achieving commercial viability, and disapproved of discrimination in favour of them by financial institutions and local authorities. Consequently, Meriden Motorcycles, Kirkby Manufacturing and Engineering and the *Scottish Daily News* were not cases with which Lawrence and the board wanted to be associated. In its first Annual Report where the views of Lawrence as an elderly civil servant came through strongly, the CDA took great pains to dispel any misconceptions the public might have about its attitude to 'rescue cases' such as these, saying:

Rescue cases

50. Public interest in industrial co-operatives has fixed almost entirely on the worker co-operatives set up some years ago to rescue failed enterprises organised as companies in the conventional form. How far all these enterprises, when re-organised, in practice satisfied co-operative principles is regarded by many in the movement as open to question. Also, the recent closure of Kirkby Manufacturing and Engineering Co Ltd may have revived doubts about the effectiveness for industrial ventures of the co-operative form. And it has reinforced a serious misunderstanding of the CDA's role, a misunderstanding which sees the Agency primarily if not wholly created to undertake rescues. On the one hand, it is seen as tarred with a rescue brush; on the other a disappointment to misplaced expectation. That misunderstanding has made our task more difficult: and we take this opportunity to remove it and to explain our policy on rescue cases.

51. Emphatic in its criticism of the application of the co-operative form of organisation in the rescue cases in question, the Working

Group's report concluded that, important though the rescue might have been on general grounds, it was far from an ideal basis on which to promote co-operation. It attempted to use co-operation to turn failure into success, but against heavy odds. Events since that pronouncement have done nothing to deny that criticism.[21]

The CDA's priority had been to promote co-operatives in other ways, less politically contentious. With a change of government in 1979, followed by a major attack on 'quangos' launched as part of the Thatcher Government's drive to cut public expenditure, this policy became even more entrenched. The CDA began to promote co-operatives as if they were any small firm with the same problems and needs, and argued they should be promoted in traditional industries, and not just in the 'alternative' sector. Lawrence claimed the main difference between co-operatives and other firms was that co-operatives were run by the whole workforce, which meant they needed greater direction to ensure the workforce would act corporately as part of a business. In every other way, co-operatives should compete in the market along with other firms. The CDA's promotional work gave little credence to co-operative philosophy. The favoured way forward was to create co-operatives through conversion, and in June 1979 a comprehensive guide was published on the mechanics of this operation.[22] However, the business world turned a deaf ear to the opportunities offered.

CDA's Relations with Other Bodies
Like other interventionist bodies, the CDA does not carry out its policies in a totally independent way. It is subject to pressures from the co-operative movement. The Co-operative Union, ICOM and the CDGs in particular, have their own view of how the CDA should do its work. Among the many small co-operatives the CDA's image is poor. This is hardly surprising since ICOM has no direct representation on the board, and since the CDA has no funds to make loans. In fact, ICOM and the CDGs were in a better position to help the new ventures. The CDA's staff were mostly inexperienced in the co-operative field when they arrived early in 1979. After a year in post they were still receiving few requests for help from existing co-operatives, despite the flood of publicity material put out by the CDA.

In October 1979 Lewisham Council awarded the CDA £5000 to study the potential for co-operatives in the borough. The study was to take three months after which the CDA would provide a free consultative and advisory service for co-operatives in the borough for two years. The Council was interested in co-operatives as a method of creating jobs, particularly for ethnic minority groups. Since then other local councils have approached the CDA to help in their own co-operative development programmes. Early in 1980 the CDA agreed to undertake feasibility studies for five co-operatives in Lambeth, paid for by the Council. Later in 1980 a scheme for assisting Haringey Borough Council was drawn up.

Councils are more likely to seek help from the CDA than from other promotional bodies. ICOM ventured into this field in 1976 but made little headway. The CDA can offer professional staff while ICOM in 1980 had only one full-time worker. With the CDA looking less certain of getting further funds after its first three years, the greater potential for getting results in local authorities was one factor leading to a review of its priorities.

Another factor was that strong criticisms were beginning to be voiced by the board that the Agency was not visible enough in the co-operative movement and elsewhere. With few achievements in its pocket this was an unrealistic demand. But lack of any real political representation on the board led to a confusion about the policies to be followed. For instance, members who had links with the retail movement needed the CDA's work to appear successful and relevant to their sector. For them the CDA had been a political triumph. A withdrawal of funds would weaken their bargaining position with the Government. It had become essential for the retail sector to develop greater political strength to maintain credibility, even if this involved encouraging new sectors such as workers' co-operatives, from which there would be few direct commercial returns for the consumer movement. The consumer interests demonstrated their political commitment to workers' co-operatives when the Co-operative Bank started a scheme to fund them by matching every pound of a co-operative's capital with a loan of a pound, up to a maximum of £25,000. Further evidence of this is given by the Bank's representation on JOL, and Camden Council's CDG.

By early 1980 the CDA had not responded to the retail movement's criticisms, and tension still remained between the Agency, ICOM and the CDGs. While the Act had envisaged the CDA would co-ordinate the interests of all the promotional bodies, in practice many of them did not share the Co-operative Union's concern with the CDA's symbolism. They saw little value for themselves in the CDA's publicity work, and would have preferred a funding body rather than a promotional body which was supplanting some of their interests.

The diverse collection of people and organisations purporting to support workers' co-operatives that has appeared over the last five years cannot hope to be extended much further. Just when the CDA has built up a solid core of expertise – badly needed by the new co-operatives – it could be axed out of existence along with many other quangos which challenge the Government's beliefs and policies. Increased cuts in local authority budgets may severely hamper the ability of councils to assist co-operatives. ICOM's funds · from the Industrial Common Ownership Act are nearly exhausted. The CPF is to be absorbed within the Co-operative Union. JOL has failed to generate a single co-operative and risks collapse.

Before the Labour Party is returned to power, years of effort to build a central pool of resources to help co-operatives could be wasted. The stronger consumer sector is facing an enormous challenge. There could be commercial and political advantages for the Co-operative Union if it maintains and develops workers' co-operatives in the vacuum left by the state's withdrawal from the field. But its ability to take a lead depends on more than an ideological commitment to all sectors of co-operation. It depends on the Co-operative Union's ability to convince the co-operators in the collective-style groups that it is sympathetic to their aims. It goes without saying that such a stance by the Co-operative Union would lead to a shift towards stronger forms of workers' co-operatives.

Conclusion

This chapter has attempted to unravel the range of perspectives underlying co-operatives today. The co-operative philosophy has appealed again to Christian Socialists whose enthusiasm and particular moral codes lie behind the rules of ICOM, the promotional organisation which has attracted most followers among the new wave of co-operatives. The co-operators themselves in ICOM firms are inclined to hold more radical beliefs. Since ICOM was formed a large number of other independent bodies have sprung up to assist co-operatives. The state too has added to the list with the national CDA and local authority-based CDGs. But there is no coherence of philosophy or strategy among these organisations or their supporters, and no political perspective. The natural home of co-operation – among socialist ideals – seems an embarrassment to many people in the movement. Chapters 3, 4 and 5 will show how the different approaches to co-operation affect the performance of co-operatives in the market.

3 Raising Money

Problems of Finance

It is widely held that the most serious problem co-operatives face is a lack of finance. Some people are in favour of the joint stock banks giving the same treatment to co-operatives as they give to any other firm. Drugged by the mystique of co-operation, but blind to its defects in the market, they promote co-operatives as just another type of company which competes alongside partnerships, private firms, public companies and nationalised industries. Other people consider there should be special funds available for co-operatives which should be given on favourable terms because of the superior nature of these ventures. Both these views ignore the fact that the capital structure of co-operatives is intrinsically weak. The movement finds it hard to admit this in case it implies co-operatives are less able to compete and less deserving of support.

In practice, finance has been difficult to find. In some cases, co-operatives have looked to their sympathisers for support. The more profitable co-operatives have lent to others on favourable terms. The Labour Government of 1974–79 saw their value in creating jobs and introducing experiments in industrial democracy, and set up a fund for co-operatives which on-lends at lower than market rates. Local authorities, where the councillors are politically motivated, have also lent on favourable terms to co-operatives to create jobs. The MSC has paid the wages of co-operators for one or two years in enterprise workshops as part of its job creation programme. All these sources are small but have played a vital role in building up the new co-operative sector.

Co-operatives and Capitalism

A co-operative is different from a private firm in that its non-refundable capital is collectively owned; in principle, there is no capitalist or manager who acts in the interests of capital. The whole workforce performs as a functioning capitalist to the extent that it must buy and sell competitively. In other respects too a co-operative is different. Its primary aim is not to make a profit and to accumulate capital. Profitability is essential to survive, but survival is only required to enable the co-operative members to pay themselves wages and to achieve other goals. In Britain these include democracy in the workplace, job security, and assistance to other co-operatives and socially worthwhile projects, campaigns or causes. The co-operative commonwealth is the aim of the movement's leaders, but strategies to achieve this have not so far included working alongside other socialist campaigns or making any major commercial links with other sectors of co-operation.

Co-operators are less concerned with social change than with achieving the objectives of their own individual firms. This leads to confusion about their business orientation. It does not automatically follow that social and commercial objectives are incompatible or that contradictions between them cannot be tolerated. The state's recent investments in industry have demonstrated regularly that viability and profitability in an individual firm can benefit the economy as well as the owners. But as far as co-operatives in Britain are concerned the worker members have seldom taken this view and have not seen the contradiction of their position in the economy, preferring to think they have freely chosen the co-operative path. Because of this, they do not accept that a relationship to capital must be worked out, and try to by-pass the 'straight' or capitalist market. For instance, rather than seeing co-operatives' growth as essential if their influence on other workers is to increase, members believe there is a capitalist quality to the concepts of growth and profitability. From this perspective they see in-built conflicts between social and commercial objectives which they must resolve internally in their co-operatives. They believe compromises are needed to balance those objectives which help the business and those which make the working lives of co-operators more worthwhile. The conflicts are starkly presented by members in meetings and their resolution becomes an unavoidable part of a co-operative's life. Over and over again, reinvestment and growth are posed against better wages and conditions.

Members believe that they, the labour power, hire capital, and that a surplus rather than profits is produced. Proof of their separateness from the capitalist market is demonstrated by their frequent refusal to trade with private firms, to borrow money from banks or, in some cases, to accept grants and loans from the state.

In fact, it is their ideology which encourages co-operatives to cut themselves off from the market and to find protection in the labour and co-operative movement. But co-operatives are a response to the effects of capitalist production and their whole existence is bound into the capitalist system. They *do* therefore have a relationship to capital. For instance, they play a role as small firms in sub-contracting and assembly work in low-paid, sweated trades which exist in parallel to more advanced production systems. They contribute to the state's job creation programmes, providing young people with rudimentary skills, giving them the experience and discipline of work and helping to create a more entrepreneurial environment in which large firms can expand. They are tolerated or encouraged as much for these reasons as for their democratic principles. If they played no part in industrial development they would die from capital starvation, exclusion from markets and refusal of credit.

It is true that choices must be made in a co-operative. Where there is no employer, the workers themselves or their elected committees must decide how profits are used. Sometimes co-operatives are cautious and find they have hoarded larger reserves than they know what to do with; sometimes the members pay themselves large bonuses finding later they have precious little to invest in new machinery. But basically the decisions are business ones made by a responsible workforce which wants its firm to survive and wants a standard of living roughly in line with other workers.

If co-operators saw themselves helping to build socialism, they would also see their relationship to capital more clearly. They can help to achieve social change only by using progressive production methods while at the same time playing a necessary role in capitalist development, and playing it collectively. They need some approval from the state, large firms and financial institutions to avoid exclusion from the market. And they need protection from the co-operative sector to offset their vulnerability in the market.

Access to capital for new starts, growth, diversification, or survival is as essential for workers' co-operatives as it is for any firm. However, co-operatives have greater difficulty in raising capital than other firms. This is less to do with their principles being in some way offensive to banks than with their capital structure. The capital of a co-operative is made up of members' shares and loans, external loans and reserves. The level of capital may be reduced by individual members calling in loans or withdrawing shares. However, where these exist they are not regarded as financial investments and are rarely removed in an opportunist manner. The funds of a co-operative are not thought to be owned individually but are considered to be a collective resource. The problem is not that there are withdrawable funds but that in many cases there are not enough member shares and loans to use as a basis for borrowing. Another reason why co-operatives find it hard to raise the capital they need is because financial institutions are not skilled in assessing the risk of lending to a firm with collective capital as they are to a single entrepreneur. Co-operatives have met reluctance from banks, and have sometimes been refused credit primarily for these reasons.

Political and ideological support for them has brought special funds, grants and other help to offset these difficulties,[1] and they have been forced to find alternative ways of competing in the market. The basic need has been to increase productivity in line with other firms. With less funds at their disposal, co-operatives must often buy inferior machinery and accept poor quality premises. To remain competitive they must then reduce the costs of labour to a greater extent than other firms and work more intensively.

Internal Capital

The capital of a workers' co-operative can be divided into internal and external capital. Internal capital is composed of refundable capital – members' shares and loans – and non-refundable capital – profits held in reserves. The number of shares a member may own is limited by law to £5,000 maximum, but most workers' co-operatives forbid members to own any more than is needed for entry; namely one £1 share. Any firm using ICOM's model rules must adhere to this principle. To get round the dire financial problems at start-up, the founders and workers of ICOM firms have usually supplied loans in lump sums, or made loans out of wages. By contrast, most of the CPF co-operatives encouraged the maximum investment of both share and loan capital from the start, only reducing the pressure on members when reserves were built up to a satisfactory level. But in many of the ICOM and CPF co-operatives, plough-back of profits into the reserves has not been adequate to replace assets at inflated costs. Co-operatives need to build up their reserves more than other firms to offset the fact that shares must remain at par value with no capital appreciation. Plough-back has often been resisted by co-operators because it seems to them to imply a greater commitment to growth and profitability than to their social objectives.

The Collectives

The members of Green City, Marble Arch Intensive English, Drym Fabricators and The Builders' Collective all own one £1 share each. To cope with costs of stock, the founder members of Green City put £4,000 of their own into the venture. Green City is a wholefood wholesale firm whose members had previously worked in a wholefood shop in Glasgow, Grassroots Wholefood and Herbs, formed early in 1977. Later that year the Scottish Wholefood Collective was formed by Grassroots workers and members of other wholefood shops in the area. They decided a wholesale outlet was needed locally to reduce costs in the shops. The Grassroots group began wholesaling from the home of one member, and in September 1978 Green City – as the firm was called – moved to a new warehouse rented to them by the Scottish Development Agency. £2,000 of Green City's start-up capital came from profits made by Grassroots, and £2,000 was in personal loans from members.

Drym Fabricators of Onllwyn, South Wales, started with a £2,000 loan from three people. Subsequently, the firm's loan stock was built up by each of the 12 or so members contributing £5 a week. This money could not be taken out without notice being given, and then only 50 per cent could be withdrawn. The firm was set up in January 1978 to make steel fences and, as an enterprise workshop, received wages and 10 per cent overheads from the MSC. Its members took very seriously the problem of achieving viability by the time the MSC money ran out. However, after a year of trading, their reserves were too low to withstand the crisis caused by the steel strike from January 1980, when steel supplies became irregular and production levels dropped. The firm went into liquidation at the end of February that year.

Members of the Builders' Collective also pay weekly into a loan fund. From the £40–£45 a week they each earned at the end of 1978, 10 per cent was lent to the firm and 10 per cent of profits were put into a reserve. The enterprise was formed in April 1978 and renovates old houses in the Leeds area.

Conversions from Private Firms

Co-operatives which converted from private firms had few problems over internal capital. Scott Bader of Wollaston, a firm making polyester resins and other chemical products, was handed over to the workforce between 1951 and 1963 by its owner, Ernest Bader. The Scott Bader Commonwealth was formed to hold the company's share capital of £5,000, and from the beginning there were hefty reserves. In June 1951 they stood at £129,750 (including £50,000 of share capital); by 1973 they had risen to £1,887,194 and in 1978 totalled £3,396,989. There was no need for contributions from the workforce. (See Appendix IV for financial details of all conversions mentioned.)

Michael Jones followed in the same tradition. It was formed in 1968 by conversion and makes high-class jewellery. Its £2,000 share capital is held in the Michael Jones Community and again there were adequate reserves at start-up. By 1973 these had risen to £26,399 and by September 1977 they stood at £63,132. This is another ICOM firm in which members do not hold more than one share each or contribute loan capital.

After Ernest Bader's initial success with Scott Bader, he initiated the formation of another common ownership, Trylon. Formed in 1967, its primary objective was to develop techniques for the artistic application of the resins produced by Scott Bader. This was to be later supplemented by the production of canoe moulds for sale or hire, together with the necessary materials for home construction. The aim of the founder was first, to create a second common ownership; next, to develop the use of his companies' products for other than the existing commercial applications; and finally, to establish another sales outlet. The founder firm provided the initial funding, and when the venture 'took off' in 1969 further loans followed; two such loans, amounting to £10,000, were converted into 'funds' to be used for donations to social projects, overseas aid, and for the promotion of other common ownerships. A further £5,000 was given as a long term loan to be paid back from 1985. At March 1980, three fifths of this had already been repaid, some five years early.

In 1973 the protracted and costly negotiations to create Trylon Community Ltd, the charitable holding company, had been completed. Trylon was finally a common-ownership company; the original owners had successfully gifted their 200 shares to the work group. The total reserves amounted to £29,171. By 1978 these had risen to £63,806.

CPF Co-operatives

For the CPF co-operatives, members' shares and loans were a vital source of finance, particularly at the time of start-up when there were few opportunities for co-operatives to receive capital on favourable terms. They welcomed members from outside the firm from among supporters of co-operation, such as trade unions and local co-operative retail societies. Members provided both share and loan capital. Though variable, this source of funds enabled firms to buy their first premises, machinery and materials. Later, it was valuable in times of crisis and as a basis for borrowing. The tangible commitment from members represented by this individual capital, say the CPF firms, is still regarded by banks as convincing when they consider whether to lend a co-operative money.

Equity Shoes is the outstanding example of a CPF co-operative which has achieved success by continuously paying attention to the needs of the business. It was formed in 1886 after a dispute at a CWS factory, and has always made high-quality shoes. Many crises were weathered in the early days through prudent management and the commitment of the workers and others to its success. Shareholders were welcomed from outside the firm and by the 1890s there was a queue for membership. The workers' contributions were even more crucial. As J. H. Plumb commented:

> In the early days of any enterprise, there are sudden demands, unexpected emergencies. When these occurred, there was always some worker ready to find ten, twenty or even thirty pounds to invest in the business . . . The Society commenced to make shoes with a share capital of roughly two hundred pounds. By the time of the issue of the third quarterly and first working balance sheet it had been laboriously increased to £310 19s 2d; by the fourth quarter, £348 18s 6d. In the next six months, share capital almost doubled itself. By the end of 1888 it had accumulated to the extent of £1,112, besides reserve funds which were steadily growing. Membership amounted to 304; these included 142 co-operative societies, three trade unions; all the rest were workers or individual members. This was the highly encouraging result of eighteen months' work.[2]

By 1973 there were 2,358 shareholders who owned £24,714 shares; loans from workers amounted to £39,806 that year and reserves stood at £233,001. (See Appendix IV for financial details of all CPF co-operatives mentioned.) In 1977 the number of shareholders had fallen to 1,300 and share capital had dropped slightly to £22,952; members' loans, however, rose to £41,647, and reserves leapt to £667,105. Profits in that year amounted to £371,676.

Leicester Printers is another successful co-operative, though its profit levels are considerably lower than those of Equity Shoes. Formed in 1892, the firm has operated as a high-class printers, always having good-quality machinery. A high proportion of workers are members of the co-operative and this, together with outside members, has enabled the firm to maintain a high level of share and loan capital. In 1973 there was £44,462 worth of share capital, and £59,473 of loans. With membership falling by 51 to 311 in 1977, share capital remained almost static at £43,520, but loans were raised to £70,268. Although profits were only £24,480 in 1977, £200,000 was spent on equipment between 1976 and 1979.

A different picture is presented by Derby Printers. Set up in 1900, this has always been a general printing firm. Members' shares were never on the same scale as 'the Equity' or Leicester Printers. From the start a limit was set at £200 on the amount of shares each member could own. Outside members helped in the early days but, as retail societies in the area closed, they left the firm, and today there are none remaining. From the dwindling membership inside the firm, £4,571 shares were owned in 1973 and £4,072 in 1977. Members' loans in those years were tiny, at £962 and £624 respectively. The co-operative regrets its past policy of paying large bonuses out of profits and its failure to build up reserves. By 1979 new machinery was desperately needed but reserves were too low.

In one of the newer co-operatives, Chieftain Industries, shares were drawn from supporters in the community. This company was formed in 1970 by Tom McAlpine, a Scottish National Party candidate in the 1979 General Election, and manufactures heaters. McAlpine contacted 500–600 sympathisers to the co-operative idea from among socialists, the peace movement, the Campaign for Nuclear Disarmament, and presumably from his own party. For every £100 they put up, £5 was given to Chieftain Community, a trust fund, as the workers' share capital. By stipulating a limit on what an outsider could own, McAlpine ensured that the workforce had a larger volume of shares which they could use as a block vote to prevent outsiders from controlling the co-operative. £15,000 of share capital was raised by outsiders for themselves and £1,200 for the workers. This scheme avoided the necessity of raising shares directly from the workers, most of whom were young and on a low wage. The device of raising capital from the community is now gaining popularity in rural areas like the Highlands of Scotland, Eire and Wales.

Occasionally workers have used their redundancy pay to start a co-operative. JOL is currently trying to encourage this in an organised manner among the Corby steel workers. But usually such long periods have elapsed before a co-operative is formed that redundancy money has been swallowed up in the waiting time. The Meriden workers, for instance, had to live on this during their long occupation of the Triumph factory. Wandtronics workers were more fortunate. They were a group of men made redundant when their factory closed in Balham. With the help of Wandsworth Council they set up a co-operative producing electronic circuits on contract to larger firms. They used their redundancy pay to help convert a factory, and later this was reimbursed to the firm by the Council. However, the firm later collapsed.

External Capital
External capital has been taken to mean loans – other than from workers – and overdrafts. The need for external capital has increased for most firms as the capital costs of industry have risen. Co-operatives have had access to a number of sources. Occasionally they have raised loans from other co-operatives but more usually funds have come from special sources or the joint stock banks. Of the 40 co-operatives considered in this study, 28 have received external capital at one time or other. Often this had led to high gearing ratios, with regular repayments and high interest rates putting a severe strain on the workers to maintain profitability and regulate their cash flow. This is a particular problem for firms with loans which are only partially secured. They have nothing to fall back on in a crisis. But in many cases the hardship has been reduced by the favourable terms offered to them, and by grants from the state.

Of the 12 which did not receive any external capital at any time up to the end of 1979, six were enterprise workshops which were not fully fledged firms, and one relied on the MSC to pay most of its wage bill. Among the remainder is Derby Printers which has always studiously avoided bank loans; Cinnamon, a very small wholefood shop in Newcastle set up and run initially by members of the Divine Light Mission, followers of Guru Maharajgi; the Builders' Collective; *Leeds Other Paper*, an alternative fortnightly newspaper; and Co-operative Build in Connah's Quay, North Wales, which only lasted the four months between July and September 1978.

Co-operative Build was the only enterprise to have totally failed to raise a loan. Its members approached the Welsh Development

Agency for £2,000–£3,000 but were refused on the grounds that they were a service and the WDA funds were available only for manufacturing industry. They also approached ICOF and the Co-operative Bank without success. However, their biggest blow was probably the refusal of credit by the building suppliers. Some of the co-operative's members had been among the 'flying pickets' arrested in the building workers' strike at Shrewsbury in 1972, and it is possible that they were victims of discrimination on account of this.[3]

From the co-operatives studied it seems that the majority aim to operate with the minimum amount of loan capital. There are a number of reasons for this. For instance, their attitude to growth differs from that of a private firm. Landsmans of Buckden in Cambridgeshire, a co-operative converted from a private firm which hires out mobile industrial units, has reached what it considers to be an optimal size for its current operation and feels no incentive to grow. In others, like Trylon and Suma of Leeds (another wholesaler of wholefoods), growth was considered to be useful only to hive off new co-operatives. The anticipated difficulties of running a democratic workplace with a large number of members has frequently been expressed. The collectives, who prefer to operate in units of less than 20, have regularly pointed a questioning finger at Scott Bader with 350 employees in 1980.

Special facilities have been available to the new co-operatives from ICOF, the Co-operative Bank and local authorities, and heavy reliance has been placed on these. Without these sources, many of the smaller co-operatives – with their weaker capital structures – might not have survived.

Industrial Common Ownership Finance

ICOF was established as a subsidiary of ICOM in 1973 as a non-profit loan fund. It began with loans from Scott Bader and other supporters of co-operation. ICOF also acts as an agent to channel money from sympathisers into specified co-operatives. The funds from individuals and firms are still important, but ICOF's scale of operations expanded considerably when, in 1976, it was granted the status of a 'relevant body' under the ICO Act, and could draw on the £250,000 of grant made available over five years for on-lending to any registered co-operative in manufacturing industry possessing a certificate to show that it is a bona fide co-operative and a letter of support from the relevant trade union. Once a loan from this source has been repaid, ICOF can use the principle again, for either manufacturing or service co-operatives, as it chooses.

By the end of 1978 advances to borrowers were £128,733. Between 1973 and 1978 ICOF made 36 loans totalling £192,924, of which 23 were still outstanding at 30 April 1979, totalling £127,576. The number of loans made annually rose steadily to 14 in 1978, and during the whole of its life up to 1980 ICOF has only made two bad debts. This represents a percentage of 3.5 per cent, which is low by the standards of other financial institutions and shows how successful administration of its funds has been considering the difficulty of measuring the risk of lending to a co-operative.

It was intended that loans made from government grants would be small, although anything up to £50,000 would be considered. However, loans of over £7,500 had to receive the approval of the Secretary of State. He has performed this task by asking the Department of Industry and the Co-operative Development Agency for their advice. In practice ICOF's average loan has amounted to £7,000. Of the six loans made to co-operatives in the sample, only one was over the £7,500 ceiling. This was a £30,000 loan to Northampton Industrial Commonwealth, a plant hire, lorry hire and building company.

ICOF lends in the short to medium term (six months to six years), and interest rates are lower than conventional sources of finance (10 per cent early in 1980). Normally, interest is repayable twice yearly, and loan repayments can be made throughout the loan period or in one lump at the end. Loans are usually given for plant, equipment and working capital, and where possible, security is required, though this has sometimes been waived for new starts. The requirements for security are the same as for banks. ICOF asks for a mortgage or charge on assets and to have first call in the case of liquidation. If the co-operative looks as if it will survive, ICOF will make efforts to find security.

Commercial criteria are used to assess the risk of lending. Under the terms of the ICO Act, ICOF must satisfy itself that the project has a reasonable prospect of success. Some of the factors examined are the same as those a bank would consider, such as the financial history of the firm, cash flow forecasts, product development, the quality of management, the degree of personal financial commitment among members, the history of industrial relations, and proof of assets against which a debenture could be secured.

On some matters ICOF is even more rigorous. Applicants are

asked to provide a prospectus of market opportunities and, in the case of new starts, they must demonstrate firm links with a sponsor common-ownership enterprise, and the availability of suitably qualified and experienced advisers on financial and management issues.

On less tangible aspects, ICOF needs considerably different skills from that of a bank. The team spirit of a co-operative must be assessed, as must its will to succeed. This is perhaps a more challenging and unusual task compared with that of summing up the commitment of an individual entrepreneur who has probably invested substantial savings in a venture. Norman Lowe, a full-time officer for ICOF, discusses an application with one co-operator and assesses where the leadership exists and the likelihood of the leaders remaining with the firm. He tries to engender a feeling of responsibility among the applicants both to himself and to a sponsor.

Despite the help ICOM and ICOF may both give to applicants in preparing them to take on a loan, the co-operatives may still lack personal capital commitments and assets. Because it is ideologically committed to creating co-operatives, ICOF will lend in some of these cases at a higher risk than would a bank. Sometimes loans are given without security, and considerable flexibility of terms is offered.

ICOF loans are given by its board of trustees, elected by the ICOF membership, after applicants have presented their case in person. The burden of administering loans is carried out by Norman Lowe and his assistant. Although they draw low wages, the administrative costs are very high because of the small size of the loans made. They are estimated to be 18 per cent of the money loaned. This is still paid for by the Department of Industry under the ICO Act, together with a contribution from Scott Bader. It is hard to see how costs could be reduced by much unless the scale of operations is increased substantially.

Without a commitment to create co-operatives, no other institution could fund them in the same way. If co-operatives were treated like other firms it is possible that most of those receiving loans would be already well-established firms. The small, new starts would fall by the wayside. There is nothing uncommercial about ICOF's activities, but it does not lend to make money; it aims to create viable co-operatives and to assist existing co-operatives, and to succeed in this task it must lend at a higher risk. For its work to continue, subsidies are essential.

Other Sources of Finance

In 1978 the Co-operative Bank began a scheme to provide start-up capital to co-operatives. As a bank, the high administrative costs involved posed more of a problem. Since its funds derive from the deposits of retail societies and others, it cannot afford to take such high risks as ICOF. At first £1 was offered for every £1 put in by the co-operative's members. The bank was prepared to offer over-draft facilities and three- to seven-year loans at about 2 per cent below normal rates. It was looking for groups of 10–20 people wanting to start a new co-operative and prepared to put up £500–£1,000 each, and anticipated that most loans would fall within this range, although higher amounts would be considered.

The bank took the view that the commitment of members to their venture would be more forcibly expressed if they put up some loan capital of their own. But to many of the co-operators in collectives – in most need of favourable treatment – the availability of finance being offered appeared no more generous than that offered by any other bank. The scheme only reinforced the many prejudices already held against the Co-operative Bank. However, the spirit behind the move was supportive and indicated that more favourable terms would be given later on. This proved to be the case when a new co-operative, Caversham Closures, approached the Co-operative Bank and ICOF jointly for a loan to re-establish a bottle-top making business which had been closed by the owners. The bank and ICOF together agreed to lend about £30,000 of medium term finance, and the bank offered a large overdraft facility on top of that.

The only other special fund for co-operatives is the Commonwealth Development Fund of Scott Bader. This was set up to fund new common-ownerships and is now administered by ICOF, with Scott Bader's agreement on each case. Any loan from this fund is usually matched by ICOF. Normally the maximum loaned is £5,000 and the period of a loan is one year, though Sunderlandia received a loan of £10,000 from the fund.

In 1978 The Industrial and Commercial Finance Corporation, part of Finance for Industry, expressed an interest in funding co-operatives. It offered loans for a period of between five and 20 years, with a minimum of £5,000. Interest rates were to be as normal for banks, and ICFC would also take a participating interest (a percentage of the profits when they occurred, or rolled up over a period). ICFC would look for good growth prospects in firms coming to them for funds, and a delegated hierarchy of management responsibility, and would expect the person at the 'top' of this hierarchy to have an entrepreneurial flair and be well-rewarded for his or her responsibility. Security would be based on fixed assets. By 1980 no workers' co-operative had accepted a loan from ICFC.

From a commercial perspective, it is clear that ICFC did not devise this scheme for short-term financial gain. Although it would not be liable for tax on financial gains made in co-operatives registered under the I & PS Acts, the small sums likely to be made would hardly be worth its efforts. Large profits are rarely made in the workers' co-operative sector as a whole. ICFC is a member of the Action Resource Centre, which is described in Chapter 4. The bank, along with other large companies, has a longer term interest in promoting small ventures in the inner city and other declining areas. It is probable that the scheme was developed with this aim in mind and to show support for initiatives being taken by the then Labour Government to involve the public and private sectors jointly in revitalising decayed urban areas.

Occasionally co-operatives have received financial help from a charity or trust as a one-off action. Little Women (liquidated), for instance, received a loan from the Wates Foundation, Commonwork Trust, given interest free for two years. Little Women was a grocery shop in Sunderland run by seven women to provide a meeting point and child care facilities which were not otherwise available. The pay they received was extremely low, at 50p an hour in 1979 and, unable to undercut the supermarkets, they lost trade as the economic crisis deepened in the 1980s, and wound up while they could still afford to pay off their debts.

Similarly, funds have been received in other cases where more was involved than creating a viable co-operative, especially where jobs were made for young people or where firms were being set up to provide a service to community groups. Tyneside Free Press was given a grant by the Arts Council to help convert the basement of their building; Wirral Ceramics on Merseyside was given £200 by Merseyside Arts and £2,000 by a local trust, Ocean Fleet; Sunderlandia was lent £10,000 by the East Midlands Housing Association; and Calverts North Star Press in London, a printshop which deals mainly with the 'alternative' sector, was given a hire purchase 'loan' from the St Margaret's Trust to buy machinery. Occasionally the new co-operatives have been funded by conventional sources. Two of the more successful collectives have demonstrated their creditworthiness in the open market. Suma received a £5,000 overdraft facility from the National Westminster Bank, and Recycles – a co-operative selling, repairing and hiring bicycles in Edinburgh – took a £4,000 overdraft from the Bank of Scotland.

A Picture of Struggle

Overall, the young firms we have been discussing present a picture of struggle. They are very dependent on state funds channelled through local authorities and ICOF, and on the paternalist philosophy and development policy of Scott Bader. For these co-operatives, where members are reluctant or unable to commit their own savings to their business, the future is most insecure.

Only a general impression of their financial position can be given. Although they were all registered with the Registrar of Friendly Societies as limited liability companies, few had submitted annual returns by mid-1978. Of those that did, Calverts North Star Press apears the most successful. With a high gearing ratio at 82 per cent in 1977, this firm made a profit of £9,305, and its rate of return on capital, or profitability, was 17.7 per cent which is only 2 per cent below the Investors Chronicle average for 18 of the largest printing firms in 1977.

But even Calverts could not have achieved this without sacrifices being made by the workforce. When they started in 1977 the workers each paid themselves about £30 a week. By 1979, wages had risen to £65 for a 35-hour week or £78 for 42 hours, and the long-term objective was to achieve the national average wage, then at £100 a week. Wage levels are particularly low because some of their potential earnings go to subsidise community groups, campaigning organisations, and so on, who have no printing budgets.

They depend for much of their work on what John Berry, one member, called 'a solid core of customers who have appreciated what we are trying to do and prefer to give their material support to a co-operative'. In return, Calverts charge three different rates, depending on the type and financial position of the customer. Initially the firm applied for an MSC grant but was turned down because it did not comply with the MSC's rules. In retrospect John Berry said, 'We were glad we did not get a grant to pay our wages, because it meant we had to survive by our own efforts. We realised that we were a "business" which had commitments to its employees in terms of conditions and security of employment, wages, etc, and also to its customers in terms of speed, quality, etc'.

It seems that the low pay and poor working conditions in Calverts are partly explained by a deliberate underpricing policy in the firm. Many of the collectives are similarly affected. For example, Publications Distribution Co-operative, *Leeds Other Paper* and the wholefood co-operatives are all keen to keep prices as low as possible, having identified their customers as people who share their own values and who cannot afford high prices. In other cases, low pay is more directly the consequence of poor profitability. Green City of Glasgow, Little Women, Recycles and the Builders' Collective all pay low wages because it is extremely hard in their labour intensive fields to make good profits. They claim they have found 'a gap in the market' but this is questionable if no private firm would consider offering the same service because of its low profitability.

The collectives use their capital in different ways from private firms to survive. Their wish to practise equality as far as possible helps to keep costs down. Most have a policy of equal pay, based on the belief that each member puts equal effort into his or her work. Experience is not rewarded financially because, to quote Marble Arch Intensive English, 'it is just as hard to be a new member as an older member'. Management does not exist as a separate task in many of these enterprises, again reducing the temptation to reward the function with higher pay, as in private firms. Typically, the workers are under 30 and rarely over 35. Few have children, so the expense of caring for unproductive members of a household has not yet affected these co-operatives.

Work is often physically demanding. Tasks must be performed which in more profitable firms would be taken over by machines or would be made easier in modern buildings. Suma, for instance, had a two-storey warehouse when it was set up in 1975; working a 40-hour week for £24, members had to move 56lb loads of cereals, rice and flour manually between floors. Where machinery does exist it is usually second-hand. Green City, for example, bought machines cheaply from a closed CWS factory for its manufacturing operations. But second-hand machines break down more frequently and, in some cases, are less efficient. To remain competitive, workers have often found it necessary to put in unpaid hours of overtime.

Less of a Problem
For the conversions and the CPF co-operatives raising external finance has been less of a problem. However, this did not make them immune from financial difficulties. Bad management and a slump in

sales caused by the recession of the mid-1970s resulted in problems for the conversion, Michael Jones. This firm expanded in 1976 by opening up a new shop just when VAT was increased from 12 per cent to 25 per cent on luxury goods like jewellery. In that year the firm had £83,959 of loan capital which, by September 1977, had risen to £106,142. The gearing ratios of those years were 101 per cent and 110 per cent respectively because the co-operative had deliberately 'frozen' share capital at £2,000. But reserves had been built up only to £44,695 and £63,132 so that the firm could not expand and at the same time withstand the slump in the market. Losses were made in both years and the co-operative was forced to make a number of redundancies before recovering.

Landsmans was also hit by the recession while trying to expand into manufacturing and had to close this side of the business, concentrating on a more specialist market. In February 1977 profits sank to £1,535 while loans were up at £26,948, and reserves were at £10,593. The firm survived by reducing the workforce from 36 to 12 and by selling off its manufacturing plant which had risen some seven or eight times in value.

By the mid 1970s the CPF co-operatives had 50 or more years behind them. Most had built up a safety net of reserves and a large number of shares. The financial problems they have faced are nowhere near as severe as those of the collectives. But only Equity Shoes and Walsall Locks could confidently look forward to a successful future. In this respect they are no different from other firms of under 200 workers, but it does appear that their capital structure has made management a bigger task.

It is possible to examine the gearing ratio of these firms to get an indication of their borrowing patterns since their rules allow them to imitate more closely the capital structure of a private firm. Derby Printers has a gearing ratio of nil as it has never had a bank loan so far. But it has failed to build up share capital and reserves and, now that loans are needed, it is in a weak position to borrow. By contrast, Equity Shoes which has also resisted loan capital so far, is in a very healthy position to borrow, should the need arise.

Queen Eleanor, Leicester Printers and Walsall Locks have all depended on bank loans for growth. Their gearing ratios – at 21.3 per cent, 29 per cent and 50 per cent – are not high for the industries they represent. The average for the 18 clothing firms in 1977 was 40.8 per cent, and for printing was 50.1 per cent. Two of these firms have expressed a desire to borrow more, but it is likely that they will have to be more cautious when financing development since members' share and loan capital is increasingly hard to raise.

Investment and Economies

Many workers in these co-operatives treat their firm like any other. Their wages, though average for the work, are low, and they are reluctant to commit a portion of these or their bonuses to the firm. Most have taken up their posts with little concern for the co-operative nature of the business. New rules have been introduced to build up share capital and to prevent shares from diminishing too quickly as members leave or die. Walsall Locks, until the early 1970s, allowed members to withdraw all their shares when they left the firm. Now the firm's circumstances are taken in account in deciding how soon withdrawals can be made.

Queen Eleanor was the last co-operative to pay a bonus to the co-operative societies which were members, but withdrew this facility ten years ago at a time of acute financial difficulty. By 1974 the firm was forced to close two of its factories and make 50 redundancies. Recently a bank loan was raised but shares were not high enough to back the loan adequately, and the retail society members had to come to the rescue by guaranteeing the loan. In addition, in 1968 a rule change was made doubling the amount of bonus that had to be used to buy shares. It is now a rule that when members have £5 of shares and before they have £50 worth amassed they can take home only half of their bonus; until they have £100 they can take home two thirds; and after that additions to their share capital are voluntary.

Workers in Leicester Printers must put the first £40 of their bonus into share capital under the co-operative's rules. In this firm, membership is high with 60 of the 80 employees being shareholders in 1978. However, contributions to share capital are not rising fast enough; it has remained between £44,000 and £50,000 for the last 15 years. The firm had plans to expand into litho-printing but needed a sounder financial structure to be confident about its ability to raise productivity, increase profits and make the loan repayments.

The old co-operatives have also had to save on the costs of wages, machinery and buildings. Although the equal pay principle is not practised, wage differentials are narrower than in private firms. While the lowest paid usually receive slightly above the average for the job (when bonuses are added), managers get substantially less than the going rate. If their posts are filled by people with a strong commitment to the co-operative ideal, this practice can be perpetuated and money is saved. In Walsall Locks and Equity Shoes there are managers who have worked their way up in the firm over many years.

Where machinery is concerned, the CPF co-operatives closely resemble the collectives. Second-hand machines have, in all but Leicester Printers, been commonplace. The decision to invest in a more up-to-date model is always a critical one. The co-operatives cannot afford to slip too far behind their competitors. Throughout its life, Equity Shoes has kept a watchful eye on the local CWS factory which also sold shoes to the local retail societies. Since this factory was known to keep abreast of change, the 'Equity' measured its own pace by comparison.

Conclusion

This chapter concludes that inadequate capital from inside and outside are a major source of concern for co-operatives. Of course, the problems of financing growth are felt acutely by many other small and medium sized businesses. But for co-operatives, which have a peculiar relation to capital, the problem itself is different. The members can only provide limited funds because they are precluded by co-operative law, in most cases, from buying unlimited shares, and in the case of ICOM firms they can only buy one £1 share each. Money raised externally must be in the form of loan capital and there are legal limitations on the rate of interest co-operatives can pay on loans. On top of this, with a smaller asset base than most companies, they may have difficulty raising the loans needed.

The co-operators themselves are not always aware of their contradictory position in the capital market; they regard adequate funding as clearly essential but tinged with immorality and the profit motive. Unless they can take a pragmatic approach to balancing ideological and commercial objectives, and unless they are supplied with capital on favourable terms by sympathetic organisations, it seems the sector's growth will be severely restricted.

4 Workers at the Helm

Management and Labour

There are other problems besides funding which may be keenly felt in a co-operative. These can be broadly termed 'management' problems. Again it can be claimed that the owners of small firms may battle for years to get their businesses off the ground, with two or three people trying to cope with every aspect of the financial, sales and production operations. But again, because of the difference in ideology and ownership, there can be no direct comparison between a co-operative's situation and that of a private venture.

Co-operatives are formed by groups of like-minded people who may not have a full range of skills between them. On top of this, the low pay managers are often expected to accept makes it hard to attract the right people to these posts. In other cases, the founder members – keen to see their visions materialise – sometimes dislike the progress being made and behave autocratically in the eyes of the workforce, interfering with the democratic process. In yet other cases, people are taken on who are less committed to co-operation than the rest of the workforce and are unwilling to make the sacrifices needed to achieve commercial viability.

Against these problems, co-operative workers have benefited from taking a greater share in running their business. Many have learnt how a firm works in its entirety and have contributed in meetings of the workforce and in elected committees to broad policy questions, gaining confidence that they, through their own efforts, can compete with private firms. For co-operators in the collectives, management skills have often been learnt on the job.

When workers join a co-operative they sell their labour power to their own firm. Since it operates in the market place, the co-operative must produce the equivalent of surplus value. Although the co-operative's aims are not capitalist, it has to set prices and wages, measure productivity and provide other entitlements to the work-force in direct and constant comparison with private firms. Pay and conditions are lowered from the average only by acceptance of the members and with the aim that the co-operative becomes profitable.

It is the workers who decide how their firm is managed and how it can act both in terms of capital and as a co-operative. In this they are bound to exploit themselves. However, the term 'exploitation' does not mean the same as for a worker elsewhere. In return for any daily hardship, many co-operatives have a better chance of giving job security, of valuing and making use of creative talents and allowing members to control their working lives.

In a sense, management and labour are one and the same thing. In the collectives, management is rarely a separate task. In other co-operatives, managers are appointed by the members or an elected workers' committee, and everyone can play some part in decision-making. In the larger co-operatives operating complex industrial or marketing processes, skills have become more clearly defined and the management function is more distinct. In the sample studied, no co-operative of over 20 workers, with the exception of Marble Arch, has avoided the need for specialisation, and where the workers in a small co-operative are mostly unskilled, as in enterprise workshops, a manager has been needed.

The Right Blend of Skills
The first problem has been to get the right mix of skills. Co-operatives formed from large occupations usually keep their shop-floor skills, but managers move on to jobs elsewhere. Meriden Motorcycles, for example, suffered from gaps in its management. Temporary help was given by GEC and GKN (Guest, Keen and Nettlefolds), and Geoffrey Robinson, MP for Coventry North West, has acted as the co-operative's unpaid chief executive from the start in 1975.

Dowlais Knitwear (now called Pandy Fashions) of Merthyr Tydfil had problems with production skills as well as with manage-ment. The co-operative was set up as an enterprise workshop, following the closure of a Kayser Bondor (Courtaulds) factory which caused several hundred redundancies. Most of the 12 women workers were making tights before they started at Dowlais in 1977, but decided they would find better outlets at the CMT (cut, make and trim) end of the trade, finishing blouses. They had to learn the skills for the job from Violet Pugh, the only woman with previous experience of the work. When more workers were taken on, the co-operative looked for women with the appropriate skills. After two years when the MSC money had run out, the firm was breaking even, but productivity was still not thought to be high enough. The co-operative suffered additionally from poor management. The first manager left, having failed to build enough outlets for the blouses. The second arrived in April 1979, a man also made redundant at Kayser Bondor. By 1980 he had established a three month order book, but the future looked far from rosy.

Enterprise workshops are occasionally vulnerable to opportunist leadership. The actions of one middle-class woman created bitter disillusion among the working-class workers – mainly women – at Brookhouse Ampersand, outside Denbigh, in North Wales. She had formed the co-operative in December 1976 with unrealistic ideas of making exclusive ladies' fashion clothes for the wholesale trade and export markets. Despite getting finance from the MSC and ICOF, extensive publicity from the local press and a fashion show at the Intercontinental Hotel in London, nothing was sold and the company fell deeply into debt. It was not until that stage that the workers discovered they were part of a co-operative! Dismissing their manager, they tried desperately to retrieve the situation. But without any business skills in the rag trade they had to learn from scratch how to find work, taking orders from any quarter, 'doing straight run production work making anything from pyjamas to dresses for other companies'.[1] They took wage cuts and struggled on, preferring any work to the dole. In February 1979 the firm finally collapsed.

Few members of collectives start with any business experience, but some have attended courses run by ICOM, Commonwork and others on various management tasks like book-keeping, accounting, marketing and internal democracy. They recognise the importance of these in a successful business, though they also believe traditionally highly rewarded jobs should be demystified and shared among the workforce. Job rotation used to be favoured, but has since been abandoned in most cases because of its detrimental effect on profits.

The administrative jobs are rotated in Marble Arch. These posts are elected from among the teachers and include the director of studies, registrar/secretary, book-keeper, publicity person, accommodation person and student counsellor. They are changed every six months because the workers believe it is valuable for all members to understand each other's work. Efficiency and profits have

improved and, in 1978/79, turnover was £136,000 and was anticipated to rise to £200,000 in 1979/80.

Similarly, where the production skills are relatively simple, such
as in Little Women, they can be rotated without affecting productivity. For the seven members of this firm, rotation of jobs introduced
flexibility into the business which was valuable since the women did
not all work in the shop at the same time. It was also valued for
giving confidence and all-round competence to the working-class
women, previously housebound with their children.

Publications Distribution Co-operative (PDC) also practises some
rotation of jobs and tries to avoid specialisation of work. Members
share management responsibilities, for instance, breaking down
financial tasks such as VAT, PAYE and wages between them, and
dividing up other work so that each person covers one region
(including foreign countries), and deals with all the distribution
aspects for periodicals, magazines, pamphlets, books, etc. for one or
more subject area. While this method of working demands greater
co-ordination among the workforce, it creates a better sense of
collective responsibility.

Commitment and Incentive

Where managers are essential to a co-operative they are usually paid
at uncompetitive rates. Large differentials in pay are considered
against the spirit of co-operative effort, and this is often resolved by
'underpaying' the managers rather than boosting the wages of other
workers above the average. However, this policy has created
difficulties for both enterprise workshops and the CPF co-operatives.
Wandsworth Council, for instance, searched for a long time for
someone to head the MSC-funded Wandtronics, described in
Chapters 3 and 6. Eventually, a retired manager was found and
persuaded to join.

It is usual among the CPF co-operatives for managers to be found
from the ranks of the workforce. In Equity Shoes, the secretary,
Sidney Pepper and the manager, Fred Dean, both joined the concern
as school-leavers in 1935 at the age of 14. Arthur Rose, the 67-
year-old current manager of Walsall Locks, also joined from school.
He was the firm's accountant before being asked to take on his
present job in 1969, and 'is only the fourth general manager in the
co-operative's 106-year history. He stepped into a minor crisis for
the lock-makers but pruning and streamlining of production

brought about a steady improvement, culminating in last year's record turnover'.[2]

The manager of Derby Printers said a similar pattern had evolved there, but commented that, although there are clear advantages in a manager understanding the firm and its co-operative principles, it is harder for such a person to keep discipline. Sometimes there is no-one suitable inside the firm and outsiders must be hired. This has happened in Leicester Printers but some management recruits have not fitted in with the peculiar nature of the business. More recently the firm was fortunate in finding a financial manager who was also an idealist.

Co-operative managers' accountability to the elected board, or workers' committee, makes their job particularly difficult. They need the trust of the workforce to have freedom in making day-to-day decisions, but to get this they must also be self-critical. The manager of Leicester Printers, Gerald Fletcher, said members were well aware that the board, however interested in its role, could never have enough detailed information about management tasks. The workers have to feel they are not being mystified by facts.

There is another labour problem which affects the CPF co-operatives and enterprise workshops. Both have employed people more interested in a job than industrial democracy. The problem did not exist in the early days of the older co-operatives. Leicester Printers, for example, helped to pioneer the 40-hour week, two weeks' holiday and other fringe benefits. But today its workers see few advantages in joining the firm. They rarely identify with the early struggles of the enterprise and see little point in contributing to the firm's decision making.

This view was echoed in Equity Shoes, Queen Eleanor and Derby Printers which all have difficulty in finding skilled labour. With some 2,000 vacancies for printing work in the area, skilled printers prefer to work in larger firms than the printing co-operatives because they have a wider range of machinery and the work is less hard. In both Derby and Leicester Printers, workers in 1978 had to compete through their physical efforts with other firms where machinery often replaced muscle power. Lack of interest in co-operation has meant membership has decreased in Derby Printers and Equity Shoes, reducing the vital share capital needed. Even where membership is still high, interest in co-operation has waned. In Leicester Printers the rule that board members can serve for only five years has been relaxed because of a lack of applicants.

Perhaps more serious are the problems of membership that some co-operative enterprise workshops have tackled. Enterprise workshops are small co-operative ventures funded by the Manpower Services Commission primarily to create jobs. (See Chapter 6). They have coped with more than a disinterest in co-operative principles. The workers, drawn straight from the lists of the unemployed, have included a high proportion of young people with no skills, no previous job experience and no long term expectations of employment beyond the MSC funding. The effects of petty thieving in some of these ventures were exaggerated because only 10 per cent on top of wages were paid by the MSC for materials and overheads. But the lack of discipline created more worries because the long term viability of the co-operatives depended on the workers learning quickly and working efficiently. While most sponsors wanted to employ the maximum number of trainees to supervisors, this proved a difficult policy to carry out.

According to Louise Ellman, Clogora in Skelmersdale has experienced these problems. This was despite the fact that the workforce was deliberately chosen to include a mixture of skilled and unskilled, young and older workers, management and labourers. However, the maximum number of apprentices were taken on, at a ratio of one to one skilled worker. At first the firm's manager thought no supervisors would be needed but, finding little motivation among the workforce, he later added more managerial staff.

Co-operation in Letter and Spirit
In the first instance a co-operative must be equipped with the right skills, whether they are for management tasks or shop floor jobs. But for a co-operative to function according to its principles, each worker must respect the value of each job and recognise every member's right to join in the decision-making on broad policy matters. According to the International Co-operative Alliance, and as agreed by all its member countries, there are six basic principles that every co-operative should follow (these are listed in the Introduction, see page 3). For an enterprise to be accepted as a co-operative by the Registrar of Friendly Societies or by the Secretary of State as eligible for government loans, these principles have to be adopted as a minimum requirement. Each of the co-operatives in the sample studied had done one or more of the following: registered under the I & PS Acts; received government loans; qualified for acceptance as ICOM members; or intended to be bona fide co-operatives.

However, there is more at stake than the principles. The spirit of co-operation can, in the new ventures, permeate the whole work-force or emanate from a few individuals who believe co-operative actions can be taught. Or else the co-operative form may be offered by outsiders. Experience has shown that commercial success is more likely where both a sense of collective commitment runs deeply in every worker, and where the future of the enterprise means jobs.

At this point two distinctive strands of the movement should be separated, the collectives and others. The class nature of each gives them a different ability to survive. Workers in the collectives are far less vulnerable in a personal capacity. Many are middle-class, with personal access to professional help, with educational qualifications that give them opportunities to find alternative employment, and sometimes a safety net in their families, should they fail. The ideology behind their efforts is of outstanding importance to them. They are more free to experiment with new democratic forms. They have a better chance of surviving but it matters less if they fail.

For most working-class co-operators, by contrast, co-operative ideology is of secondary importance to the wish for employment in a harsh economic environment. Without the co-operative they would be on the dole, or in a worse situation such as in home-working activities. Once they have formed a co-operative they value the principles because they allow the workers to determine their own future. And that means commercial viability, however stretched the rules may have to be. So democracy within a co-operative is vital for different reasons, whether they are collectives or other types. Once a sense of an employer existing in their midst creeps in, workers will begin to act in defensive ways. With morale slumping and a sense of helplessness, productivity can only fall.

Apparent Exceptions

The fortunes of the conversions tend to distort what has just been said. While they are criticised for being not truly co-operative, being run by paternalist leaders and generating suspicion among the workforce about their leaders' motives, they have all survived. But the tiny number formed this way in this and the last century puts them in a different category altogether. They must be regarded as very far removed from the labour movement inspiration behind co-operatives which can be claimed for all the others. It is no use turning worshipfully to the colourful history of Scott Bader. This is a highly successful business, with a profit of £1,398,640 in 1979, seven subsidiaries, and 350 workers. The momentum generated in its 'private' days in terms of entrepreneurial spirit, invention, and respect for hierarchy and customers, has carried the democratic experiment along as a rich embellishment.

What the conversions do suffer from is called the 'founder member problem'. On more than one occasion the founders have behaved in an autocratic manner offensive to the workers. The history of Scott Bader before it became a co-operative was long and conventional and engendered so much respect among the workforce that Ernest Bader's ideas, increasingly more eccentric in his old age, were usually debated and his presence tolerated under worker-ownership. When Ernest Bader retired in 1966 he left his son, Godric Bader, as Chairman of the Board for life, indicating that power was never really passed to the workers. The firm has a very complicated democratic structure which tends to defuse conflict and makes it hard to see exactly where decisions are being made.[3]

In his book, *The Case for Workers' Co-ops*, Robert Oakeshott, himself a pioneer of Sunderlandia, comments on the characteristics of Trylon, the offshoot of Scott Bader. In many respects Trylon resembles its parent, he says. Its constitution is almost exactly the same as that of Scott Bader, and in other ways too, the values of Ernest Bader were stamped firmly on this company. For instance, they could be seen in 'its structure, its small size and implied commitment to "small is beautiful", the nature of its origin, the character of its first manager, Roger Sawtell [and] its products'[4] – all of which are likely to make the firm 'have more appeal to people with middle-class outlooks than with traditional working-class attitudes'.

These claims seem hard to justify. The smaller size of this co-operative made it easier for the 28 workers to understand its democratic structure. The founder member resigned his post and the whole workforce interviewed prospective candidates for his replacement. All the candidates on the shortlist held Christian beliefs but this reflected the values of many people in the firm. In fact the co-operative runs by Christian as well as co-operative principles: for example, there is no Sunday working except for commercial expediency. Michael Angerson, the second general manager, admits that the two-tier structure with its interrelating committees, board of directors and trustees was clumsy. But at the time no alternative existed and to change would be both difficult and costly. There was no lack of interest in discussions, and participation has increased in the firm.

While criticising the 'high-minded' character of Scott Bader and Trylon, Oakeshott himself demonstrated a similar founder member's attitude to Sunderlandia. The firm was started with a structure permitting no permanent hold on power by the promoters. As he says, 'the constitution was informed by the democratic, libertarian, Left tradition'.[5] When the workers did finally take over membership of the board, excluding the promoters, and when at the same time the co-operative faced grave difficulties over productivity, Oakeshott remembers feeling 'in the helpless position of someone who has moral responsibility but no authority'.[6]

Lessons from History

Some of the enterprise workshops and the co-operatives being formed by local authorities are, perhaps, the least democratic. Again it is emphasised that this matters from the point of view of their survival. The combination of the democratic ideals among their sponsors and the rules of the MSC governing its funding were responsible for their 'peculiar' emergence in the history of co-operation. It is a lot to expect that the workers in these enterprises will quickly grasp the concept of co-operative democracy when few have had experience of private firms or of any work at all. The promotional bodies have welcomed the job creation projects but have done little to influence the way they are set up.

Co-operative history has taught the movement surprisingly little. The variety of co-operative types today has induced a bemused and unassertive attitude to what will work and what will probably fail. It seems irresponsible to allow so many tiny firms to spring up on government subsidies which are so vulnerable that a puff of wind will blow them away, leaving their workers disillusioned with frozen hopes. The economic crisis has produced the means to set up co-operatives more easily than ever before with the aid of government funds. But it is arguable that the co-operative movement should take a more responsible view of what is happening instead of opening up a developing sector to well-intentioned opportunism. The will of the people who are in control of their work is a vital ingredient to co-operatives' survival. Goodwill from outside is no real substitute.

If the workers must take the major responsibility for their own future, they often need advice on particular aspects of their trade and benefit from the lessons learnt by other co-operatives which have evolved a democratic structure to suit them. Help has been available from many sources. Of course, it is partisan in that those offering advice have their own objectives in encouraging co-operatives.

Advice and Assistance

In the last ten years ICOM has been the dominant source of advice on legal matters, wanting to steer new firms onto a common-ownership path. From the sample studied, most of the ICOM co-operatives had received help in registering, but in many cases, contact had ceased after that. ICOM has also offered its members a range of courses, and now runs Beechwood College, an educational institute. But the problem of finance has always been a constraint. The new college was expensive to convert and lacks sufficient tutors. For the ICOM co-operatives themselves, the train fares to Leeds and the time away from work often prohibit them from attending. To a lesser extent the regional branches give guidance to new ICOM co-operatives, and advisers have been supplied through a central register of talents to individual firms.

More recently local authorities, together with CDGs and the central CDA, have begun to play an important role in this field, being available on the spot to co-operatives and able to give a more continuous service. Where a local authority by itself sets up a co-operative the officers of the council may be able to supply most of the entrepreneurial skills in the start-up period. This will be described more fully in Chapter 6. The CDA has found its most sympathetic response from local authorities and, at a fee, undertakes feasibility studies for co-operatives within their boundaries. By calling on the CDA's expertise in marketing, for instance, the local authority can supplement the range of advice that can be offered to new or existing co-operatives. Although local councils and the CDA have different reasons for supporting co-operatives, both are equally concerned to make co-operatives viable businesses. The CDA, however, can offer expertise on a wider range of matters than councils by themselves. After 18 months' experience, its officers could tackle problems of co-operative structure as well as those of a commercial nature.

Another source of assistance has been the private sector itself. The motivation behind bodies like the Action Resource Centre (ARC), local enterprise trusts (LETs), the London Enterprise Agency (LENTA) and individual large firms varies according to the co-operative. The member firms of ARC 'offer expertise – through secondment from businesses and industry – to projects and initiatives which come under the heading of WORK'.[7] ARC explains its philosophy by saying 'It is a person's right to use one of his basic skills (to make an effort) for the benefit of himself, his family and his community. No community can be healthy long-term, either materially or socially, if the vast majority of its members are not committed to the principle of putting in at least as much effort as is needed to earn the reserves they draw out'.[8]

ARC, LETs and LENTA

In November 1977, four years after ARC was formed by a small group of senior businessmen from major companies, it was supported by 173 firms or organisations, including Barclays Bank, BP, Cadbury Schweppes, GEC, GKN, ICI, Lewisham Council, Marks & Spencer, and Scott Bader. ARC offers a free independent service to companies which wish to second people to community projects, acting as a 'broker'. It offers specifically management expertise to small firms, treating any business problems a firm may have – whether a co-operative or not – as management problems.

No help has been given by ARC to the co-operatives in the sample, but there are a number of cases where co-operatives have benefited this way. The House of Lambeth, for instance, a MSC-funded project making wooden items like bread boards and cutlery trays on contract to larger firms, was assisted for a year by an executive from Rank Xerox. A planning, operations and support manager, he was responsible for finance, marketing and production, and for fostering and establishing links with a Training College, the local Employment Office and local business. The MSC provided £70,000 to the scheme, £12,500 was donated from private enterprises, and a training course was run for the workers by the London Furniture College. A finance manager was also seconded to the enterprise by BP for two days a week.[9] The management of the House of Lambeth and personnel from the Lady Margaret Hall Settlement, which also assists the project, intend that it will become a co-operative. This is the only option available since it will not be profitable enough to attract a private investor when its grant runs out.

For the large firms involved, secondment is useful for several reasons. It gives young executives a chance to broaden their skills and prove their ability in a challenging situation; it also gives the firms an opportunity to hive off unwanted staff – where the alternative of redundancy would be costly – into community projects. The firms benefit from this policy over the long term because it improves their relations with government, helps to reduce tension within the community created by mounting unemployment and helps to widen the country's economic base by creating alternative sources of wealth and taxation, ultimately increasing living standards and purchasing power. All this adds up to a long term commercial objective.

There are a number of LETs which operate in a similar way. These are groups of large and small firms in a particular area which, together with the local councils and other organisations like colleges . of further education, are collectively offering assistance to small-scale enterprises, including co-operatives. The Community of St Helen's Trust is one such example, formed in 1978 and backed by Pilkington Brothers, local businesses and local authorities. Large firms like Pilkingtons are becoming involved in these initiatives because they are conscious of doing nothing to create jobs themselves. In fact, one quarter of the jobs in St Helen's would have been lost when a £25 million new technology development was introduced into the glassworks, had the unions not negotiated to reduce working hours.

In London, LENTA was also formed in 1978 and launched its own social programme with seven firms at the helm which were heavily involved in London's economy: Shell, BP, British Oxygen, IBM, Marks & Spencer, Tesco and Finance for Industry. The scheme was formed in response to Peter Shore's inner city policy of 1976 which encouraged a greater involvement by the private sector in the regeneration of inner areas. Shore had invited the chairmen of the largest multinationals in Britain to a dinner in Downing Street to discuss his proposals. The companies decided collectively to set up an organisation which would offer business expertise to small firms and projects. London was chosen to start this experiment because it so obviously needed help of this kind and because the manpower resources of the multinationals were concentrated in the capital. LENTA has been run on a low profile with very little publicity, suggesting its political and commercial importance for the firms involved.

The Skelmersdale and Fife Experiments
One of the more promising methods of developing strong co-operatives which do not suffer constant uncertainty is to form a linked

system of co-operatives with access to many central resources. This had been the aim of JOL since its inception. The idea was based on the Mondragon system in Spain where a central bank provides capital and all kinds of advice to the co-operatives. JOL has not yet found a way of generating central funds, but a number of activists in the labour movement in Skelmersdale have begun one experiment of this kind.

The Skelmersdale scheme was provoked by massive redundancies at Thorn and Courtaulds in 1976. Unemployment at that time was around 25 per cent in the town. First, a textiles co-operative was suggested to help regenerate the economy for a population bitterly reliving the Depression. An action committee was formed of Courtauld's union representatives, members of the textile unions and county council members. With the help of the Department of Industry, a feasibility study was undertaken to assess the viability of such a co-operative. Although it looked possible, the co-operative would only have created 300 jobs, so another scheme was devised.

In 1977 a holding company was set up to foster a number of co-operatives. Clogora Woodcraft Co-operative, Cotastone and Hawkesbury had, by 1979, grown out of this experiment. Clogora, employing 39 staff by the Spring of 1978, began by renovating school desks for Lancashire County Council, but hoped to move on into more profitable activities such as antique and garden furniture making, with the co-operative retail societies as a major outlet. For the first two years the MSC paid the wages in this 'enterprise workshop'. It is too early to know whether the firm has successfully survived the transition as an unsubsidised business (see Chapter 6).

Among the founder members of this job creation effort were Louise Ellman, chairperson of Lancashire County Council's Labour Group, and James Mason, her predecessor, president of the Blackburn Co-operative Society and CWS board member. Alongside the holding company a trust fund was formed to act as a watchdog. Its board of directors comprised representatives from the TUC, the Co-operative Union, and the founder members of the scheme. The idea was that surplus generated by individual co-operatives was to be channelled through the holding company to regenerate old co-operatives and develop new ones.

A similar approach was taken by Fife Regional Council. In 1977 the careers officer, John Morrison, generated interest in co-operatives among the council when he first produced a scheme to assist their formation. His scheme was to set up Fife Enterprises, a limited liability holding company without share capital, which would initiate the establishment of co-operatives, administer loan finance and provide business management skills and other help. Fife Enterprises was to have 500 members, these being the council and the co-operatives as they were formed. It would act as a revolving loan fund,[10] lending at bank rate plus up to 2 per cent, with 20 per cent profits ploughed back into the holding company to set up new co-operatives, and 60 per cent re-invested in the co-operatives.

The project foundered through the scepticism shown by officials in the Scottish Development Agency and by the Director of Finance. After pressure to continue was exerted locally and nationally, a compromise was suggested: that the parent company should be dropped and only a few co-operatives formed. But John Morrison felt the protection of Fife Enterprises was needed for the co-operatives to succeed.

A second scheme emerged in 1979, again coming from John Morrison, and this time it got off the ground. Inwork was formed as a company limited by guarantee. Its five board members were all experts in various fields of business: a project development specialist from a GEC college, an economist, a publicity and personnel manager, a specialist in product design and evaluation, and a property expert. The Council – with a much reduced role – agreed in June 1979 to give Inwork a grant of £33,000 under the 2p rate provision. Inwork was to act as an umbrella company which set up subsidiaries of three kinds: limited liability companies which aimed to make large profits quickly; trusts employing 50 per cent handi-capped people, which were 51 per cent owned by Inwork and 49 per cent by the workers; and co-operatives. Profits from the first type would be used to assist and start up co-operatives and trusts, and 25 per cent would be ploughed back into Inwork as loans for the subsidiaries.

Again, it was hoped funds could be raised from the EEC, the Department of Industry, etc. Tax would be avoided by group accounting devices and by using profits to buy fixed assets as security against future borrowing. Loans would be at favourable interest rates. Product ideas from the previous scheme would be used. Also, local colleges would provide help and it was hoped the GEC involvement would generate contracts for work. It was felt that a lot of contract work would be available while the electronics industry changed over to micro-processing techniques during the 1980s.

Wandsworth Council has also been heavily involved in building a mechanism for funding and advising co-operatives. The Wandsworth Enterprise Development Agency, formed in 1979, will be described in more detail in Chapter 6. Apart from the community co-operatives, so far these are the only examples of schemes to protect co-operatives, particularly in their vulnerable, early stages of life. But they may form prototypes for the CDGs, eager to set up local funds using the community's resources and to employ full-time advisers. The principle behind these experiments is not to create unprofitable companies which are subsidised by the public purse. Commercial viability will be sought as quickly as possible, but in the meantime co-operatives are seen to be at a grave disadvantage in the market, where the small firms' sector as a whole rests in a fragile state. It is too early to assess the results of the schemes in operation. But the protection offered to co-operatives by the centralisation of resources and the commitment to group survival must surely give them a greater chance of succeeding.

However, there is one major ingredient missing from the Skelmersdale and Fife ventures which puts a question mark over their future. Both grew outside the mainstream of the workers' co-operative movement and were invented by union leaders, councillors and a careers officer, in response to mounting unemployment. The stimulus did not come from the workers themselves. In Skelmersdale morale is low among the workers, who have been offered jobs but on low pay and in semi-skilled work. Where the co-operative idea is foisted on men and women expecting to work under organised trade union conditions, it is hard for them to take it on board without a degree of scepticism. The workers are used to selling their labour, not a product.

5 Producing for Capital

How to Proceed?

At first glance, there seems to be a wide range of goods and services produced by workers' co-operatives today. Co-operatives form a sector producing quality women's shoes, household radiators, motorcycles, car locks and chemicals, selling expensive jewellery and hiring building plant. At the other end of the market there is office cleaning, cut, make and trim, printing, wholefood retailing and school desk repair. Does this range of goods and services imply that co-operatives can break into capital-intensive industries? Or are there just idiosyncratic exceptions in an otherwise labour-intensive field of activity? With so many new co-operatives being set up now by promotional bodies and local authorities, the question of what they should do is a crucial one.

The apparent diversity results from a number of factors including the way co-operatives are formed, their capital structure, their access to funds and the character of their labour force. All these affect the range of products and services that co-operatives can provide. A close examination reveals a sector where growth is mainly in labour intensive fields and where competition is high and large profits are hard to make. Goods and services provided are usually cheap, and are sold to people and industries who cannot or will not pay more. The most successful co-operatives are those which have developed specialist lines. Co-operatives are emerging in a declining economy where spending power is reduced and where technological changes in industry are introduced alongside, and are dependent on, sweated trades.

But the promoters of co-operation are still overwhelmed by the desire to build a strong sector of the economy which can successfully challenge private firms. They also want to shift the labour movement from its faith in municipal enterprise and nationalisation to a belief in the co-operative commonwealth. The limitations of co-operative enterprises are conveniently glossed over. Unrealistic claims filter down from orators to the community, to local councils and trade unions, where palliatives or even solutions to unemployment are sought like gold dust. The co-operatives which fold are always the exceptions, the pioneers, they say; it couldn't happen like that again.

Vulnerability in the open market has led some co-operatives to seek refuge in protected markets. Paradoxically, they do not regard trade with their friends in the co-operative and labour movements as a protection so much as an escape. They prefer to trade with friends for ideological reasons and to create an alternative system of production and exchange. Despite their shortcomings, co-operatives have many opportunities to grow if they recognise that capitalist markets should be courted, not shunned, and if, wherever possible, they make positive efforts to develop protective mechanisms and campaign at a political level for favourable treatment from the state. The capitalist system, which brought co-operatives into existence, is the one with which they must come to terms if they are to survive. This is the factor which workers' co-operatives have most often disregarded over 150 years. It is certain that greater political commitment to co-operatives by central and local government, and by other sectors of co-operation, would widen their scope for development. And publicity for the idea – although it has failed so far to win over the working class – is not fruitless. But to make false claims about what is possible can only harm the co-operative image, as history has amply shown.

By failing to exploit opportunities for assistance the new co-operatives are providing a service to consumers and to private, large-scale industry at a cost to themselves. In many, the pay is low and conditions of work are primitive. Work space is often cramped and badly heated; long hours of work are needed if the firms are to survive, and in many cases co-operators have worked overtime without pay and taken a cut in their wages in times of crisis. Machinery is usually second-hand and inefficient, but must be made to compete with the latest designs and technology in larger firms. For the workers, all this is worth the struggle. It provides work where none would otherwise exist; it might pay better than outwork or a 'woman's wage'; or the chance to control the production process may be better than working in any other job. But the fact remains, it is sweated labour.

Competition and Dependence

The co-operative creature which has emerged in the last ten years has been nurtured in some cases by large firms. (Telegraph Textiles Co-operative in Lewisham, for instance, was given advice by Marks & Spencer on how to sell clothing products.) They have recognised the value to themselves in a body of workers which will apparently exploit itself to the extent that it can easily be exploited by others. Groups of workers, already in a weak position with nothing but their skills and a collective spirit, may have to accept whatever contracts for work are available. They could become a valuable resource for large firms, taking their work overload in peak periods, experimenting with new lines and accepting short runs. Already there are co-operatives which sub-contract from industries which are suffering from foreign competition, and from those which are rationalising and restructuring their most profitable sections.

The promotional bodies dislike what is happening and encourage co-operatives to develop a range of markets to avoid overdependence on one or two firms. They feel co-operatives must be encouraged wherever they are accepted in the market since there are many cases where outright hostility has forced closures, prevented entry or caused other difficulties. ICOM, JOL, the CDA, and local CDGs, have all talked of co-operatives developing in Britain's major sectors of the economy. As co-operative movements in Europe have shown, it is indeed possible for them to succeed in some capital-intensive and competitive fields, but in Britain where they are developing almost from scratch, the position is different.

The most vulnerable co-operatives have been those which offered no specialist product or service and faced heavy competition from other firms. Wandtronics had little protection in a highly competitive field. This co-operative worked on contracts to larger firms, making stereophonic amplifiers and other electronic equipment and looking for work wherever possible. Nothing was refused. Contracts were won with the BBC, Rank Xerox and a number of smaller firms. This was the firm's bread and butter work. The manager, George Dilworth, said they needed a specialist product of their own to bring in more profits and survive. A car lock device for car manufacturers was being designed, but the lead time before production was estimated at one to two years, while the skilled technical drawing and market research were carried out, the contracts arranged and the prototypes made. In the meantime a regular flow of work was hard to maintain, and in the second year of Wandtronic's life, not long after its MSC funding ran out, the firm collapsed.

Similarly, co-operatives have found a niche in the building industry where small jobs are needed and hand work dominates. The Builders' Collective found a market in renovation work among the older, owner-occupied property in Leeds. Co-operative Build turned more to the public sector. The Direct Works Department around Connah's Quay engaged solely in maintenance work and the co-operative rightly identified a gap in the market for renovating local authority property. Sunderlandia was bigger than either of these, and found it was squeezed both by the larger, more efficient firms and by the smaller firms which could undercut through having very low overheads. The firm has survived by reducing in size to about 14 from between 40 and 50 workers earlier on. The type of work done has not changed much since 1973 when Sunderlandia was formed, involving building for housing co-operatives, and improvements to older property in the private sector.

In some traditionally 'women's jobs', such as cut, make and trim in the clothing industry, low wages have held back investment in more mechanised processes, and, with cut-throat competition, good profits are hard to make. Early in 1980 Telegraph Textiles was started by Lewisham Council and the voluntary sector, making expensive fashion clothes. But profits were only raised to an acceptable level by one specialist line – bullet-proof waistcoats. A competitive model had been developed for the co-operative, and an outlet was found in the Ministry of Defence. Debates on the ethics of producing garments for use in wars were resolved in favour of commercial expediency.

The fate of Doon Valley, a co-operative of 12 women in Ayrshire, demonstrates how vulnerable cut, make and trim work can be. In 1978 the owner of a large clothing firm made a section of the work-force redundant, then suggested they form a co-operative, offering to sub-contract work to them. Living in a rural area with few job opportunities, the women took up the challenge but failed to make their co-operative pay.

Finding a Market
Craft work was chosen by a number of enterprise workshops, such as Wirral Ceramics and the Warrington Industrial Trust. With a small outlay on equipment and with the MSC paying wages, both had a chance to build up their skills and add more machinery to become profitable by the end of their funding period. Wirral Ceramics

started work in April 1977 with 15 people, including two trainees. Ceramic manufacture had died out in the Liverpool area and the workshop found a market existed for domestic items like cups and bowls, and a smaller proportion of decorative work, among the cafés and individuals in the locality and beyond. Their nearest competitors were in North Wales. Here was a gap in the market which any firm might have filled. With only one kiln and one wheel, productivity was low at first. The kiln space was too small to keep pace with the flow of pots from the wheel. The firm intended to slim down in size when the MSC funds ran out, leaving a rump of skilled potters. Extra wheels and a new kiln were bought or made by the workers, and profitability looked certain. The workshop planned to register as a limited liability company with share capital, but claimed its co-operative principles would not be abandoned.

Warrington Industrial Trust started a year earlier, in 1976, at first making wooden toys and sewn goods. When a new manager took over, he introduced a range of new items such as garden furniture, upholstery and curtains, and school desk renovation. John Lewis placed an order for the workshop's 'West Virginia' range of garden furniture; and a market for renovation and fitting-out work was found in two colleges of education. The projects were all part of a linked programme of 'work areas', and the intention was to float them off as co-operatives when they became viable.

Co-operatives are increasingly springing up in the field of maintenance and repair work. In most cases there is a market for the service but the prices customers are prepared to pay are low. Sometimes a customer will pay above the market rate as a mark of support for the venture. For example, a small window cleaners' co-operative, a Klean Concern, was formed in Sheffield in 1979 by the South Yorkshire CDG for unemployed young people and was given contracts by the Northern College, Barnsley, and other labour movement organisations. For the Northern College it was worth paying a high price for the window-cleaning service because the organisation was an educational institute for the labour movement, sympathetic to the co-operative idea and the need to create jobs, and because Klean Concern was willing to conform to trade union standards of health and safety at work. However, the firm collapsed in January 1980 through lack of sufficient work.

The public sector was also closely involved with Clogora's formation for the same reason. Lancashire County Council, in September 1979, awarded the co-operative a contract for £128,000 from the education budget to repair school desks. However, this was not a commercial deal since it would have been more economic for the Council to buy new desks instead. From Clogora's point of view, desk repair has such a limited local market, and would result in overdependence on a few customers, that it was only regarded as temporary work while the workforce was trained and while products were developed for sale. Even during the start-up period, its sponsors complained that reliance on the council caused problems. The cuts in public expenditure meant further contracts became more infrequent, and early in 1980 the workforce had to be laid off for several weeks.

Where a service is aimed at the private market no such protection can be offered. Milkwood, in Milton Keynes, another enterprise workshop, began in 1976 by repairing wooden pallets but found that a solid market was impossible to build up since firms will repair their own pallets whenever crises occur. Milkwood soon had to abandon that line of business, turning to the manufacture of simple wooden goods. But profits were still too low and the firm quickly collapsed.

Sometimes repair work has not been the main line of a co-operative's business but has been carried out to attract customers, although it has not been profitable in itself. Recycles, for instance, started a bicycle repair service, but found it did not make enough money to keep its three founder members. To this were added the more profitable activities of bicycle hire and sales. The repair service was expanded as far as possible, but soon reached a plateau. This, it was explained, was due to the small premises and a fluctuating demand, and to the separation between the repair shop and hire/sales shop which shared stocks of spare parts.

With bicycles becoming more and more popular, particularly among tourists and students, Recycles buys and hires out bicycles over the summer and winter and sells them six months later for their retail price, cashing in on high second-hand values. After dealing with Raleigh and other major bicycle firms for hire, it eventually won the confidence of these firms and can now buy for sale. In 1979 it had a turnover of £100,000 and was reputed to be the 'second' bicycle shop in Edinburgh. Its market is still growing although, without a high-street location it cannot attract the full range of customers. Expansion has been considered by opening up a second outlet in a country park at Dunbar, 30 miles away.

Specialist Goods and Services

Goods manufactured by co-operatives are rarely in dominant markets. Competition from firms able to mass produce has pushed some co-operatives towards specialist goods of high quality which can be produced in smaller batches. The most famous example of this is Meriden, which specialises in 750 cc Bonneville motorbikes. Meriden, formed after an occupation by the workforce, is all that remains of an industry which once held 50 per cent of the world market. Now the market is dominated by the Japanese, who produce a range of bikes and are pouring investment into new designs.

Painfully undercapitalised at the top end of the market, Meriden is selling what is basically a 30-year-old design which is not as sophisticated as some of its Japanese counterparts, and has no prospect of updating its models without a major capital injection, estimated in 1975 at up to £50 million.[1] In 1979, sales in the USA were lost through the falling value of the dollar against the pound, and the worst winter for years coincided with a petrol crisis, boosting the popularity of smaller bikes and knocking down sales for the co-operative. By July Meriden had agreed to cut production from 300 to 200 Triumphs a week to avoid a stockpile of 8,000 unsold bikes by September. Unless it can diversify, the co-operative's future looks grim.[2]

Co-operatives formed in less adverse circumstances, like Equity Shoes, Walsall Locks, Trylon and Marble Arch Intensive English, have found more lasting positions in the market. In the shoe-making, lock-making and canoe businesses, there is still room for the small to medium sized firms producing specialist lines, and providing a personal service to individual customers. Equity Shoes has suffered many crises in its 94-year life in a trade which has always been highly competitive. Apart from a brief and unsuccessful trial period making fashion shoes, the firm has stuck to good quality women's shoes. A steady market was found among the co-operative retail societies in the early years. But, with the closure of many of these outlets, customers had to be found in the private sector. In 1979, 40 per cent of 'the Equity's' shoes were being exported to Scandinavia. But by then the firm was in a healthy state, recording good profits every year.

The product range of Walsall Locks has narrowed over time. In particular, the number of locks made to individual requirements has fallen. The firm now concentrates on supplying special locks which can command higher prices. It is unable to touch the more risky, mass-produced range of locks. At the specialist end of the market there are few competitors, and Walsall Locks ranks as sixth in size, with good growth prospects.

Car door locks are the firm's main line of business. Among these, anti-burst locks are its speciality, and 2,000 a week were being made in 1979. With infrequent changes in the designs, these are profitable products. In addition, old locks – such as for ships – are made to order for the Ministry of Defence, produced in lots of 50,000, and locks are made for the Customs and Excise, like those for whisky vats, and for the National Coal Board and Gas Boards. The firm also makes agricultural locks, trace chains, cow ties and harnesses for export, for instance to Kuala Lumpur, Barbados, Florida (USA), Quebec, Eire and parts of Australia. Some of this work is very specialised, being brass-plated and forged.

After some limited assistance from Scott Bader, Trylon was able to identify its own products and market, and in fact pioneered the use of plastics in education so that today these techniques are a vital element of the craft curriculum in most schools. The firm has been able to get itself appointed the approved supplier for many County Councils, notably in Scotland. There has been little real growth in this market since the mid-1970s when public expenditure cuts started to bite into local authority budgets. Despite this, general demand is growing steadily.

The canoe market remains very important to Trylon as a supplier of moulds for hire or sale, with materials and accessories, to schools, youth clubs, canoe clubs and private individuals. In addition, canoes are made for sale, as well as a range of other glass-fibre products. The profit element on moulds is not large but is seen as the stimulus for material sales, which is the profitable side of the business. The joint service offered is unusual and Trylon are market leaders in this. Canoe designs are regularly updated and by February 1980 nine designs were available, catering for most aspects of canoe sport. The designs are also made available to commercial manufacturers under a royalty arrangement. Despite fairly stringent controls, pirating still exists, but legal action against offenders is not thought to be worthwhile.

A disturbing event for Trylon occurred in November 1978 when Scott Bader bought Strand Glassfibre. Strand had always been regarded by Trylon as a major competitor as it maintained shops in most major towns. Scott Bader argued that the purchase was made for commercial reasons as it wanted more outlets for its materials and to increase turnover. Strand Glassfibre is now almost totally dependent on Scott Bader for its principal raw materials, whereas Trylon has reduced its dependence. In the event, the purchase has had no effect whatsoever in the short term but Trylon still remains concerned for the future.

Marble Arch competes in foreign language teaching with both small concerns and large companies like Berlitz and Davies's. The co-operative concentrates on general English teaching as this fitted the members' skills and demand was known to be massive. London is a world centre for English language teaching. Students can easily be recruited because Marble Arch is recognised by the Department of Education and Science, which means it can belong to the Association of Recognised English Language Schools. They provide good publicity by sending brochures listing recognised schools to all British Councils and Embassies in the world. Reasonable profits can be made by the co-operative while at the same time its workers can be paid an average wage for the job, far better conditions of work are provided than elsewhere, and students are offered a good teacher/ student ratio (at 12 to one compared with 15–20 to one in the worst schools) and low fees.

Occasionally, co-operatives are involved in main line activities, but diversifying into new lines may be their only way to survive crises in their own markets. Metropolitan Motor-Cab Co-operative Society of London, formed in 1927, was recently hit by inflation and its own failure to build up reserves. The cost of taxis soared from £5,000 to £7,000 in one year, between 1979 and 1980. Fuel prices also rocketed with the oil crisis, and the lease ran out on its cheap, archway garages. Lambeth Council found the firm new premises and it began negotiating for a bank loan. But to meet its higher expenses the co-operative had to expand into car repairs, used car sales and MOT testing. Without a solid capital structure, however, its future looks uncertain.

The 'Alternative Movement'
More than half of the 300 or so co-operatives existing are engaged in some aspect of the 'alternative movement'. Most common are the wholefood shops and distributors, bookshops, publishers and printers. While profit levels have been hard to raise, the survival record of these ventures has been good. They have a special position in the market due to the strong ideological backing they receive from their members and many of their customers.

They are concerned about the progressive nature of their businesses – keeping prices down, making their goods and services accessible to the less privileged and community groups with small resources, and contributing to socialist causes. Sometimes this is at the expense of their own wages and conditions. But by entering these particular markets they do find some commercial protection. Many people and organisations buy from co-operatives specifically because they share the same values. In return the co-operatives treat their customers sympathetically.

A large sector in wholefoods has appeared which cannot easily be broken up by large firms. This is partly because the sector runs on low profit levels, and partly because much of its custom is based on contacts with the libertarian and left supporters of the 'alternative movement'. Wanting to increase their influence in society, they are loath to see any co-operative isolated in an environment hostile to co-operative principles and to the sector's capital growth. The wholefood movement has defended itself against competition by forming federations and by trying to set up co-operatives at every stage in the food business from farming through to sales. Wholefoods are defined by Lizzie Vann[3] from CENA[4] as 'unprocessed foods, grown without synthetic fertilizers, hormones or pesticides. If any processing is done, nothing like preservatives, emollients, colourings or flavourings is added, and nothing of nutritional importance is taken away'. 'Most of the products in wholefood shops', she says, 'are dried beans, grains, fruit and nuts, as the shops cannot cope with perishable goods, but the definition could also include free-range meat and animal products, and organic fruit and vegetables.'

The simplest method of forming a food co-operative is for a group of households to take responsibility for buying and distributing food bought from a cash and carry warehouse. A second method is for the group to order in bulk at a meeting, and for people with transport to collect for the group. During the 1960s many of these food co-operatives grew up as informal arrangements. But in the 1970s most of these groups were replaced by co-operative shops with limited liability.[5]

The primary aim of the shops was to develop a practical alternative to consumerism. Anna Whyatt, co-founder of Suma, explained what was meant. From the start, she said, they were committed to 'small scale production and distribution, collective practice, and an extension of the function of 'shop' in an industrial society to being part of the community. And although such an analysis was rarely articulate, they became increasingly concerned with some of the

implications of their demands in terms of world economies. They
became information centres, community meeting places and education centres for food issues on an *ad hoc* basis.'[6]

But it was not a logical step for the founders of this movement to
extend their influence by forming co-operatives at more than one
point in the food chain from farming to the retail shop, i.e. through
vertical integration. The alternative movement is based on personal
alienation and encourages an 'ostrich attitude to politics'.[7] But the
founders realised that the viability of the co-operative shops could
not be maintained without forming a distribution network to raise
efficiency and lower costs.

The Federation of Northern Wholefoods Collectives (originally
the Northern Wholefoods Co-operative) and Suma, a distribution
warehouse, were formed in 1975. The FNWC became a loose federation of some 50 co-operative shops, restaurants and market stalls in
the North of England which brought representatives together from
its member co-operatives at meetings held every six weeks. It levied
money through the warehouse from the shops to provide credit for
small shops in poorer areas, and occasionally made loans to
co-operatives in difficulty. At first the levy was 0.5 per cent based on
food costs. Later it was raised to 1.5 per cent to help a York
restaurant, Aardvark, and then was dropped back to 1 per cent and
was based on turnover, at the shops' request. The FNWC also
arranged a worker-exchange system between shops and an open-
book system to ensure the continuous free exchange of business
knowledge and information. More recently, similar federations have
been formed in other regions, such as the South Coast, the Midlands
and the Southern Wholefoods Federation. The North was divided
into four regions, but the North East later detached itself from the
FNWC to become independent.

Much of the co-ordination for the FNWC was done by CENA.
This independent workers' co-operative was set up in 1976 as an
educational, information and action centre involved in the politics of
food production and distribution. The shops had always intended to
play a part in these activities themselves, but the energy they were
putting into their businesses left no time for anything else. CENA
was sponsored by the FNWC, which paid for the weekly wage of one
worker and for materials, for the production of a newsletter and the
cost of organising meetings. CENA provided a link with other
federations and stimulated discussion on a proposal to form a trade
association, the use of the levy as loan capital, and other matters.

Early in 1978 the FNWC was wound up and the seeming potential for better trade links in the wholefood movement was lost. The movement had been divided between people who favoured expansion for political reasons, and others with a more insular approach. The FNWC collapsed over the question of using its levies. Without a collectively agreed political framework, the differences of opinion could not be resolved.

Suma was the first warehousing venture, but again this was followed by two more in the North of England and one in Scotland. Suma has offered a 5 per cent discount to co-operative members of the FNWC. Shops pay for their goods on delivery to reduce Suma's capital needs. Prices are tied to the time of payments but are kept as low as possible by pressure from the shops. The average mark-up on goods is 15 per cent. Before the FNWC collapsed, the shops played a large part in Suma's policy-making since they account for 80 per cent of its turnover. Day-to-day decisions, however, are left to Suma's members. Deliveries are made in Suma's trucks once a week to shops throughout their area, and an attempt has been made to integrate the distribution of other co-operatives' products in their rounds. Publications from PDC are taken to bookshops wherever possible. While social and political links with other 'alternative' groups in the country are well established, it has been harder to build them around an economic basis.

Eventually, a trucking co-operative is envisaged to reduce costs for the wholefood movement in all regions, and to assist the creation of an alternative sector, including bookshops, printing, publishing and some professional activities. But this has been slow to materialise, probably because other groupings have not yet developed to such a sophisticated level as the wholefoods movement. Suma's members would like to buy stocks from firms with similar values to their own. But there is little scope for choice between suppliers. There are only 12 major suppliers of grains, and only one for nuts.[8]

Protective Trade Links
Co-operatives in the 'alternative movement' have not been alone in receiving help from sympathisers. For most of the CPF co-operatives, similar trading links have been recorded. Usually the co-operatives sold goods to the co-operative retail societies, benefiting both types of enterprise. The stores were more clearly symbols of a socialist ideology at the turn of the century than they are today, and welcomed good commercial relations with reliable suppliers. The

workers' co-operatives for their part chose to support the stores even when private outlets were offered. Often the co-operatives' prices were competitive, but, as explained in Chapter 1, even when they lagged behind those of the CWS factories and private firms they made up the difference by awarding the stores bonuses from profits each year.

Leicester Printers was heavily involved with the retail societies and trade unions, although these ties have been loosened over the years, and the firm now relies more on private markets for its more specialised work in the leisure industry. The co-operative stores, however, are still the main outlet for Queen Eleanor's clothing. This represents a substantial commitment by the societies today. For instance, Queen Eleanor expected to sell £10,000 worth of goods to the London Co-operative Society in 1978, and £29,500 in 1979. Although the stores no longer receive a bonus, they benefit in other ways from Queen Eleanor. For example, clothes are made to order – outsize, or very small clothes in small numbers – even though the service is more costly to the co-operative.

The more successful co-operatives appear to be in two categories. First, there are those which are closely tied to the labour and co-operative movements, where trading links have been made of value to both supplier and customer. Then there are those which have developed the rudiments of an integrated structure of production and distribution. Huge economies can be made in such a system and the weaker sections can be given special support unobtainable else-where. Failure can usually be avoided. The wholefoods movement offers an example of what can be done. At the moment, opportunities for other co-operatives to follow suit are limited because – apart from the bookshops and printers where some efforts at federating are in hand – there are not enough firms in the same industry.

The tendency for many of the ICOM co-operatives to pay too little regard to their business expertise and commercial interests has reduced their level of profits. But at the same time they have often followed the pattern set by the CPF co-operatives, developing strong trading links with people and organisations – including other co-operatives – whose ideological beliefs they share. Unlike the many co-operative experiments of the 19th century, the protection offered by the labour and co-operative movements and the 'alter-natives movement', or 'libertarian Left', does not amount to by-passing the capitalist market. It helps co-operatives to ride over the rougher periods and provides some stability in their markets. Those which have not formed such links, having set up with more concern for job creation than ideology, have been more vulnerable. Unless the state's support for them compensates for their isolation they are more likely to collapse.

Conclusion

The sample illustrates that there are co-operatives in a wide range of industries but, because of their basic weaknesses, they are often tied into the economy on the bottom rungs. Their very existence is a comment on the state of the economy. There is surely a link between the growth of co-operatives in assembly work, repair and maintenance, and cheap crafts, and capital's increasing need for firms performing these tasks for multinational companies.

Sympathisers who will make regular purchases from a co-operative are vital to these enterprises. But there may be dangers in a refusal to trade elsewhere. Co-operatives need to experience the discipline of the market place. Few can be expected to sympathise for long with organisations which charge uncompetitive prices. They also need a greater number of outlets than their sympathisers can offer. There will never be enough co-operative stores, trade unions or labour councils – also operating within a capitalist framework – to form a closed market for a growing co-operative sector.

6 Living with the State

Local and National Support

Co-operatives have received growing support from the state since 1974 when the Government put up £4.75 million to help form Meriden Motorcycles Co-operative. This followed the famous occupation by the workforce of the Meriden plant, which had been threatened with closure. The then Secretary of State for Industry, Tony Benn, was the driving force behind two similar rescue operations, Kirkby Manufacturing and Engineering (KME) and the *Scottish Daily News*. Since then, support for individual co-operatives has mushroomed among local councils and other bodies like the Scottish Development Agency and the Local Enterprise Development Unit in Northern Ireland. The Manpower Services Commission (MSC) has also assisted co-operatives under the 'enterprise workshops' label. Apart from this direct support, aid from central government has been channelled through independent co-operative promotional bodies like ICOM, ICOF, the Scottish Co-operatives Development Committee (SCDC) and through the government agency set up to assist co-operatives, the Co-operative Development Agency (see Chapter 2).

The total amount of money made available to co-operatives through all these means is estimated at some £14 million, given in grant and loan capital. But from this sum, £11.6 m was accounted for under Section 8 of the 1972 Industry Act for Meriden, KME, SDN, Bardrec and Sunderlandia; £0.8 m went to some co-operatives under the MSC programmes; and £1.35 m was earmarked for assistance for the sector under ICO and CDA Acts. Local authorities' contributions amount to only £0.25 m although these have been given in small sums and are spread among a number of co-operatives and on development work.[1]

State aid to co-operatives is extremely small compared with assistance given to private firms. Nevertheless, it has been very significant for the development of co-operatives in Britain. Of the 300 or so registered co-operatives in 1980, more than 100 had received help directly or indirectly from the state.[2] With Meriden still in existence and employing around 500 workers – more than any other co-operative – it could be claimed that the number of jobs saved or created through state intervention was around 900. This is equal to more than half of all the jobs created in co-operatives since 1970.

It appears that state assistance is helping to develop a larger co-operative sector, though it is not always associated with the strongest co-operatives. With their weak capital base, co-operatives have more need of external finance than private firms, and demand favourable terms on loans, and other forms of financial aid. Banks and other financial institutions have been unwilling to provide the help needed. In many cases they also need management advice, especially during the start-up period.

Local authorities have increasingly taken a positive stand in providing the support demanded. At the national level there is more uncertainty. The Labour Party has talked about a Minister for Co-operatives and a budget for co-operative development. The Tories, however, have considered ending funding to the CDA after its first three years. Aid may still come from a Conservative government, but it would be given on the grounds of expediency.

First Cases of State Aid
State aid to co-operatives arose first at the national level. The struggles at Meriden, KME and the *Scottish Daily News* were widely publicised in the press. Central government assistance to these firms became associated with 'lame ducks', sometimes blackening the image of co-operatives in the public eye and among organisations which could offer them help. These were co-operatives formed by men and women desperately trying to stave off unemployment by running their enterprises themselves. They were quite unlike the collectives and conversions.

They were all grossly undercapitalised and had little chance of long term survival without a major injection of finance. But the co-operatives also achieved some positive results. They brought the co-operative idea back into the political arena and were a tangible expression of a more democratic method of running a business. Many more people in the labour movement have since begun to realise the need for working people to be re-educated to take more

control over their lives as an essential part of the future battle for
socialism.

These three 'rescue cases' followed in the wake of the Upper
Clyde Shipbuilders' work-in, when there was wide support for
practical experiments in workers' control. The co-operatives were
'self-selected'[3] and, in 1974, seemed to offer a chance of success.
Despite their unfavourable starting conditions, and contrary to the
advice of civil servants, they were funded by the Labour Government of 1974–75, which could not withstand the pressure put on it to
save jobs in the politically sensitive areas of North-West England,
the Midlands, and Scotland's central belt.[4]

The co-operatives were encouraged by a leading protagonist of
industrial democracy, Tony Benn, who was responsible for allocat-
ing grants under the Industry Act of 1972. But he was by no means
the only person responsible for the formation of these co-operatives.
He was 'educated and inspired'[5] by the Upper Clyde Shipbuilders
and other shop floor demonstrations of the right to work during the
early 1970s. In a determined effort to work positively with the unions,
he responded enthusiastically to the demands of the co-operatives.
The Benn co-operatives burst into the limelight at a time when there
was little experience in the labour movement to advise and assist
them. They were underfunded, isolated in the market and frightened
of exposing their internal problems for fear of bad publicity.
Although they were respected and admired by left-wingers in the
trade unions and the Labour party, only Meriden was in an
important position in the economy.[6] For this reason it was able to
attract sympathy and help from wider sources.[7] The other two fought
to their deaths alone, blindly, and in wild optimism.

It is not inevitable that co-operatives formed this way will fail.
Indeed, Meriden has proved that, after a long period of uncertainty,
some of the jobs there are likely to be saved. Early in 1980 the
co-operative looked as if it would be rescued by Japan's need for
more foreign outlets.[8] However, in June discussions were under way
to sell the co-operative to a British firm. In the early 1970s the new
co-operatives symbolised left-wing ideology. It was not appreciated
that they could offer only limited opportunities for effective production under workers' control. The unease they engendered was caused
by the fear that trade unions would make further demands for the
support of workers by the state in similar circumstances.

Central government entered the field of co-operation a second
time by supporting 'enterprise workshops'. These are community

projects which aim to provide jobs for the unemployed and to become self-financing by the end of a period of MSC funding, thus creating permanent employment. They were first formed in 1976 under the MSC's Job Creation Programme (JCP). The majority were run as co-operatives from the start or were working towards co-operative status. Their reception has been mixed. ICOM eagerly embraced them as a way of swelling the number of co-operatives in an embryonic sector, but their heavy failure rate raised many questions about their value to the co-operative movement.

Some 40 co-operative enterprise workshops were formed by 1980, out of which one third have survived. About one quarter are now running without the help of government grants. Some of these receive financial assistance from other sources, but most are struggling to maintain viability. Although this record is probably no worse than the failure rate of small firms in general, it has been resented and criticised by the co-operative movement and community organisations. It is widely believed that if governments are serious about creating permanent jobs, they should do more to ensure that co-operatives can successfully transfer from MSC funding to a more independent existence. However, a sympathetic attitude towards enterprise workshops has persisted as the problems of unemployment have deepened. They are accepted as an innovative initiative which offers scope for experimentation and as worthwhile for men and women who would otherwise be without work.

> They do . . . represent an opportunity for a much wider range of people to attempt self-help job creation and to learn about the process of production and self-management. They are also perhaps a more creative way of spending (MSC) . . . resources than some of the short-term projects that have been funded.[9]

Job Creation Programme
In 1975 the Labour Government was committed to public expenditure cuts in response to the crisis, seeing the need to reduce public spending as part of the solution to reducing inflation and stimulating private sector investment. But unemployment was rising fast, particularly in inner cities and development areas. Among young people (16–17-year-olds), unemployment rose by 120 per cent between January 1972 and January 1977, compared with a rise of 45 per cent among the worker population as a whole.[10] Job creation and training programmes were thought to

. . . reduce the official unemployment figures without reflating the economy (and) . . . enable the government to keep the unemployed in contact with the disciplines of work at the lowest possible cost.[11]

The Job Creation Programme was one among a large number of measures to create jobs, give work experience and increase training opportunities. It was launched in October 1975 with a grant of £30 million, subsequently raised in stages to £180 million. It was operated under the power vested in the Secretary of State for Employment by Section 5(1) of the Employment and Training Act 1973 as amended by Schedule 14 of the Employment Protection Act 1975 for the purpose of providing temporary employment for people without jobs. The MSC was authorised to operate the programme on the Secretary of State's behalf under a separate grant.[12]

The JCP aimed to provide short-term jobs of social value, to create benefits for the community and to provide jobs primarily for people under 24 years of age and over 50. The MSC was responsible for operating the scheme and, in doing so, was asked by Government to:

pay particular attention to the needs of the young unemployed and to encourage training where practical;
give priority to projects which would assist urban renewal;
achieve the co-operation of local authorities and health service authorities invited to help sponsor projects in personal social service and other fields;
encourage public bodies, including the nationalised industries, private employers, voluntary organisations, charities and community groups, to sponsor suitable projects.

The scheme was a reactive one, relying on sponsors coming forward with applications for funds. The criteria for approval are listed in Appendix III. The MSC paid the agreed wage bill and up to 10 per cent on top of that for administration costs, equipment and materials. Wages were paid at the locally agreed rate for the job, subject to a maximum laid down by the MSC. Initially this was £50 per week but was subsequently increased in line with the incomes policy of the day. The scheme was administered from the Central Unit in the MSC's head office and from 10 area offices, each of which had an action committee. Action committees comprised influential representatives from local industry, trade unions, local authorities and academic institutions, and they had independent chairpersons. All schemes had to have the approval of the committee.

With unemployment remaining at a high level and continuing to rise among the 19-and-under age group, all the MSC's and Department of Employment's programmes were revised from September 1978. The new programme was divided into the Youth Opportunities Programme, for 16–18-year-olds, and the Special Temporary Employment Programme (STEP) for unemployed adults aged 19 and over.

Under the JCP, enterprise workshops were subject to the same criteria as other projects. After 1978 they came under the STEP programme, but the funding conditions were modified to enable them to run for a maximum of two years, with a review after the first year, and they did not need to employ predominantly young people. The failure rate of enterprise workshops under the JCP was considered by the MSC to be too high. The main reasons for this were said to be:

(a) lack of setting-up and operating capital;
(b) lack of management expertise – particularly management accounting;
(c) failure of the sponsor to identify the right product, market and price;
(d) failure of the sponsor to give first priority to becoming self-financing.

Had authority existed to create permanent rather than temporary jobs in this way, it would not have been necessary to graft the idea of co-operative enterprise workshops on to JCP and it would have been possible to design funding and approval criteria more suitable to their needs. However, in the context of the JCP and STEP programmes, all that could be done was to relax some of the criteria for funding the schemes. The MSC announced that:

(a) the work to be carried out need not necessarily be of community benefit;
(b) greater flexibility may be used in the requirement that preference be given to the long term unemployed preference groups;
(c) income from sales or services provided may be retained;
(d) any net profits may be retained at the end of the funding period for reinvestment in the scheme;
(e) any plant, equipment or other assets purchased wholly or partly with STEP funds may be retained provided the enterprise continues to provide useful jobs.

Under the Tory administration of 1979, cuts were applied to STEP amounting to £44.6 million. From June applications were confined to Development Areas, and criteria for approval were tightened. This meant the number of places on this programme was cut from 30–35,000 to 12–14,000. Enterprise workshops are still being funded within the STEP budget but no new ones are being started.

Problems of Survival
It is remarkable how many enterprise workshops have survived, given the problems that any co-operative faces in the market and the additional difficulties these government-funded ventures have had to contend with. One factor responsible was the tremendous dedication and enthusiasm that the sponsors, managers and supervisors brought to the workshops. The idea attracted a number of talented individuals from the community who took on these roles with great imagination and ability. However, this in itself was not enough to bring about commercial success. As the MSC reported, too often they placed great emphasis on co-operative principles, tried to help those most in need in the community, and were reluctant to trim the labour force to a viable level, even when it became clear that income was not going to be as high as expected. Self-financing was rarely the sponsors' first priority. But – as the MSC has pointed out – a failed workshop is no good to the community.

The financial limitations on enterprise workshops were severe, and few funds were available to buy plant and equipment. Sometimes contributions to their needs were donated by local authorities, such as rent-free periods at Milkwood and Wandtronics and reduced rent at Wirral Ceramics, or special concessions were granted by private firms, such as the hire-purchase terms given to Clogora (based on personal contacts). Occasionally the workers contributed money of their own, but in general the workshops had few assets and little collateral as a basis for borrowing. This, together with their requirement at first to employ mainly young people, resulted in low-skilled or unskilled activities which were labour intensive and used low technology. In these circumstances profits were hard to make.

Occasionally enterprise workshops were able to develop specialised products of higher value, such as Wirral Ceramics (now a private firm), which makes ceramic ware for the British and foreign markets. But mainly they have found 'gaps in the market' on the margins of the economy in both services and manufacturing industry. For example, Wandtronics competed with a large number of small firms in electronics assembly work; Dowlais Knitwear, Brookhouse Ampersand (liquidated) and Doon Valley (liquidated) were involved in the cut-make-and-trim market, notoriously exploited by large firms; and Clogora renovates school desks for a local authority at below-market rates.

These financial difficulties – hardly affected by the MSC's relaxation of rules – were compounded by the requirement that enterprise workshops were not allowed to compete with other local firms. The official reason for this was that they were wholly subsidised by government grants and the worker-owners were therefore not taking any risk, so should not cause jobs in commercial businesses to be lost. The rule of all JCP and STEP schemes was that jobs and businesses should not be at risk as a result of the schemes. The co-operatives were being treated as subsidised community projects while at the same time they were expected to find a place in the market.

There were other problems too. For instance, assistance on legal, financial, marketing and other aspects of business were usually needed since the workers rarely had enough of the necessary management skills between them. The Central Unit of the MSC which dealt with all applications for enterprise workshops had only two people responsible for the scheme. They provided what help they could, but it was spread thinly across the workshops and was short-term and not continuous. Dowlais Knitwear attracted assistance from the Open University, and Wandtronics and Doon Valley both received help from the local authority. But none of this assistance was a real substitute for internal management skills. The limited salary paid to managers (relaxed later in the scheme) may well have contributed to the problem of attracting suitable people to these posts. In Doon Valley's case, a manager was not found until the project had been in operation for some time, and this was thought to be the major cause of its collapse.

In some of the workshops, outside help was discouraged. As co-operators, the workers were reluctant to request advice from people who did not have the same convictions as themselves, and the co-operative umbrella organisations, like ICOM, were too small to be able to bridge this gap. Also, the co-operative ideal sometimes encouraged the workers to oppose traditional management structures and to attempt job rotation or to share work generally recognised to be a skill best done by one person, at least while the enterprise was still unprofitable.

The composition of the workforce, often taken straight from the unemployed register, made it particularly hard to manage and supervise the workshops. Milkwood suffered badly from having too few carpenters in relation to unskilled young people. Discipline was a constant problem. The products and services of the workshops were often of poor quality and productivity was very low. Another factor criticised by most enterprise workshops was the timespan within which they were expected to become viable. One year under the JCP was not thought to be enough by any business standards. This was relaxed later so that two years of funding under STEP could be provided. But even this was a short time, particularly as the workshops all started with around ten workers, far more than most small businesses, which generally grow very gradually from one or two people at start-up.

Underlying all these difficulties, however, is a more fundamental factor. The co-operatives were created for unemployed workers. Work was provided at relatively low pay and in physical conditions that were often poor. The strange concept of co-operation was imposed on the workers and a great responsibility rested on them to make a success of their own firm. Often enormous dedication existed among workers who were older, but in other cases a different attitude prevailed. Many felt they had a right to work and to the jobs paid for by the MSC, and had little commitment to their ventures as businesses.

No attempt has yet been made to offer education courses on co-operative principles to these workers. While older people and middle-class people recognise more quickly the value of co-operatives as perhaps their only hope of employment (or acceptable employment), young people – indoctrinated with traditional values – often approach the idea with casual indifference.

Local Aid

Local councils and New Town Development Corporations have a better record of assisting co-operatives. Reacting to pressure from, local community groups, and often with the enthusiasm of council officers, some 11 councils have assisted 17 individual co-operatives. A further 16 have provided finance for co-operative development or given advice and other assistance. To a smaller extent, New Town Development Corporations have also been involved. These interventions began in 1975, becoming more numerous from 1978 to 1980. Their objectives are similar to those of central government in support of the Benn co-operatives and enterprise workshops. The decision to help co-operatives was in all cases motivated by a concern for growing levels of unemployment in their areas. This led to a commitment to economic planning and to various forms of intervention to assist individual firms. However, they have paid far more attention to the commercial aspects of co-operatives, which they aim to make viable and profitable.

Wandsworth, one of the authorities which have assisted co-operatives, published a paper in 1976 called 'Prosperity or Slump' which recorded a drop in jobs from 20,000 in 1971 to 16,000 in 1975, and a rise in unemployment of 6,000 to 8,000 between 1975 and 1976. Co-operatives were attractive to this and other councils principally because they could provide permanent jobs for little financial outlay.

There are other reasons why co-operatives have been singled out for special assistance. For instance, they are thought to be capable of responding to the needs of underprivileged groups in the community, like ethnic groups, young people, women and handicapped people, and can make better use of worker potential. They have been preferred because of the nature of their internal decision-making, based on democratic principles; because they show a willingness among people to help themselves; because they are more likely to produce socially useful goods or services and because their profits are ploughed back into the local area. Also, local councils can create jobs themselves by forming co-operatives. Beyond these considerations it has to be admitted that the novelty and idealism surrounding co-operatives have helped councils to divert attention from the collapse of employment. They have gained a local reputation for innovation and for a positive approach to the problems of rapid plant closure and job loss, on the strength of creating ten or twenty new jobs.

Stemming Industrial Decline
Support for co-operatives has arisen in the context of the changing role of local councils in the economy. An awareness is growing among local authorities that they must play a more active part in stemming industrial decline and job loss. Between 1945 and the late 1960s, attitudes to local investment were different. In this period, councils were content to attract and facilitate industrial investment by providing land, buildings and infrastructure for industry and offices.

This was at a time when the economy appeared to be buoyant and there was mobile industry and investment capital that could be drawn across local authority boundaries by aggressive promotional work.

Economic planning was then the province of central government and regional authorities who were concerned with adjusting regional imbalances in investment and employment opportunities. Since then the state at all levels has found it necessary to offer financial packages of assistance to individual firms to help them out of temporary difficulties, encourage them to grow, or improve their capital structure. This has primed the pump for private investors. Schemes for giving loans and grants, and occasionally acquiring shares, were developed by local councils in parallel with the work of the National Enterprise Board, the Scottish and Welsh Development Agencies, the Northern Ireland Development Agency and the Highlands and Islands Development Board. This change in policy represents a new role for the state at the local level. Councils no longer consider it enough to provide the general conditions for accumulation and to claw back profits when they are in a strong bargaining position.

By the 1970s, few jobs could be created by offering gifts to the private sector as inducements to invest locally or, by reducing the disruptive effects of large-scale development – traffic congestion, pollution, noise and the degradation of landscapes, to create an efficient and attractive environment for industry. Positive action to initiate investment was required. More attention was paid to small firms. For too long they had been discouraged, or even obliterated through housing renewal and central area redevelopment. The interventionist policies towards small firms have a commercial objective, but the state's role as a financial institution is different from that of the private sector. Finance is provided because it is not available in the right form from other sources. The state will take a higher risk and wait longer for a return on its capital or the repayment of a loan, and may sometimes give grants.[13]

Where co-operatives are concerned, local authorities will lend at an even higher risk. This does not mean a bad risk will be taken. Only those co-operatives which have a good chance of repaying their loans and interest are funded. The risk is high because interest rates are well below those that a bank or other financial institution would charge, and loans are regularly given which are not fully secured. In addition, the terms of the loans are more flexible. Councils will wait longer for repayments and sometimes will give grants to co-operatives to ease the burden of repayments, for instance by giving rent-free periods or by waiving interest rates altogether. They aim to get their money back through good management. Extensive help may be given in the co-operative's start-up period and further assistance may be available later on. Every effort is made to create a viable firm. However, the councils' objective is not simply to get their money back. Discrimination in favour of co-operatives has occurred because councils have faith in them as firms which offer social benefits as well as jobs.

So far it has been very largely Labour authorities who have assisted co-operatives. Tory councils sometimes express a willingness to fund them on the same criteria as small firms, but in practice it is exceptional for them to do so. Local authority officers can, in some cases, give advice to co-operatives, and small sums for promotional purposes can be granted from council budgets allocated for industrial development. But often the kind of help needed is more substantial. For instance, help for rent payments and loans for working capital, plant and equipment may also be needed.

Financial and Legal Constraints
The ability of local councils to offer a package of assistance to any kind of firm is seriously constrained. First, they may not have the expertise to give all the advice needed, and limited budgets mean new appointments of co-operative advisers can rarely be afforded. Only in one case has a council paid the CDA to advise local ventures. There has never been a systematic assessment of local authorities' role in economic planning despite the demands made by councils for new powers for this pupose, and despite central government's exhortations in DOE Circular 71/77 to local authorities to be more sensitive to the needs of local industry. Specific powers exist under the 1963 Land Act to lend for building construction, and under the 1972 Local Government Act to offer rent-free periods or reduced rent on industrial buildings, or to offer a range of assistance under the 1978 Inner Urban Areas Act. But for other purposes, such as giving loans and grants for plant and equipment and working capital, local authorities must rely on local Acts of Parliament or ancillary powers, such as the 2p rate provision (Section 137) in the 1972 Local Government Act (England and Wales)[14] or the 1974 Superannuation Regulations.

All these powers have been used by local authorities, and the 2p rate provision has become increasingly important. But since it was not originally intended for industrial development,[15] its use has been limited by nervousness on the part of many councils that their actions may be challenged by ratepayers and lead to an examination by the District Auditor, so incurring the risk of heavy fines. Although there are ample examples now of councils using this provision, they cannot be taken as precedents. Any use of S.137 must be justified on its individual merits, and a local authority must demonstrate that it has considered all competing claims on the money. It must show why co-operatives or other small firms are so much more important than other things. In other words, a local authority must be seen to be exercising its discretion.

A number of councils have now taken legal advice on the use of this power. Only Fife Regional Council was told the power could not be used for a particular scheme to start small firms and co-operatives, on account of the council thereby obtaining unfair inside information on commercial matters. Other councils, reassured by the results of their enquiries, have gone ahead and provided loans and grants.

The needs of co-operatives are different from those of other firms. Most of those seeking help from the council are new-starts. Usually their members have little capital between them. They are not in a position to ask for loans to build factories, and few expect to show a rate of return high enough to attract pension fund investments. In the majority of cases, the powers permitting rent-free periods, and S.137 of the 1972 Local Government Act, have been the only suitable powers for funding them. Apart from Cumbria, which used the 1964 Cumberland County Council Act, and Lewisham, which used the 1978 Inner Urban Areas Act, S.137 has been used in all cases where loans have been granted to co-operatives.

S.137 loans have been given when no other source of finance was available on the right terms to the co-operatives concerned. Councils offer better terms because it is a political decision to fund a co-operative. Once a commitment has been made, a large amount of assistance may be given to the co-operative to ensure the loan is paid back. To get Wandtronics launched, for instance, council officers helped with the accounts, marketing, product identification, premises, and with any other management matters needed. All this amounted to a very expensive administrative cost. But it was not charged up to the co-operative in interest rates because the job was considered part of the officers' normal duties to create employment.

Councils will wait longer for a return on their capital than banks or other financial institutions, again because of a commitment to job creation. If a large number of loans were being made out of the rates, then stricter criteria about repayment might be adopted. But it is easy to be flexible where small sums are involved. Interest charges have been very low. In Lambeth, loans given in 1979 were at 10$^{1}/_{8}$ per cent. This was about the same as for ICOF loans of one to five years, and around 7 per cent lower than an equivalent bank loan.

Grants and Loans

On top of these advantages to a co-operative, a local authority can also give grants. In a number of cases, grants have been made indirectly, for instance by reducing the rent charged on local authority-owned buildings in which the co-operatives operate. Grants, however, are not a sign that councils will act uncommercially. They are only given when a co-operative could, by no other means, become viable. A local authority must be seen to be acting in a businesslike manner. This requirement – which applies to all local government aid – can be traced back to common law, and tends to introduce a large element of caution into the actions of council solicitors and treasurers. Sometimes peppercorn rents, rent-free periods or reduced rents are given in lieu of renovation and preparatory work on local authority buildings which have not been made suitable for industrial letting. In these cases the council probably benefits from the labour of the co-operators.

While it would not be possible for a local authority to give a grant if a co-operative could become viable with a loan, there are other reasons why a loan is usually considered more appropriate. It puts the co-operative on a normal commercial footing, giving a greater incentive to achieve viability as quickly as possible. Also, the 2p rate product is finite, and it is obviously better for a local authority to get its money back for further use.

The lack of security co-operatives can offer is a major stumbling block when loans are needed. Most co-operatives, as has been stressed earlier, are formed by groups of young or unemployed people with little capital, except perhaps some redundancy pay, who are unlikely to own a building and frequently start production with second-hand machinery. Finance is required for plant, equipment and working capital, as well as for rent, wages and other costs. But the co-operators have little to offer for security beyond the commitment of their own labour.

Where loans are given to established co-operatives the security offered is rarely much better. Workers' co-operatives in Britain are not required by law to build up workers' loan or share capital from their wages, and there are few recent examples of this happening. The influence of ICOM on new co-operatives, most of which use its Model Rules, has exacerbated this problem. ICOM's lenders have placed great importance on the concept of collective capital and equality among the co-operators. Members of an ICOM firm, as we already know, are limited by the rules of the organisation to a £1 share each, and members' loan capital is small or non-existent · because differential amounts are thought to give members an uneven commitment to the financial success of the venture. But in any case, the wages paid for several years after start-up are usually very low, making it difficult to accumulate reserves.

In high-risk, unsecured circumstances, some councils will not lend more than half of the total investment needed. Members of co-operatives are expected to find the other half themselves to demonstrate commitment to their enterprise. Members of ICOM firms often argue that their labour should be regarded as equivalent to a financial commitment, especially if they have worked for nothing in the early stages of start-up. But labour has never been accepted by banks as a good enough demonstration of commitment. Strong political will is needed for a council to go this far.

Wandtronics and WEDA

Wandsworth Council helped to form Wandtronics after the closure of Philips Medical Systems in Balham in March 1977. The co-operative started with seven skilled workers and a manager. A successful application was made to the MSC for a grant under the Job Creation Programme to form a co-operative to carry out work in electronics. The council, then Labour-controlled, gave the workers part of a derelict council building which they started to convert for use before they officially began operating, using up £3,500 of their redundancy money in the process. This was later repaid to them by the council. They were also granted a rent-free period from the starting date of October 1977 until April 1979 to cover the rest of the costs of repair work and the installation of central heating. In addition, they were given an interest-free loan of £4,500 over one year under S.137, and a £350 grant for initial expenses, such as a patent search and the building of a prototype. The workers' willingness to use their redundancy money to improve their building and to put in time unpaid to do the conversion work influenced the council's decision to back them.

The co-operative started by making printed circuits. This involved low-level assembly work and sub-contracting. The idea was to create a firm basis for Wandtronics to build upon during which time a more balanced workforce would be assembled and additional skills introduced. Early in 1978 they were assembling stereophonic amplifiers for export to Canada and considered taking an order to put microphones into helmets, using the machinery of the firm which had given them the contract. They aimed to sub-contract for a wide market to build up a good reputation in the electronics field, and eventually to manufacture and market their own product. A car lock device was being designed and tested which was expected to have a very wide market.

While there were many competitors in the field, Wandtronics felt that the demand for small firms to do this type of work was exceptional. Large firms cannot afford to employ a flexible work-force to cover peak workloads. Also, they tend to develop very specialised skills and look to small firms when other abilities are needed. Despite the co-operative's optimistic outlook, profitability was low and the firm was wound up in 1980. Since Wandtronics, no further co-operative has been funded, though the council has recently agreed to set up the Wandsworth Enterprise Development Agency which, it is said, will be concerned specifically with creating and assisting common-ownerships. With a Tory council in power since 1978, this is evidence that co-operatives can shed their left-wing image and offer the prospect of jobs and a stronger small firms sector.

The scheme was engineered by the first secretary of ICOM, Manuela Sykes, who has been an employment liaison officer for the council since 1977. While WEDA will probably remain an exception among Tory authorities, mounting pressure on councils to alleviate the problems of unemployment is likely to result in local develop-ment agencies or municipal enterprise boards[16] being formed which will assist all kinds of firms. Already, Greater Manchester has its Greater Manchester Development Association, formed by a Tory council in 1978 to offer a range of assistance to firms. Other councils are investigating the idea, and discussing the use of local authority pension funds to provide the investment capital needed.

WEDA will receive £46,000 a year for five years from Urban Aid money, and has been granted small sums from a trust and the

Council to cover start-up costs. It will employ six full-time workers, two of whom will be seconded from the London Enterprise Agency through the Action Resource Centre. They will work to a board of directors representing ICOM and ICOF, the London Chamber of Industry and Commerce (LCIC), two councillors (one each from the Labour and Tory parties), co-operatives as they are formed, and others. With the emphasis firmly on creating viable companies, the LCIC member – a local businessman – is important. For the same reason it is hoped a representative from a bank can also be found to join the board. The Agency will work independently on business· matters but will be accountable through the board to the council, and council officers will co-ordinate WEDA's work with departments responsible for providing resources to co-operatives, and with subsidised training projects which may be seedbeds for co-operatives. An interesting feature is the provision made for new co-operatives eventually to have a majority on the board. The democratic principles of ICOM have been uncompromisingly adopted.

More Examples of Aid
The two schemes devised by John Morrison of Fife Regional Council have already been described in Chapter 3. A development agency similar to Wandsworth's was originally envisaged, but the Inwork scheme which was eventually approved is independent of the council. It is accountable to a board of business experts, mostly drawn from the private sector. This does not mean the council's employment objectives will be overriden, because public and private sector interests in co-operatives have much in common. But there will be no ideological input from ICOM or other sectors of the co-operative movement, as there will be in Wandsworth.

Lambeth Council in 1979 gave loans to three co-operatives – Kennington Office Cleaners, Arkwrights, and 50 Products. The loan to the cleaners' co-operative was the most contentious. It was for working capital and was wholly unsecured since the women workers, all from the same council estate, had no capital of their own. Political pressure from the trades council, the local MP – John Tilley, and others persuaded the Council to support the loan application. In fact, the co-operative is running profitably, with one contract from the labour movement – the Labour Research Department – and six others from charities such as NACRO. By 1980 it employed 15 women. Only a small part of the £8,000 loan the Council offered has been taken up. The Council also paid £7,500 to the CDA to do feasibility studies for four co-operatives or 'would-be' co-operatives: Metropolitan Motor Cab Co-operative, Arkwrights, Flypress and Badger, and the House of Lambeth.

Lewisham Council also in 1979 paid the CDA £5,000 to make a study of the potential for co-operatives in the Borough. The CDA's study concluded that the greatest scope lay in the service sector, in areas such as vehicle repair and maintenance, provision of day nurseries, security services, office and window cleaning, waste recycling, contract gardening, and building. These are all labour intensive activities. Manufacturing was considered difficult to start in the present climate with falling demand and high interest rates. A new type of co-operative was proposed to provide these services, called the Neighbourhood Service Co-operative (NSC). It would be a self-financing commercial organisation which would recognise a wider responsibility in providing services to the community. The CDA devised new model rules for the NSC and applied to the Registrar to have them recognised.

Lancashire County Council assisted Clogora in a different way, by providing surplus equipment at a nominal price for its wood-working activities, and a market for its products during the start-up period while commercial outlets were being found and viability achieved. The co-operative repairs and refurbishes school furniture for the council (see Chapter 3).

There are few examples of councils giving co-operatives contracts for work like this. It appears that only Newcastle and Gateshead have given contracts on a commercial basis. After tendering for the work, Sunderlandia obtained modernisation work on council houses from these authorities. Milton Keynes New Town Development Corporation has also given contracts to co-operatives at competitive prices. The Corporation was concerned to generate 3,000 jobs a year over six years since 1976, to provide employment for the people it was housing. The target looked hard to reach, so innovative ideas were tried, including support to co-operatives. While loans could not be offered, nevertheless the Corporation's support in the shape of buildings and reduced rent gave confidence to its own bank, which was willing to make finance available.

Milkwood, an 'enterprise workshop', was given small contracts in 1976 from Milton Keynes Development Corporation to make park benches and bus shelter panels after the wooden pallets made in the beginning had failed to find a solid market, but this effort to help was too late to save the co-operative from liquidation. While

Milkwood suffered from supervision problems and a lack of money for equipment, the inability to market its main product was probably the foremost reason for its collapse. In 1978 the same development corporation gave a contract to Bradwell Signs, to make road signs. The small co-operative was particularly suitable for this type of work because the product was not a standard design and was needed in small quantities over a short period.

Promotional and Advisory Subsidies
While few councils so far have given contracts, loans or grants to co-operatives, grants for promotional and advisory work have been more common. In 1978, Tyne and Wear gave a grant of £5,000, using S.137, to the Northern Region Co-operative Development Association, taking the view that co-operatives might contribute towards the area's economic development, employment creation and investment, and help to diversify employment opportunities.

The council also has a representative on the NRCDA. In the same year, two local councils in Scotland, Strathclyde Region and Central Region, gave £2,000 and £1,500 respectively from their industrial development budgets to the Scottish Co-operatives Development Committee towards a campaign to advertise co-operatives throughout Scotland. The SCDC's intention was to build up a 'register of talents' which listed people, and their skills, who were interested in starting up their own business on a common-ownership or co-operative basis. The aim was to bring individuals together so as to complement their skills; then the SCDC would help them develop their business ideas. Some 70 people expressed interest by taking part in the first meeting where it was hoped skills would be matched. But a second meeting drew only 12 people.

West Glamorgan, Strathclyde, Hackney and Brent councils in 1978 and 1979 sponsored Urban Aid applications for funds to support full-time officers who would promote and advise co-operatives. Camden Council in 1977 took another approach. By themselves they began a campaign to promote co-operatives by advertising the idea on a poster displayed throughout the borough. Out of a £200,000 budget for industrial development, around £50,000 was allocated in both 1977/78 and 1978/79 for co-operatives. By 1980 money had only been spent on the campaign.

The organisers of these initiatives feel the concept of a co-operative is not widely understood. But despite their efforts, potential co-operators have not been queueing up at the town hall for help. It seems doubtful that people – other than those in particularly distressed circumstances – will respond to the presentation of an abstract idea, even if it is backed up with generous offers of business help and finance. Co-operatives have been presented by local councils and others as an alternative way of setting up a firm, as a third sector alongside private and publicly-owned industries, and as a challenge to people who want more control over their working lives. However, in only a few exceptional, though influential, cases have co-operatives been formed as an alternative method of organising working life. After all, it is not easy to form a co-operative. The effort of making democratic decisions at work is difficult for people who feel more comfortable in a traditional hierarchical structure. Furthermore, co-operatives demand more personal commitment in time and money than workers normally expect to give. As already stated, most workers prefer to fight for better conditions in other ways, principally through collective bargaining.

Experience has shown that co-operatives are formed out of strong ideological principles and often when no other solution seems possible bar unemployment. Advertising co-operative principles may establish the idea more widely in the public mind, but more is needed before people will grasp hold of the principles and put them into practice. They must first be alienated by traditional work practices, or see real benefits from a co-operative, or want to save threatened jobs. Possibly the campaigns have been aimed at too broad an audience.

More success has been achieved where promotion has been linked with a development role. In Lewisham, a local neighbourhood councillor identified a group of homeworkers who were persuaded they could have higher wages and more control over their work by forming a co-operative. The Telegraph Textiles Co-operative opened in 1980, employing 20 women making clothes. Kennington Office Cleaners was formed after a community worker identified the potential that existed among women who met at the same social club and had said they wanted to start a business. Hackney Housing Co-operative has taken the same approach. In 1979 it received Urban Aid money to establish Hackney Co-operative Developments, which employed three people to promote workers' co-operatives. It plans to interest, for instance, ethnic groups of men and women attending clubs in forming co-operatives, and to form a textile co-operative from among the unemployed machinists in the area.

However, in these cases an enormous amount of developmental work has gone into a small number of new starts.

Conclusion

The recent wave of new co-operatives bears the marks of various types of state assistance. The number of co-operatives existing in 1980 has been boosted significantly by this help, but in many cases the ventures supported are far from commercially sound and many have collapsed. Those given funds between 1974 and 1978 by central government under the 1972 Industry Act, and by the Manpower Services Commission, are the weakest. Job creation was the primary objective in funding them, and the promoters were unable to give adequate attention to their commercial future.

Local authorities began to assist co-operatives from 1977 onwards, either by themselves or by funding local promotional bodies. Although employment was again the driving force behind these initiatives, councils and promotional bodies were in a better position to build viable businesses, giving a wider range of assistance on a continuous basis to the co-operatives in their area. They have been able to offer accommodation, grants, loans and management expertise. Where help has been given to new or existing ventures it has always been on favourable terms, in recognition of the financial difficulties faced by co-operatives. This form of positive discrimination has been accepted largely by Labour councils. However, despite their enthusiasm and willingness to stretch their resources to make co-operatives succeed, councils have lacked an understanding of their voluntary nature. Too often they have underestimated the degree of commitment needed by the workforce.

At this stage the pay-off in terms of jobs from pump-priming capital and other help has been small. Despite this, governments and councils of the left and right have gained political advantages from the support they have provided. However, these political gains may be short-lived if co-operatives fail to give measurable benefits to the economy itself. With a few exceptions, co-operatives have made little impact on any industrial or service sector. There is no doubt that they have contributed in individual ways as small firms to the needs of national and multi-national companies. But state assistance given to co-operatives in Britain has been too inadequate to enable them to be of any clear and lasting value to economic development. From this perspective, the future of co-operatives in this country looks very uncertain.

7 France: A Shield from the Establishment

The development of workers' co-operatives in France has similar characteristics to the British experience. Periods of rapid growth have been closely associated with structural changes in the economy, and co-operatives have been formed as an ideological response to the effects of these changes on employment opportunities. But there are two major differences. First, a business-like approach to capital has been developed since the middle of the 19th century. Members' share and loan capital has always been encouraged throughout the movement, and a co-operative bank has provided funds to co-operatives since 1938. Secondly, central government has supported co-operatives as viable firms rather than as a means to create jobs, providing markets for them since 1888 for products and services which are essential to the economy.[1] Job creation may have been a secondary aim, but – with a few exceptions – it has never interfered with the commercial aims of the co-operatives.

The French Co-operative Movement

The foundations of the co-operative movement were laid by intellectual idealists, such as Charles Fourier, Philippe Buchez and Louis Blanc in the first half of the 19th century. Like Owen in Britain, they made numerous attempts to form co-operative communities and workshops.[2] The last 30 years of the 19th century saw the first major expansion of co-operatives, but it was not until the late 1960s that interest again developed in co-operative ventures. However, the co-operative ideal never lost the respect of trade unionists and the labour movement, and there was never a spectacular decline in the number of co-operatives.

During the revolutionary struggles of 1848 and the Paris Commune of 1871, co-operatives were encouraged enthusiastically. Later still, in 1876, they were accepted by the first trade union congress as progressive enterprises which were complementary to trade unionism.[3] The major landmarks in the history of co-operation from this early period are all associated with state intervention to encourage them. In 1867, during the reign of Emperor Napoleon III, a legal form for co-operatives was established. There were a number of reasons for this. Napoleon conceded to the co-operatives' demands because he was keen to win working class support by introducing social measures. The pressure for organisation among workers was a key issue at that time. Napoleon thought he could contain some of the militancy among the population by encouraging co-operative societies, though a proviso was added to the new law, preventing societies from holding meetings to propagate their views or recruit members.[4] In practical terms this meant little. Co-operatives were in any case subject to regular police harassment and administrative obstruction.

At this time major building programmes were being carried out in Paris and elsewhere in France. It was Napoleon's ambition to complete and expand the work of his uncle in 'beautifying' Paris, giving it the monumental character considered fitting for an imperial capital.[5] Economic expansion and capital accumulation were encouraged by the building of canals, roads and railways throughout the country. Another aim of these public works projects was to cut unemployment. Between 1850 and 1880 industry provided 34 per cent of France's total production, while 12 per cent came from building activity.[6] It was in this sector that workers' co-operatives were to become valuable to the state. With a reputation for efficiency and quality of work, they won many contracts for public building and later played an important part in reconstruction work after the two World Wars. They have continued to dominate among co-operatives in France.

Co-operatives first received contracts from the state in 1888. This considerable benefit resulted from the publication of the Waldreck-Rousseau report, commissioned by the Minister of the Interior in 1883. The law was subsequently broadened to allow co-operatives to undertake a wider range of public work. The second outcome of the report was the formation, in 1884, of the Chambre Consultative des Associations Co-opératives Ouvrières de Production, a central organisation for assisting and co-ordinating the activities of co-operatives, at first comprising 29 affiliated societies. In 1937 it took on a greater promotional role and was renamed the Confédération Générale des Sociétés Ouvrières de Production.

In 1893 the co-operatives themselves set up an institution specifically to lend money to co-operatives, called the Banque Co-opérative des Sociétés Co-opératives Ouvrières de Production (now the Banque Française de Crédit Co-opératif), which operated as an arm of the Chambre Consultative.[7] In 1938 the Caisse Centrale de Crédit Co-opératif was set up by the government – with its financial backing – providing a more substantial source of external capital for new or expanding co-operatives, and for forms of co-operation other than agriculture. In 1970 the Banque Co-opérative des SCOP fused with the Banque Française de Crédit Co-opératif and was taken over by the Caisse Centrale de Crédit Co-opératif, consolidating the major sources of external finance into one organisation. SCOP then began to build up another fund of its own.

Comparisons with Britain

The types of co-operative (or SCOP as they are sometimes referred to in this chapter) existing in France are in some respects similar to those in Britain. There are co-operatives formed 50 or more years ago in printing and in specialist crafts like furniture making, clothing and leather manufacture, and recently the bulk of new starts has been by middle-class idealists in areas like computing, market research, acting, audio-visual teaching and wholefood retailing. They reflect a growing desire by industry for specialist services, disillusionment among educated white-collar workers in large-scale industry, a fear of job loss from redundancy, and a wish to experiment with new forms of democratic organisation.

CERIA[8] is an example of the new type of co-operative. Formed in 1965 with four skilled engineers, it provides a software computer service to other firms in the Paris area where it operates. The originators had previously worked for a large electrical engineering company. They suffered from insecurity in an industry hit by closures, and from lack of control over their working conditions. The co-operative from the start prepared its own computer programmes. By the end of 1969 the number of workers had grown to 15, and by 1978 to 30 – thought to be the optimum size for democratic decision-making in this type of firm. After facing financial difficulties in 1972–73 (caused by its relationship to another company) CERIA decided to diversify and now also produces software for microcomputers. This has placed the enterprise in the favourable position of having few competitors, and profits have increased.

There are also examples of co-operatives formed out of workers' occupations. The number of requests made to SCOP for help when factories close has been about 30 a year for the last four years. Only a few co-operatives have emerged from these situations, but the pleas for help are expected to grow. Considering the stigma attached to Meriden, KME and the *Scottish Daily News,* this different French experience is revealing. Co-operatives are formed in this way because they are accepted by the labour movement and because they are effectively helped by SCOP and government. For instance, in the case of Manuest in Châtenois, a co-operative making furniture formed after the collapse of a private firm and an occupation in 1974, two full-time advisers were sent by SCOP to produce a feasibility study. When a favourable report was produced, the co-operative received finance from the government and banks, and support from the unions involved. One SCOP adviser stayed on as manager because of his commitment to the co-operative.

Conversions

The impact of conversions is larger and more important in France than in Britain, but conversions have not been ideologically motivated. They have arisen out of a variety of situations. One quarter came from collapsed firms. Only one tenth were formed when the owners with no successor to run their business sold it to the workers. SCOP Cogné of Le Mans is such a case. The Cogné family firm had made clothes for women and children for 53 years. The last owners had put their lives into it and wanted it to continue. They thought a co-operative would stand more chance of success than would a sale or bringing in a manager from outside.

The workers were non-militant and were used to a hierarchical management structure. Few of the workers – mainly women – were union members, and no union was involved in the co-operative's formation. It took two years of discussion before all the workers would agree to the transfer of the firm to their ownership. The SCOP regional office at Rennes advised the Cognés on their project, and they benefited from a new law which relieved them of the necessity of paying any tax on the transfer arrangement. Like Scott Bader, this type of co-operative is exceptional in being inspired by the beliefs and needs of a family firm. However, SCOP believes there is scope for creating many co-operatives this way in future. Research has shown that the owners of 70 per cent of firms employing between

20 and 500 workers have no successor and no chance of selling up to competitors or others.

Major Co-operatives

Easily the biggest group of co-operatives in France is in the building industry, involved either in building work or the manufacture of building materials. In 1978 there were 261 in these trades representing 40 per cent of all co-operatives, and 43 per cent of those affiliated to SCOP. In that year there were 240,000 building firms in France (including subsidiaries), of which 200,000 were very small – one to two persons. Most of the co-operatives are also small, but both L'Avenir de Lyon and L'Hirondelle employ over 1,000 workers. L'Hirondelle undertook some of the construction of the Charles de Gaulle airport.

Outside the building industry there are three large co-operatives which are of major importance: L'Association des Ouvrières en Matériel Électrique (ACOME), L'Association des Ouvrières en Instruments de Précision (AOIP) and La Vérrerie Ouvrière d'Albi, a glass producer. Each of these is a major competitor at the national level. The importance of AOIP, ACOME and the building co-operatives is accounted for by their relationship to the economy and to the state. While central government has contributed to an effective legal, administrative and financial framework for co-operatives to develop, it has rarely assisted them directly with finance. But by giving contracts to co-operatives because of their superior performance, the state has been a key factor in the movement's survival and growth.

Other Strands of the Movement

There are two more strands of the movement which have, in some areas, made links with each other. Since 1978 the government has made funds available, in a similar way to the MSC in Britain, for job creation projects in areas of high unemployment. Small groups of two to three young people have obtained these funds to cover their wages and to start enterprises in building, toy-making, fish-breeding, car repair and the like. Usually they are middle-class, have a 'libertarian' perspective and are outside organised political parties and trade unions. A number of these ventures exist in Brittany.

At Plougrescant, in Brittany, there is a centre called Avel Nevez, where some of these small enterprises run on co-operative lines have received advice. Avel Nevez was founded in the mid-1970s by a group of friends of mixed ages and backgrounds who wanted to set up an alternative university where modern philosophical issues could be discussed. Its establishment as a legal association was made easier by forming a SCOP. The activities carried out at Avel Nevez have evolved according to who was living there in different periods. It succeeded in its aim of attracting members – from all over France – who came for reflective and exploratory discussions. A number of more concrete activities also developed, which included support for the local SCOPs. Their aim was to help these ventures by holding courses at Avel Nevez in alternative living and work practices, and by putting the SCOPs in touch with one another. No commercial expertise was offered. A similar centre was started at Grenoble, and another is being formed in Paris.

So far the number of people involved in this kind of work is very small. But, as one of Avel Nevez's founder members said, 'Its actions are perhaps more symbolic than real. Nevertheless, they are serious and challenging, and have already had some effect on the conventional co-operative movement'. They have criticised the older co-operatives for being bureaucratic, centralised and undemocratic. They also accuse them of offending in other ways – by making armaments and by stifling debate on important issues at co-operative congresses. Some of these idealists would like the whole co-operative movement to ally itself more closely to the labour movement. At the 1974 Congress they persuaded the movement to adopt a statement saying that co-operatives were socialist in concept – an achievement in a movement which has consistently waved the banner of political neutrality. But most are more concerned to make progress on their own doorstep than to influence the political direction of the co-operative movement.

Recently, the trend has been towards the formation of service co-operatives. About half the newest co-operatives are in two branches of the service industry – 'material services', such as cleaning and security, and professional services. The movement is keen to promote the material services as a progressive policy because there are few union members in these fields and wages and conditions are poor. However, success has been limited because the sector has many foreign workers, such as Algerians, for whom co-operation is an alien concept.

Growth, Distribution and Size

The number of co-operatives in France increased during the 1970s, though the explosion was not so marked as in Britain because co-operatives have been forming continuously since the 19th century. Nevertheless, 50 per cent of those existing in 1975 were formed after 1950, and one third were less than ten years old.[9]

Growth in Workers' Co-operatives since 1885

Pre-1885	fluctuating widely
1885	40
1919	120
1928	280
1936	400
1939	440
1970	600

Source: A. Antoni, *La Co-opération Ouvrière de Production*, by the Confédération Générale des SCOP, 1970, p. 15.

SCOP has estimated the number of co-operatives, the turnover, employment and distribution in 1975. Although there were 802 societies altogether, only 576 were registered as members of SCOP. Of the remainder, 200 were thought to be registered for tax purposes and were not genuine co-operatives. This means that the total number was 602. In 1975 the total turnover of SCOPs (members of SCOP) was over 3,500,000 Fr. By far the greatest concentration of co-operatives is in the Paris region (204) with others scattered throughout the ten other regions. In 1980 SCOP claimed there were 750 true co-operatives and the rate at which they were being formed was still on the increase, with 119 created in 1979 alone.

Geographical Distribution of Workers' Co-operatives, 1978

Regional Union of Paris	204
West	82
South East	66
North Picardy	53
Provence	42
South West	37
Centre	35
Atlantic	18
Burgundy	18
East	13
Champagne	8

Source: *The Workers' Productive Co-operative Societies* by the Confédération Générale des SCOP, 1978.

Number of Workers' Co-operatives in each Industry, 1978

Building and public works	258
Building materials	3
Printing and paper trades	69
Metal working	47
Furnishing of brain work	86
Furnishing of material services	46
Furniture	12
Glasswork	5
Foodstuff and agriculture	21
Leather and clothing	18
Miscellaneous	11

Source: *The Workers' Productive Co-operative Societies* by the Confédération Générale des SCOP, 1978.

Finally, a comment on the size of co-operatives. It has already been pointed out that the building firms employ between four and 1,200 workers. But only two employ over 1,000 and the rest are small. Apart from the three other large co-operatives already mentioned, a few are medium size, employing between 20 and 500. These are mostly in the printing trades or are co-operatives recently formed from ailing firms. The typical French co-operative has less than 20 workers. In the 19th century Paris had few large firms. In 1886, 60 per cent of the industrial workforce was employed in workshops of less than ten workers. Co-operatives existed among these. Since then capital has become vastly more concentrated and centralised, and the percentage of employees in small firms has fallen. But the size of most co-operatives has remained small. Also, they have remained labour intensive. Greater specialisation has occurred as the financial difficulties for this sector have grown.

Legal Provisions

The law is important in providing an adequate framework within which co-operatives can operate successfully. All co-operatives are registered as a form of limited liability company in France. They are a special type of 'société-anonyme', called 'sociétés anonymes à capital et personnel variable', as laid down in the law of 1867. This law covers such matters as the minimum number of associate members, responsibilities of presidents and directors, the election of officers, delegated powers, the presentation of accounts and balance sheets, the holding of annual general meetings, and taxation. The law of 1867 and subsequent laws were consolidated and extended by the Act of 1947 in which the Code du Travail lays down the fundamental principles for the operation of all forms of co-operation.[10] Since 1947 there have been further additions and modifications to the law specifically governing workers' co-operatives. There are several legal provisions which shape the financial structure of co-operatives and have no equivalent in British co-operative law. They have encouraged greater growth and financial stability than in Britain. The laws governing British co-operatives leave many more decisions to the co-operatives themselves and to the Registrar of Friendly Societies.

To begin with, the minimum amount of capital needed to form a co-operative is 10,000 Francs, which cannot be reduced during the life of the enterprise. This regulation was introduced in recognition of the tendency of new co-operatives to lack funds. For the same reason a co-operative must put 15 per cent of its annual profits into a reserve fund until it equals the amount of share capital. Since most start-up capital is in the form of workers' shares, this guarantees a doubling of the capital available to the enterprise as early as possible. Also it is especially useful in being non-withdrawable.[11] There is a provision for further reserves to be created at the discretion of the enterprise. Another important law prevents a co-operative from paying back shares to members who leave the firm 'if the effect of doing so would be to reduce the capital below one quarter of the greatest sums of capital raised since its constitution'.[12] For a co-operative there is less capital available for new starts, growth and survival than for other firms; the picture in France is similar to that in Britain. However, the pragmatism of the law and the centralisation of resources provide a stronger basis for the co-operatives.

Share Capital

Like the CPF and ICOM co-operatives, the non-refundable capital of French co-operatives is not owned individually. It is used as a collective resource. Co-operatives are often short of refundable capital, relying more on reserves and external loans. But it appears that great importance is placed on the workers' shares and loans. SCOP considers that the strength and stability of a co-operative depends more on the non-refundable capital but that the workers' funds retain a special value.

Until the Caisse Centrale de Crédit Co-opératif was set up in 1938 share capital was a vital source of finance, and when members ceased to work for the co-operative they were encouraged to keep their shares in the firm. Shareholders from outside were also welcomed. The disadvantages of this category of member were thought to be outweighed by the need for working capital and investment funds. The co-operatives still encourage their members to acquire as many shares as possible. The share capital, although variable, provides a basis for borrowing and can be useful when there is a financial crisis. It has a further advantage. It implies worker-commitment to the enterprise. Where managers and supervisors are shareholding members they often accept a lower than average salary for the job. Also, commitment to the firm may lead to a more flexible approach to the production process. For instance, demarcation lines between jobs are less strict than in competitor firms, and workers take a broad interest in the financial and marketing plans of the enterprise so that long term objectives are not overturned by short term gains. Sometimes a smaller than usual number of administrators (including managers and supervisors) are needed, and savings can be made.

L'Association des Ouvrières en Instruments de Précision (AOIP)

Over time the level of commitment in the older co-operatives has declined, and there are few existing where all the eligible[13] workers are also members with share capital. The second, third and fourth generations of workers taken on are not always enthusiastic about co-operative principles in the same way as the originators. AOIP is an example of such a firm. This co-operative began as a small company in 1896 making cameras and sextants. Unemployment was high everywhere and the workers at AOIP sacrificed a great deal to keep their co-operative viable, including selling their own furniture to provide capital for the firm. Since 1906 they have produced telephone equipment.

In 1978 the co-operative employed 4,650 workers of whom 35 per cent were members, giving 5 per cent of their annual wages to the co-operative as share capital. The co-operative can still reduce wage costs by maintaining narrower pay differentials than in competitor firms. Managers accept a low wage for ideological reasons, many having worked their way up to management positions over a long period. But otherwise the firm functions like any other. In the 1970s the demand for mechanical equipment was replaced by a demand for electronic machinery. The co-operative found itself in a fragile position with little flexibility to diversify and establish new markets.

The management of AOIP believes that in future, the success of the firm against national and international competition will only be ensured if large loans are raised, a higher quality of management is brought in at market rates, and major investments are made in new products. In other words, unless major changes are introduced, AOIP will soon be functioning as a declining firm but with the 'disadvantage' of being a co-operative – it cannot easily make redundancies, for instance.

The management believes that share capital is still crucially important both as funds and as a symbol of commitment to co-operative principles. The firm is now considering introducing some radical changes to increase its membership rate. One possibility mentioned was a plan to divide the enterprise into smaller units where co-operative education and an identification with the firm is more easily attained.

L'Association des Ouvrières en Matériel Électrique (ACOME)

In contrast to AOIP, all the eligible workers at ACOME are members of the co-operative. Founded as a small firm producing copper wire after the collapse of a private company in 1932, ACOME grew to employ 760 workers in 1978. After three years every worker becomes a member by choice, and through recognised procedures. Most workers remain in the company a long time. The level of commitment seems to have characterised the firm throughout its life. Workers have not felt the need to join a trade union and negotiations on all matters are carried out internally.

The enterprise has consistently made profits. They have been especially good over the last ten years and reserves have grown about 20 per cent a year. The workforce has also expanded fast. In 1960 ACOME employed 207. The number rose to 360 in 1970, 630 in1976 and 760 in 1978. Output rose from 735 tonnes (of copper wire) per year in 1970 to 1,760 tonnes in 1976. This record was achieved alongside heavy investments in technological change, a growing international market in the public sector, and the payment of above average wages to both workers and management, with additional bonuses.

All investments have been made from reserves (or non-refundable capital). It has not been necessary for workers to own large numbers of shares. In 1976 the firm's share capital stood at only 4,000,000 Fr, compared with 59,000,000 Fr in reserves. Neither has the firm borrowed from banks. ACOME is a highly successful workers' co-

ACOME: Wages and Bonuses p.a. 1976/77

	Wages		Bonuses (% of profits)
	Workers	Management	Workers and management
Average for industry	45,000 Fr	74,000 Fr	
ACOME	45,000 Fr plus 46%	74,000 Fr plus 28%	17.6%

Source: ACOME

operative which has been a net investor in joint stock banks and the Caisse Centrale. While its success can partly be attributed to a continually growing market for copper wire in France and elsewhere, productivity has been raised by making large savings on administrative costs which have resulted from the continuous application of co-operative principles.

Sources of Loans
Workers' co-operatives in France can borrow external capital from three main sources: the Caisse Centrale de Crédit Co-opératif, the Banque Française de Crédit Co-opératif (BFCC) and the joint stock banks. Only if they have a strong capital base will they be able to borrow from the joint stock banks and where this occurs, the co-operatives usually borrow from a group of five banks, of which one will be the Caisse Centrale and one the local bank – an 'associété de développement régionale'. The joint stock banks find difficulty in assessing the risk of lending to small co-operatives because they are not owned and run by entrepreneurs; the directors with whom they negotiate any financial transaction can be dismissed by the owner-workers. Therefore, for most co-operatives, the Caisse Centrale and the BFCC are the only sources of capital. Where a co-operative has a very weak capital structure, SCOP has a fund from which it can make small loans. Once confidence has been shown in an enterprise by this central organisation, the Caisse Centrale may then be able to make a loan.

The Caisse Centrale and the BFCC currently make loans on an assessment of the risk involved and nothing else. However, there are two important differences between these financial institutions and others. First, they advise co-operatives on how to organise their capital structure in order to present a case successfully. Secondly, they are more sensitive to co-operative principles and can assess the risk more accurately than can a joint stock bank.

The Caisse Centrale and the BFCC

The Caisse Centrale de Crédit Co-opératif is a semi-public body set up in 1938 with a special statute so that it is constituted as a union of co-operatives. It aims to carry out 'any banking operation meant to facilitate the administration or creation of non-agricultural co-operatives or mutualist institutions or such institutions providing social services'. It is governed by a general assembly in which member societies have one vote per 50 members with a maximum of 50 votes, and is administered by a council which is elected by the general assembly, with each member serving for six years. The activities of the Caisse Centrale are administered by the state in a number of ways. Its statutes must be approved by the Ministers of Finance and Labour; its president and directors are nominated by government; and its affairs are subject to government audit. Also, government commissioners sit on the board of government representatives and submit an annual report to government on the activities of the bank. Borrowing, lending and guaranteeing loans are all subject to the advice of a council of credit made up of representatives from each of the ministries of the interior and from the BFCC.[14]

The Caisse Centrale de Crédit Co-opératif manages four main sources of funds: the funds of its member societies; borrowings from public or private bodies[15] and from the issue of bonds to the public (with government allowances, guarantees and approval of terms); commercial borrowings; and advances made to it by the state for particular purposes. From its total funds the bank lent only 1 per cent to workers' co-operatives in 1976, and 2 per cent in 1977. Despite its small scale, this part of its work has caused some major problems. After 40 years of experience in this field, expertise is still being developed and any loans to workers' co-operatives are still considered high risk. However, the bank is willing to lend in this high risk area since workers' co-operatives are the bedrock of co-operation in France.

Recent events[16] have proved that this risk must be reflected in the bank's overall lending policy to co-operatives. Instead of concentrating loans in a few large firms, the Caisse Centrale now spreads its finance more widely. Currently, most co-operatives have loans from this bank. Of the 100 largest – which account for 86 per cent of total turnover – 64 have loans from the Caisse Centrale and for most of these it is their only source of capital. Only nine have no long term loans from this source.

The Caisse Centrale lends in the medium term (two to seven years) and in the long term (eight to 15 years, and occasionally to 20 years), and interest rates are lower than other sources of finance. Loans are rarely made which exceed the co-operative's funds. Where necessary shares may be bought to balance the capital structure of the firm during the loan period. Most commonly, loans are from five to seven years for equipment, particularly for new co-operatives. Leasing, guaranteeing and other facilities are offered by subsidiaries of the Caisse Centrale. The requirements for security are the same as for other banks. The Caisse Centrale asks for a mortgage on assets and to have first call on assets in the case of liquidation. Sometimes they ask worker-owners to sign an agreement to repay a loan should the enterprise collapse. This happens where the co-operative is very labour intensive and has few assets for security. In other words, if the Caisse Centrale believes a co-operative will survive, it will find the security needed.

The Banque Française de Crédit Co-opératif is a subsidiary of the Caisse Centrale de Crédit Co-opératif. It now includes the funds of the Banque Co-opérative des SCOP which was managed by SCOP. After the collapse of several building firms, these funds were weakened to the extent that the government intervened by encouraging the Caisse Centrale to take them over. The BFCC is small and in 1978 provided working capital to a maximum of 30–40m Fr., the same as other banks. If necessary it can draw on the funds and skills of the Caisse Centrale and this has reduced its vulnerability. Also, to strengthen its funds it lends to organisations other than co-operatives, such as sports centres or public hospitals, where the risk can be assessed more easily. The funds are generally used for overdrafts at a high rate of interest – 14–16 per cent in 1978 – or for discounting, and are lent to a variety of co-operatives including old co-operatives, new-starts and co-operatives formed out of collapsing capitalist firms.

From this description it is obvious that the Caisse Centrale and BFCC offer similar facilities to other banks. However, there are differences in the way their funds are managed. To begin with, some co-operatives – particularly new-starts – do not apply to the Caisse Centrale without first getting advice from SCOP. Secondly, a broad range of factors are taken into account before loans are made. Half the risk is thought to rest on the following factors: the history of the co-operative, its commercial position, its methods of operation, the quality of management, technical aspects, the means of production (age of machinery, layout, etc) and the 'social climate'. The latter includes things like the history of trade unionism, demarcation organisation, and the age structure of management. For example, if all the managers are nearing retirement at the same time, problems might be created both by their leaving and their withdrawal of share capital. The other 50 per cent of risk is thought to depend on financial factors. To assess this, a financial analysis is made jointly by the co-operative and the Caisse Centrale. This involves presenting, for example, a three to four year forecast, investment programmes (for large co-operatives), profit and loss accounts for the best three years, a history of growth, the availability of working capital, and the existence of overdrafts, credits and shareholders' funds.

Without the Caisse Centrale and the BFCC co-operatives would still exist. But these well co-ordinated and centralised sources of funds have increased the size of the movement and strengthened sections of industry where co-operatives are important, for example in the building industry. Nevertheless, the availability of special funds has not obliterated the financial problems of co-operatives. Their peculiar structure has always made it hard for banks to assess the risk of lending to them, and this itself has curtailed borrowing. The capital available has not made any significant difference to the size of co-operatives, or to what they do. Most are small, labour intensive, make specialist products, operate in industries where technological change is slow and where markets are steady. Only where conditions are exceptionally favourable have co-operatives grown large.

State Contracts
The state in France has intervened in another way to help co-operatives. It has given finance for certain projects and provided a market for products made by co-operatives. Consistent with its help in providing a legal framework and a bank, the state has never deliberately favoured individual co-operatives over and above other firms. But where they have provided goods which are essential to the economy at competitive prices, the state has facilitated their growth and development by offering them contracts. Support for co-operatives has never been regarded as a social service or a subsidy –

except for small scale job creation projects, as support for 'lame ducks' or as experiments in industrial democracy. Finance and contracts have always been given on strictly commercial criteria.

Contracts for co-operatives have been most important in the building industry where they have been awarded since 1888. In 1978 there were 258 co-operatives in this industry. Contracts for work are currently regulated by the Code des Marchés Publics, which lays down that a *lot réservé* can be offered to co-operatives by public authorities. The Code states that if it is practicable, one quarter of the work involved in a project will be temporarily reserved for co-operatives to undertake at the average price of the other three *lots*. If several co-operatives compete for a single *lot*, the choice is made by means of a ballot.[17] For a co-operative to qualify for a *lot réservé*, three quarters of its members must be working permanently for the enterprise, and it must produce written evidence that it is on a register drawn up by the Minister for Social Affairs and published in the official journal of the French Republic. In addition, the contract must not exceed 150,000 Fr.[18] These contractual favours have helped to ensure the survival of a large number of co-operatives which have provided services to the state when they were required, but without the state taking any responsibility for them.

The building co-operatives' work is spread between private contracts, contracts for the state and contracts for the Locales Collectives. There is no emphasis on any one sector, although certain co-operatives work only for the state while others work only for the Locales Collectives or for the private sector. The large scale building programmes in France under Napoleon III and after the two world wars, have meant the supply of work has been consistently high until the cutbacks in public spending recently.

Public Sector Dependence

Co-operatives in other sectors also rely heavily on the public sector market. AOIP, for example, began making specialist mechanical equipment and in 1906 was given a government contract to make telephone switching equipment for the PTT (Poste Télégraphe et Télécommunication). The contract was renewed annually and by 1976, 200 telephone exchanges had been produced and installed by the firm throughout France. By 1977/78, 90 per cent of AOIP's production was being sold to the PTT. However, it was not the sole supplier of this product to the state. It only supplied about 11 per cent of the telephone equipment market in France. In other words, its competitiveness is also maintained by the sale of licences to other firms for the manufacture of its products.

The telephone system in France was mechanical, so many parts of AOIP's production process were labour intensive, such as relays, wiring, testing and electro-mechanical systems. Recently, the government decided to change to an electronic system. This will require less labour and will involve a completely different production process. The electronic equipment itself will not be produced by the co-operative since it would require new skills and major capital investment. These are not possible for a co-operative to acquire or undertake. In future, AOIP will import parts from the USA at a high price and assemble and test the final products. It will be left undertaking the least skilled and least profitable parts of the production process. The PTT market could be removed altogether from AOIP should it become more profitable to integrate all the production processes together in the USA.

AOIP is in a vulnerable position and has been forced to diversify its products, develop new markets and reduce its sales to the PTT to around 50 per cent. It is now beginning to make different specialist mechanical products such as measuring equipment, navigation instruments and mechanical industrial equipment. New markets have been found, for instance among large shipping companies and the Ministry of Defence. The training school attached to the co-operative could help it to survive. Large investments are being put into this and into research and development to adapt the firm's training programmes to new needs and to develop new products. Other important factors influencing its future are its large size and its good profit record, which means external finance can be raised fairly easily. However, the co-operative's size is at the same time problematic. Only 35 per cent of the workers are members, and this is thought to have lowered productivity.

The example shows that AOIP's growth over 70 years was due to a steady market in the public sector for a specialised product, no major technological changes, and labour intensiveness. The introduction of new technology into the telecommunications industry will enable the PTT to provide a service at a lower cost, but AOIP cannot make the investments and redundancies necessary to restructure itself and adapt to the new production process. It has been forced into the less skilled end of the market. It has tried to keep its workforce continuously in productive activity, find other products with similar public sector outlets as a replacement for the manufacture of telephone equipment, and retrain its workforce for new tasks. It is also looking for ways to increase its co-operative character to raise productivity and reduce labour costs.

Co-operative Federations

Two sectors of co-operation – the building and printing industries – are large enough to support a federation. In the building industry the Fédération des SCOP du Bâtiment et des Travaux Publics is an advisory body which represents the co-operatives in negotiations with the public sector, employers' organisations, professional bodies and SCOP. It also communicates useful information to member societies on technical and legal matters and investigates new markets. For the 75 or so printing co-operatives, a similar federation was formed in 1964. It compares experiences in member firms on matters such as technical problems, prices, contracts and management. Flexibility has been introduced into the industry through a work-exchange scheme, and the federation also negotiates with banks on behalf of the co-operatives.

Like the printing co-operatives in Britain, many contracts are made with the sympathetic labour movement, but the prices charged for work are the same for every customer – they are at competitive rates. Monsieur Gérard Collet, currently the permanent secretary of the federation and president of a printing co-operative – Cootypographie of Asnières in Paris, pointed to a situation in the printing industry which is very similar to that facing some of the CPF co-operatives in Britain. The printing industry is in a crisis. Unemployment exists, but at the same time it is hard to attract young people into printing firms or to find anyone who wants to join for the co-operative principles. On the positive side, the co-operatives have usually appointed managers from the shop floor, and so have avoided hierarchical practices being introduced from outside. Also, wage differentials are generally low (for instance, in Cootypographie the highest wage is two and a half times the lowest) and labour costs have been kept down. But unlike British co-operatives, their French counterparts have good access to outside loans and they pay better wages than the industry as a whole.

Conclusion

The early co-operatives in France were in similar industries and formed in similar ways to the older ones in Britain, but their development has been less isolated. The state has had no illusions about the value of co-operatives to the economy. Since the last century contracts have been awarded to these enterprises on a competitive basis for building and manufacturing work. Their reputation for quality, reliability and efficiency made them suited to the job of providing infrastructure for the economy – houses, roads, bridges, telecommunications networks, wire, and armaments. Both central government and the municipalities have given them contracts, and central government in 1938 backed up its support by forming the Caisse Centrale. With this type of aid, co-operatives in the building industry have grown to represent half the co-operatives in France, and two of the largest attribute their growth to their reliable state markets. The most recent trend is for local authorities to show more and more interest in encouraging all kinds of co-operatives in order to create and save jobs in their areas.

The Caisse Centrale, the BFCC and SCOP between them provide a well co-ordinated advisory service on finance and enable the co-operatives to borrow on favourable terms. While the weaker capital base of co-operatives is recognised, in all other respects co-operatives are treated in a strictly business-like way, tendering for contracts with other firms and charging competitive prices for their goods and services. Only in a few cases so far have co-operatives been formed with temporary state funds to create jobs. Even Manuest was seen as an important producer of furniture as well as a major employer in the locality.

For its part, the co-operative movement has produced a strong, centralised service for advising co-operatives on other matters, and for negotiating on their behalf with outside bodies. Also, it has formed federations in the building and printing industries which contribute to the commercial and co-operative development of their members. Since 1970 co-operative firms have been contributing one third of their shares to SCOP, building up a reserve of central funds. By 1980 25m Fr. of collective capital had been accumulated in this fund and the total is increasing annually by some 4m Fr. The fund is expected to reach 50m Fr. by 1985. It is used by SCOP to give start-up capital to new co-operatives and to strengthen older ones. However, the movement still feels vulnerable enough to see advantages in political neutrality. The leadership of SCOP has made no political alliances. But this may change for two reasons. First, the increasing number of collapses among large firms, and the worker resistance from *L'Affaire Lip* onwards,[19] has resulted in a number of co-operatives being formed from the wreckage. This has needed trade union support, and in future could lead to a stronger link with this organ of the labour movement. Secondly, more radical and political ideas have recently been surfacing among the new co-operatives in the professional services, and those like Avel Nevez – now the fastest growing sector. The core of the movement, dominated by the older firms, is slowly giving ground. Despite these conflicts, there is nothing like the fragmentation of perspectives that exists in Britain. The roots of the movement are more firmly in socialist traditions, and at the same time its supporters approach with realism the business needs of co-operatives in a capitalist economy.

8 Italy – A Political Strategy

Italy has many more workers' co-operatives than Britain or France. Their strength can, to a large extent, be attributed to a planned programme rather than to the actions of individual co-operatives, or to the availability of capital. A political awareness pervades the movement. Idealism has not disappeared; the Italian movement considers that it is impossible to build a co-operative movement without it. But the co-operatives have staked their future alongside other sectors of co-operation and the labour movement. They have woven together in a network that protects them from companies which oppose their ideology. At the same time, their competitiveness has won them favours from the state, and they have offered progressive working conditions which trade unions have welcomed and encouraged.

A History of Political Support

Co-operatives have been actively supported by political parties since the last century. The Lega Nazionale delle Co-operative e Mutue (Lega) was set up in 1893, and from the start was closely associated with the Socialist Party, formed in 1892. By 1919 a Catholic-supporting section of the Lega broke away to form the Confederazione Co-operative Italiane (Confederazione). A second split occurred in 1945 when the Associazione Generale delle Co-operative Italiane (Associazone) broke away from the Lega. During the Fascist period from 1922 to 1945 the Lega and Confederazione were made illegal and dissolved. The movement almost collapsed. But the militant spirit among the co-operatives prevented their destruction; a number of co-operatives became organising centres for the resistance. After 1945 the movement was re-established and has continued to grow, constantly expanding into new areas of the economy. This all happened with minimal support from either the state or any of the major banks.

Today there are three major political divisions among them. The Lega is predominantly supported by the Communist Party, Socialist Party and Republican Party; the Confederazione is supported by the Christian Democratic Party; and the Associazione is supported by the Social Democratic Party and the Republican Party. The Lega and the Confederazione are strong and offer a wide range of business expertise to co-operatives through central and regional offices. Since the late 1960s the federations have loosened their ties with the parties and act more autonomously. This was not to relinquish their political allegiances, but to develop stronger links with each other, to encourage a wider political base for their support, and to build a forum for negotiating collectively with public and private agencies.

The movement emerged first in the North of Italy as a reaction against unemployment, low wages, poor working conditions, poor quality goods and high prices. Italy became industrialised later than Britain and France, and there is no record of co-operatives existing until 1850. In Emilia Romagna where the movement is strong, the first co-operatives appeared in the building trades. In a pre-dominantly agricultural economy, workers were drawn away from the land into construction work to improve land-drainage and infra-structure. Co-operatives were formed to compete for public works.

Growth of the Movement

The size of the workers' co-operative sector is hard to discover. Little detailed information is available for the whole movement. However, the confederation in April 1979 claimed to represent 1,780 workers' co-operatives. Among these, building construction firms dominated with 860, followed by 473 in services, 322 industrial co-operatives, and 125 *artigiani* (small workshops). One month later another 115 had been added to the total. The Lega report that there are 3 million members in all types of co-operative affiliated to it; 2 million are affiliated to the Confederazione; and 200,000 are affiliated to the Associazione. According to the Confederazione, co-operatives are formed in three ways. 15 per cent are set up spontaneously. This is particularly common in the building industry where workers are not employed full-time and look for better working conditions in co-operatives. Also, young professionals have recently formed co-operatives of architects, engineers, and the like. One quarter are

converted from private firms. These are not philanthropic hand-
overs. Sometimes they occur in the building industry where taxation
laws make it easy; at other times they occur when private firms are
in trouble and, with the help of the federations, the owners sell up to
the workers.

The majority of co-operatives, some 60 per cent, have been
promoted by the federations. In some cases, the federations join with
the trade unions and state development agencies to form a co-
operative as the best way of providing a certain function. For
example, in 1979 a large co-operative producing fishing nets was
formed by the Confederazione, the state agency ENI and the
National Federation of Fishing. Equally important are the co-operatives formed out of the ashes of collapsing firms. This drains the
resources of the federations, and viability must look certain before
the effort is made. However, extra commitment is given to a group of
workers who have fought to keep their jobs and want to run their
own firm. In these cases the federations can call on finance of their
own through the solidarity among members in the co-operative
sector. But the opportunities to act in this way are limited because of
the financial burdens placed on the movement.

In these cases, trade union support is crucial. Since the early
1970s the unions have lost some of their traditional suspicion of
co-operatives, and no longer see them as diverting attention from the
wages struggle, or as a 'last resort' for workers in collapsing firms.
This change has come about because the policies of the trade union
have broadened from strategies for raising wages to include a more
positive approach to economic development. And – reminiscent of
the co-operatives' aims – they demand more participation and information for workers, and planning agreements on investment targets.
At a time of falling rates of profit in large firms, some companies seek
to hive off their less remunerative parts. Attempts have been made
to set up co-operatives in these weaker sections and for the 'parent'
firms to provide them with contracts. At first, these opportunities for
expanding the co-operative sector looked attractive to the
federations. But now they are treated with more caution, and
supported only if the workers want and can have self-management,
and if the co-operative movement, and not a private firm, is in
control of the co-operatives. For example, the federations had an
offer from Louisa Spagnola, a clothing and knitting firm, to form a
co-operative from the collar and button-making section. Louisa
Spagnola wanted to keep their label in the market and to control

prices, leaving the co-operative with little autonomy. The offer was turned down.

In ten years the workers' co-operative sector has grown rapidly and turnover has increased twelve-fold. After a lot of mergers and the appearance of consortia to service the co-operatives, their strength in the economy has grown.[1] The average number of workers in an industrial co-operative is said to be around 200. Growth has been especially fast in the service industries and in manufacturing and professional services. There are co-operatives, for instance, of railway workers, home-helps, scaffolding erectors, and earth . movers, and co-operatives involved in engineering, brick production, ceramics and furniture making. Apart from the federations' attention to their business needs, success has been attributed to several factors. Most obvious is the large pool of labour affected by the failure of private enterprise to provide jobs or satisfactory working conditions. Many people in this pool are attracted by the co-operative idea.

Seizing Opportunities

It is claimed that the productivity of co-operatives is better than in other firms, and absenteeism – said to be high in Italy – is lower in co-operatives. While the current economic crisis has created problems for co-operatives, particularly in restricting the money supply, it has also opened up more markets for them in the public sector. Co-operatives can clearly survive where private firms fail. They have made a success of the remnants of capitalism in crisis conditions, adding to their number while capital in general is contracting.

By the early 1970s workers' co-operatives were strong in the economy and could take advantage of the opportunities opened up by the crisis. It is said that only 5 per cent die each year, while as many as 25 per cent new ones are formed. Already in a position of strength, and with a long history of association with political parties, the federations have been able to take a broad perspective of their potential role in the economy. Led by the Lega, they have devised a common programme for developing the co-operative sector. They recognise that the current economic crisis is caused by structural phenomena and should be confronted by a structural solution. Reorganisation for production along co-operative lines, they claim, would enable industry to avoid the massive waste of material and human resources at present occurring among public and private firms. Also, they argue that more democratic businesses would satisfy the personal needs of individuals in Italian society.

The programme aims to initiate new co-operatives which use natural resources, and to stimulate their formation in sectors where there is a continuous home demand and where Italian investment has been sluggish. They include the building industry, the service industry, and industries associated with agriculture, animal husbandry and fishing. And they are keen to promote co-operatives which help to overcome some of the problems caused by the economic crisis, such as unemployment and inner city decay. In other words, the programme aims to contribute to the country's social and economic recovery.

The Lega

The Lega itself devised its own three year strategy from 1978–80 which went further than this. While giving priority to the sectors already outlined, it planned to stimulate co-operation in all sectors of the economy, and in all regions, particularly in the South of Italy where co-operation has been slow to develop. It held that the various sectors of co-operation should inter-trade to make co-operative activity self-sustaining as far as possible, and should develop close links with the state through contracts for goods and services. In this way, the Lega considered that the movement could be built to a size which would give it greater force in negotiations with government, private firms and other bodies, for finance, contracts, and legal and taxation advantages. This would further strengthen the efficiency and competitiveness of co-operative activity and would provide products and services for the Italian market.

The Lega's outlook is important because the federation is dominant among workers' co-operatives. The Lega appears to be achieving some of its objectives. In Emilia Romagna, for instance, co-operatives are concentrated in firms which produce building materials, in the building industry itself, and in services such as hospital transport, school-bus and taxi transport, goods distribution, and office, factory and school cleaning. They also produce specialist goods for the home and foreign markets. In the building industry the co-operatives trade frequently with the housing co-operatives and with each other; and many are now undertaking work on contract to the local authority.

Although there are philosophical differences between the Lega and the other federations about the role of co-operatives within society, they all agree that co-operatives should be profitable concerns, able to compete with public and private firms. This is no idle boast. The sector is not dominated by the least profitable and most labour intensive industries, and neither are co-operatives treated as a welfare service for job creation. Co-operatives have demonstrated that they can achieve objectives beyond those of capitalist firms and still be profitable. When restructuring has been necessary, or when closures have occurred among them, redundancies have been avoided; retraining programmes have been carried out within the co-operatives and production has been , diversified, or else workers are redeployed in other co-operatives.

Co-operative Imolese Reconstruzione (CIR) is a Lega firm which has grown without sacrificing the interests of its workers. It has expanded steadily since 1947/48 from 200 to the present level of 365. During this period it developed a number of products, diversifying into new areas when opportunities were identified so that the work-force could be retained and moved to different activities when slumps occurred in the demand for one or another product. The co-operative was formed from an existing munitions factory which was threatened with closure. Three products were made to begin with: metal parts for building work and small repair vehicles for the Italian railways, specialised wooden frames, and moulds for ceramic presses. Production of the moulds was discontinued in 1953/54 and the machinery was adapted to produce high quality dentists' chairs. More recently, a further product – a safety door – was introduced.

The window frames have been sold mainly to the home market where CIR competes with other co-operatives as well as private firms. Fluctuations in the building industry have been common throughout the co-operative's life, created by material shortages, cuts in public expenditure, and falling profit rates in the industry. It has been important for CIR to expand production into safety doors and dentists' chairs which have different markets. Dentists' chairs, for instance, are sold to the Italian health service and to the Jordanian army. Diversification helped to provide continuous employment for the workforce to offset slumps in the building industry and the effects of introducing new machinery. As well as having job security, the workers have been retrained without a drop in wages.

The Lega emphasises that the achievements of this or any other co-operative should not be seen in isolation from the broader political objectives of the movement. Co-operatives have a greater chance of success – in both commercial and social terms – if their actions are co-ordinated within a movement which is working towards common objectives at national and regional levels, at the sectoral level and at the level of the individual firm. For all three federations, the outcome of negotiations for more favourable treatment, and the future of the movement, will depend more on the economic contribution that co-operatives make. If they can invest where private investment is weak, create new jobs and bring foreign currency into the country, they cannot easily be ignored by a government facing grave economic problems.

Signor Carpanelli, head of the Lega, comments that the co-operative movement did not create the capitalist system and has no choice but to work within it. As businesses which are competing in this system, co-operatives are primarily a sector of the economy and not a force for building socialism. The role of the co-operative movement, he says, is to change people's attitudes towards work and production, encouraging demand for greater participation and democracy. Also, the co-operatives can show how profits made are not divided up among their members, but are reinvested to create employment and to reduce the exploitation of workers.

Problems of Finance

Lack of finance has been the greatest single constraint for Italian co-operatives, exacerbated by recent events. There is no special source like the Caisse Centrale de Crédit Co-opératif in France. Of course, co-operatives can compete with other firms for loans from the joint stock banks. But their weak capital base means they need more sensitive treatment. Only the Banche Populari has shown some sympathy, but relations between the co-operative movement and all the banks are slender. For the co-operatives affiliated to the Confederazione, slightly better interest rates are given from the Casse Rurali because of the historical link between the two. Also, Coopercredito was set up as a special division of the Banca Nazionale del Lavoro to give credit to co-operatives. But the funds at its disposal are restricted to endowment funds and reserves, and exclude savings, so they are limited.[2]

The state has softened this generally hostile response by providing loans on favourable terms for co-operatives. But they are only given for certain purposes, like house building. Applications for these loans are made through the medium credit banks, and are granted if the government considers they are in the national interest. Since

1945 building co-operatives have most frequently received state loans because of the recognised severity of the housing shortage in Italy, and because of the well-known efficiency of co-operatives in the building sector. One co-operative, Matisa of Bologna, believes it is overdependent on the state. It has received state loans and other assistance for its work on the railways. But unlike the building co-operatives, Matisa receives all its finance and contracts from the state – at the same time having to compete with other firms in the field. The building co-operatives like Edilfornaciai, also of Bologna, are less vulnerable to changes in government policy. They produce a variety of goods which are sold to different markets, including the state.

The federations are currently putting pressure on the government to release more funds. In particular, the Lega argues that Coopercredito should be allowed to accumulate finance through bond issues by increasing its endowment funds and by forming a revolving loan fund for converting failed businesses into workers' co-operatives. It also argues that the bank should be made more responsive to the co-operative movement by having elected members on its board, should develop a better planning function for lending and should have regional offices. But, more importantly, the Lega believes that loans from Coopercredito should be made available at normal interest rates. Co-operatives, they say, should be treated like other firms and given loans on the basis of the risk involved. If this was achieved – the argument runs – workers' co-operatives would be able to demonstrate that they aim to be profitable and are as capable of repaying loans as other firms. This attitude is markedly at odds with the belief held in both France and Britain that co-operatives need more favourable terms if they are to form a strong sector. Despite the Lega's view of an ideal state of affairs, Italian co-operatives have often benefited from government loans which, in 1979, were as low as 6.5 per cent.

Raising Money

The only way out of their capital problems is for co-operatives in Italy to raise money from their members and to set up their own centralised sources of finance. Borrowing and raising shares from members has always been important. Before the crisis of the mid 1960s onwards, these were usually the only sources of finance available to a co-operative. Raising internal finance is now helped by the high level of membership – said to be at 80 per cent of all workers in co-operatives. With no restrictions on the rate of interest on loans that French and British co-operative law imposes, there is more incentive for workers to lend to their firms. In fact, some co-operatives have given higher rates than the banks. But in the face of heavy demands for capital to cope with changing technology and expansion, members' shares and loans fall far short of their needs.

The Lega in 1970 established its own financial institution – Fincooper – which aims to negotiate on behalf of co-operatives with banks and the government's Financial Commission. It intends to own assets and to underwrite loans to individual co-operatives, and to enable loans to be given at slightly beneficial rates. Intercoop has also been formed as an import/export company for the small to medium sized co-operatives; Unipol and Unifina are the movement's insurance companies whose funds are held entirely by the co-operatives and trade unions. In its turn, the Confederazione has also set up a body to provide loan capital in special cases of need.

Reducing Labour Costs
Besides developing closer links with the state for contracts, Italian co-operatives have made other moves to strengthen their competitiveness. They have, like co-operatives anywhere, reduced labour costs as far as possible. For example, they have kept the number of supervisory and management posts to a minimum. This does not mean they underestimate the importance of management skills. Co-operative law says there should only be one 'white collar' worker to every 12 'blue collar' workers. The law recognises the necessity of reducing the number of non-productive workers and of avoiding a heavy management bias which could, in the author's view, weaken the ideals of the 'shop-floor' workers and increase the co-operatives' outgoings. More people are needed today in a management role than the law permits, but – with the aid of commitment to the co-operative ideal – the co-operatives get round the law by paying some managers a 'blue collar' wage.

Matisa practises this cost-saving device, paying managers as if they were top category production workers. Managers in this firm are estimated to receive about 20–30 per cent more than other workers. Similarly, Edilfornaciai, which makes tiles and prefabricated concrete panels for buildings, also pays its managers as top-line blue collar workers. All the workers are members of the co-operative and own share capital. It was started in 1920 from the collapse of a private firm by workers wanting to keep their jobs. Throughout the

Fascist period the co-operative stopped production, but resisted being controlled by the Fascists and played an important part in the struggle against Mussolini. After the war, it began trading again and made prefabricated structures, mainly ceiling panels. But by 1965 a major financial and management crisis had developed. The firm only survived after sackings, reductions in workers' wages, the introduction of new management techniques and major investment. It is probable that this history of struggle by the workers led to the high level of ideological development among the workforce today, and to the acceptance of small differentials between managers and the shop floor.

Again, in Manuten – a co-operative which cleans offices, schools and factories, makes disinfectants, renovates buildings and distributes petrol – managers' wages are well below those in competitor cleaning firms. However, shop-floor wages are above average for the work. This is because Manuten is in a traditionally low wage service industry. The co-operative movement has deliberately entered this field because there are public sector markets to be tapped, and because of a political need to raise wages and provide better conditions in the cleaning industry. In most other co-operatives the production workers get the average wage for the job.

Consortia – an Important Development
An important development has been the formation of consortia. These are servicing co-operatives which act on behalf of co-operatives in different sectors, centralising functions such as acquiring raw and semi-finished materials, negotiating for finance and contracts, selling finished goods, and lending expertise. They have sprung up since the 1960s because there was a need for new trading structures to make co-operatives' production more efficient. As well as increasing the competitive power of co-operatives, consortia have helped to overcome their expansion problems by enabling two or more co-operatives to work to one contract. Many estimates have been made of the optimum size of a co-operative. It is clear that – whatever the size – the larger it becomes, the more difficult it can be to function democratically and to sustain ideological commitment.

The first of the new consortia was ACAM, formed in 1960 in Bologna with 24 member co-operatives, of which 19 were in the building industry. ACAM was preceded by ACEPLA, a union of co-operatives in the building trades, formed in 1955 with 50 members. But this had a more limited function. It co-ordinated the political and economic objectives of the co-operatives and – as a secondary aim – it provided some specialist business assistance to members. ACAM, however, was formed specifically to lower costs through the collective acquisition of materials, to develop common commercial policies among members and to improve relations with public and private bodies.

Between 1961 and 1970 its membership increased to 73, and during this time the importance of providing a pool of management skills also became apparent. Experts were appointed to act on behalf of the co-operatives in negotiations for finance and contracts, and could be 'lent' to co-operatives for short periods. After ten years the marketing function became so specialised that it was separated from ACAM into a subdivision. In 1971 a special sales section was added, but two years later this too was hived off to form a separate office. In 1974 the first branch of ACAM was set up in Florence for the co-operatives in Tuscany; then a second one appeared in Rome in 1975, and a third in Ravenna in the same year. Later, branches were opened in Palermo, Mantua and Milan, and so on.

One of ACAM's member co-operatives is Ceramice of Imola, a Bologna firm making tiles and ceramic crafts. Business efficiency has increased through its involvement with the servicing centre. Some of Ceramice's tiles are sold through ACAM to the Italian market and abroad; 20 per cent of its profits are made this way. ACAM pays a fixed annual price for the tiles. If the firm undertook all its own sales, prices would fluctuate constantly and make financial planning difficult.

Another important function of the consortia is to facilitate inter-trading between the co-operative sectors. For example, they sell products made in industrial co-operatives – like TV sets, vacuum cleaners and other electrical goods – at a discount through their own shops. In the agricultural field, co-operatives have recently moved into the processing side, producing tinned and frozen foods. These are also sold through the consortia's shops. To assist the agricultural co-operatives even more, the consortia sell tractors and other equipment made in the industrial co-operatives to the co-operative farms. In the building industry similar exchanges are arranged. Regional Planning Centres have been set up in each region of Italy which house co-operatives of 11–35 architects, engineers and other professionals. The building consortia draw on the services of these groups for their member co-operatives. They also arrange for the co-operatives manufacturing building materials to sell them to housing co-operatives.

The co-operative movement is not trying to cut itself off altogether from the private market through these devices. In fact the leadership considers it would be unwise to follow such a course because proof of competitiveness in the open market can encourage governments and banks to take co-operatives seriously. But without the new business structures and inter co-operative trading, the individual co-operatives would be isolated and vulnerable against the highly organised multinationals. The co-operative movement is trying to strengthen production in areas of basic need like housing and food. This, it believes, will make a positive contribution to the economy, and increase political support for co-operation. But only by being self-sufficient in these sectors can co-operatives hope to compete with the private sector. This means that the industrial co-operatives must make everything needed for a new house, or hospital or school, and all the mechanical equipment needed by a farmer. Without a clear political perspective of their role in the economy and the labour movement, no such cohesion would be possible.

Diversification and Restructuring
Aside from business matters, co-operatives have to make funda-mental decisions about growth, diversification and restructuring. Sometimes the consortia and federations can help here too. In making major investment decisions a co-operative can be in difficulty, because labour is considered to be at least as important as profit-ability. Redundancies are avoided wherever possible. If closure of a co-operative or a part of its operations is inevitable, the movement will often come to the rescue, relocating redundant workers in other co-operatives. Ceramice of Imola is one co-operative that has sought help from the movement. It was forced to introduce new machinery in the 1960s. In 1969 a new factory was built, and by 1978 the most modern machinery for ceramic production had been installed in both the new and old factories. In this industry technical advances are so rapid that machines can become obsolete in four to five years. Investment was costly, and the workers also had to be trained how to use new machines, and it was necessary to employ young, highly skilled managers. But this co-operative, producing both mass-market, low-price tiles and specialist craft goods, has demonstrated that with the help of the movement it can operate competitively, at the same time keeping its workforce stable.

The federations have encouraged mergers to make co-operatives stronger. In the case of Graficoop, a merger occurred in order to improve the standard of production in two firms engaged in printing. Both were operating on low profits and could not afford to invest in better machinery or new plant. The merger took place in 1974 between Steb and Assoguidi. Steb was formed in 1945 and by 1969–70 had reached a crisis point; 133 out of its workforce of 200 were made redundant. Assoguidi, an older co-operative formed in 1880, was also in difficulties at the same time. By merging, a more viable business has been created with a workforce of 175 in 1979. The firm is now the second largest of its type and very competitive. Matisa, also, resulted from the merging of three co-operatives; two joined together in 1945, then another joined in 1951. Finally, a firm was created which was capable of maintaining railways over a wide geographical area, and large enough – with 260 workers in 1978 – to operate a highly specialised activity involving huge investments. The formation of large, successful co-operatives has not automatically led to deskilling and production-line techniques. The quality of work in a co-operative is always an important matter. In the larger building co-operatives, for instance, craft skills are maintained as far as possible.

Diversification has often helped survival, and merging sometimes enables this to take place. Edilfornaciai, for example, merged in 1969–70 with a small co-operative making bricks and tiles. This enabled the firm to break into a new market, at the same time providing the investment for modernisation needed to save the jobs of the smaller co-operative. Then, in 1977, two other co-operatives producing prefabricated panels merged with Edilfornaciai. The number of workers employed rose from 250 to 680, and the firm became a major builder for the municipality, housing co-operatives, and the private sector.

Cooperative Imolese Reconstruzione also diversified its products over time, as explained earlier, to increase the stability of the firm, and has also diversified its markets. It exports building frames to France and Arab countries, and – as already mentioned – sells dentists' chairs to the Jordanian army. The dentistry equipment is considered to be high technology and needs frequent investment in new machinery; the other products are less sophisticated. While this type of diversification would be done to accumulate capital in a private firm, it is done to provide job stability in a co-operative.

Legal and Other State Aid

The co-operative sector has not simply relied on its own resources for development. The state has facilitated growth in a number of fields, though its influence has been more limited than in France. The first co-operative law was passed in 1934. This was followed by additional laws in 1951, 1963 and 1978. A further law is being considered which will make conversions easier, and will provide money for them through Coopercredito at 9–10 per cent, about half the normal interest rates, instead of 18–19 per cent, and special funds will be available for loans of up to 50m lire at 5 per cent (1979 interest rates).

Co-operatives have been given special status in relation to government departments. A forum for consultations with state bodies has been created in which they can negotiate for legal, taxation and financial advantages. Under Article 45 of the 1947 Constitution, co-operatives are recognised as a form of enterprise under the protection of the Ministry of Works and Social Security.[3] The Ministry was enabled to take positive initiatives to:

(a) develop co-operatives;
(b) spread co-operative principles; and
(c) set up courses for the professional training of co-operative directors, through the three National Associations (federations) separately or in collaboration.

The Central Commission for co-operatives within this Ministry is the main focus for consultations between government and co-operatives. There is also an interdepartmental committee which, through the Banca d'Italia, makes policies for co-operatives in consultation with the Banche Populari and the Casse Rurali.

The newest laws have been very important to the growing movement. In 1977 politicians from the Communist Party (PCI), the Socialist Party (PSI) and the independent left, in consultation with the federations, prepared amendments to co-operative law which they presented to the Senate. The reformers attempted to define a co-operative more clearly by establishing precisely the democratic principles which it must demonstrate. They sought a broader recognition of co-operative types of enterprise. Under the heading of 'workers' co-operatives' they grouped agricultural, commercial, craft, professional, technical, cultural and manufacturing co-operatives. They also sought to abolish restrictions on internal capital holdings.[4]

Recently, co-operatives have been far less reluctant to develop close links with the state. The federations argue that this in no way signifies a weakening of the movement's autonomy. Links are being forged because of the mutual benefits. During the economic crisis co-operatives have provided products and services more reliably than other firms. As a result they have won contracts for work and government loans at favourable interest rates. In most cases they have retained their independence by bidding for work or finance in competition with other firms, and by selling only a proportion of their goods or services to the state.

Co-operatives are attractive to local and central government for reasons other than their competitiveness. They have shown a more 'responsible' attitude towards labour than other firms. It is a deliberate policy of some of Bologna's co-operatives in the building industry to reinvest profits to create new jobs rather than to distribute them. It is this attitude which has led to an increase in the number of jobs in co-operatives during the crisis. From the federations' viewpoint, establishing markets in state bodies could provide more stable outlets for their goods and services in the longer term. Closer business relationships with the state also provide them with opportunities to bargain for better treatment.

Links with Local and Central Government
Contracts for work and assistance in arranging finance have been given by both central and local government. Most contracts or covenants have been between local authorities and building co-operatives (or consortia, on co-operatives' behalf). 20–25 per cent of the building co-operatives' work was for the public sector in 1978. But recently other types of co-operative have landed state contracts. Manuten, a cleaning co-operative which employed 860 workers in 1976, offers a more reliable service to the Bologna municipality and does not charge higher prices than its competitors. It has achieved this, as well as paying better than average wages in the industry and offering better terms and conditions of work, by undertaking profitable activities alongside the cleaning work – such as manufacturing disinfectants used in the cleaning, and renovation work for the local authority.

At the regional level, the state intervenes in the economy in a number of ways. Emilia Romagna, for instance, has provided land and infrastructure for industry in general, and gives special assistance to the small, craft workshops – the artigiani. Investment grants are available to them for new installations, interest on running costs and for setting up in new locations. A regional agency, ERVET, was set up early in 1978 to undertake market research for local firms and to circulate technical information among industries. Umbria and Ligoria regions are making similar attempts to encourage investment in industry through these means. But few positive powers exist anywhere to assist industry except in the five special areas with severe problems, such as industrial decline and ethnic tensions. Emilia Romagna – not a special area – considers the state's assistance is unsatisfactory. In particular, it would like to provide investment finance for small firms, whose closure rate has risen dramatically in recent years. In the context of all this, few privileges are offered to co-operatives by the regional authorities. Co-operatives are almost always in competition with private firms.

At the national level co-operatives have received more help. Matisa, employing 260 workers in 1978, has worked on contract to the state railways doing maintenance and construction work. The government makes certain its prices are competitive by making the firm compete for contracts. But – as it has already been explained – since there is no other market for its service, and since there are no explicit long term plans for the railways, the co-operative is in a vulnerable position. It means some workers must be hired and fired locally according to need, and the whole workforce cannot have the same level of job security. In 1978, 40 of the workers were employed casually.

Like other firms, co-operatives have been affected by reduced profit levels, increased interest charges and pressure to introduce technological change.[5] Their needs for capital and credit have been great, but their access to external funds has been poor. However, this is not the reason why the state has given them loans at low interest rates. Only certain co-operatives receive these loans, and only for certain purposes – all associated with providing basic needs for capitalist development. These include road and rail construction, public transport, house-building, school and hospital building, cleaning of public buildings, school desk manufacture, and so on. There are no criteria for giving these loans; each case is looked at on its own merits.

Conclusion
Italian co-operatives have rarely put their principles before the need to be profitable. But they have discovered new ways of competing

with other companies which enable their principles to be maintained. Rather than growing to an unwieldy size, for instance, the new consortia can arrange for two or more co-operatives to work together on a contract. The movement has also found that co-operatives can be more competitive if they combine within vertically integrated industries – providing all the inputs and excluding the private sector. And they have welcomed any concessions made by the state.

To achieve all this, the movement has developed a common political outlook. Although the co-operatives are affiliated to three federations which are allied to different political parties, they do not see co-operation in vastly different ways, as do the promotional bodies in Britain. Idealism still exists, but it is tempered by realism. First and foremost, co-operatives are regarded as a third sector in the economy, and they are encouraged wherever opportunities open up. Within this broad, pragmatic policy there is room for differences in emphasis, and a greater or lesser belief in the contribution that co-operatives can make to achieving a socialist society.

9 The End of the Dream

The Utopian Legacy

Workers' co-operatives in Britain, in both this century and the last, have been inspired by utopian dreams of a new, socialist society. They have provided a practical demonstration of how labour can protest against gross exploitation at work, and the failure of capitalism to provide stable employment. Through running their own firms, co-operators have been able to challenge capitalism and create a radical means of awakening the working class. However, the utopian drive behind co-operation has seriously hindered its growth.

The leaders attracted to the co-operative idea have easily seen their goal of a co-operative commonwealth, but failed to develop a strategy for achieving it. Often, they have been blind to the need to integrate co-operatives closely in the market. Above all, their inability to raise capital has restricted co-operatives to certain sections of industry. But few people in the movement have doubted the potential of co-operatives to spread throughout the economy. Encouragement in unrealistic circumstances has led to many disastrous failures. This must have seriously weakened the appeal of co-operatives among the working class either as a solution to capitalism or even as a minor victory.

In all the major periods of the movement's expansion middle class philanthropists have encouraged people to form co-operatives. Professional, skilled and unskilled workers have responded. In the last century they were usually the more conservative members of the working class. Radicals preferred to involve themselves in the political struggles of the Chartist and trade union movements. Today the middle-class drop-out from organised politics is the typical co-operator. In the first quarter of the 19th century co-operatives were very influential when other forms of association were forbidden, and while the working class was in an embryonic form and poorly organised. But as other movements developed they lost their lead.

The utopianism of co-operation promised people a better future, an escape from the severe hardship of the industrial revolution and, in the 1970s, from unemployment and alienation. The day-to-day experience of running an enterprise was not romantic but has given people confidence and educated them about the nature of capitalism. It has offered them a chance to fight against the principles of capitalism in a fundamental way, and provided some clues to the type of society that could be built under socialism, and the problems associated with it. And it has helped them to understand human nature, and to see how strongly the social and economic environment influenced people's characters.

However, instead of building a political movement around the idea, the leaders from Owen, Ludlow and Neale to those of the present day, have been apolitical in outlook. They have paid little regard to theories of social change and have ignored the class nature of society. Abstract notions of a co-operative commonwealth have continued to be put forward even when the evidence of 150 years' experience shows that the goal is no closer, and when it is clear that the labour movement has put its reliance on other strategies for developing socialism. The idealists have believed they could persuade governments, industrialists and other establishment figures to encourage co-operatives out of the logic of their arguments, and have done little to link their practical work to the activities of other mass movements. This problem has been compounded by the huge amounts of energy needed by the co-operators to make their enterprises viable. Like the leadership, they have turned their attention inwards.

Carried away by their enthusiasm for principles, co-operators and their leaders in the first half of the 19th century persistently refused to reconcile themselves to the essential features of the capitalist market. They tried to carry on business in isolation from the market, setting their own prices for goods, raising capital where they could from sympathetic sources, and sometimes selling goods through co-operative outlets. However, without a large enough outlet among their supporters, and without a large source of capital, they were often exposed to the private markets where they could not compete. The Owenite communities, the Labour Exchanges, the co-operatives affiliated to the Society for Promoting Working Men's Associations, etc, all failed to generate a strong, viable co-operative sector. Besides their refusal to exist side by side with private firms, they had numerous other problems to deal with peculiar to co-operatives.

They had to find ways of giving incentives to workers brought up in a capitalist culture and to operate democracy at work against all the hierarchical traditions in industry. They were trying to achieve impossible objectives.

Successes and Failures

By the late 19th century a more realistic approach had been adopted, and many co-operatives formed in this period lasted longer. For it was by no means inevitable that co-operatives would break up soon after they appeared, or that they would be less profitable than private firms. Those established in craft industries like boot and shoe manufacture, furniture making, and light engineering, often survived for many years. They were easier to set up. Second-hand machinery could be bought for them cheaply, relatively little finance was required, and there was a market for good quality, hand-made products of this type.

But by this time the influence of the co-operative movement was dwindling and being replaced by other forms of working class organisation. Success for a co-operative has to be measured against the success of any firm in the 19th century. Before limited liability was introduced any enterprise was in a precarious position, and for some time afterwards a great many new firms were formed which lived for only a short time. It was not until the period 1850–1875 that banking capital began to play an important part in funding firms; before that firms were largely family concerns, without access to a lot of capital.

Also, the average firm, until 1871, was small, employing fewer than 100 workers. Even the cotton factories only averaged 180 workers at that time.[1] While the development of capitalism meant the gradual concentration of capital into large firms, it also required a large number of small firms to undertake vital parts of the production process. The division of labour and the need to use skilled handwork alongside more mechanised processes were responsible for the continuation of a large, small-firms sector.

Successful co-operatives, existing for a number of years profitably, were generally small and in craft industries. They were operating in the most low paid areas of the economy, sometimes employing outworkers, and using the same tactics to raise profits as other firms, such as short time, wage cuts and child labour. Co-operatives in the cotton industry were larger, most employing over 200 workers, reducing their capital needs through sub-contracting and hiring machinery. But conditions in these factories again were mostly horrendous. Co-operatives persisted not because of their superiority in terms and conditions – though there were important exceptions – but because work in a co-operative was preferable to no work at all.

Co-operatives struggled against difficult odds. Their close relationship with the retail societies was crucial to their survival. The stores were normally their main sales outlet and sometimes took goods at high prices because they were reimbursed by the share they were awarded in the co-operatives' profits. Also the societies were committed to helping the producer units survive because many of their members were keen to get jobs there. While the pay and conditions in the workers' co-operatives were often poor, this was only during hard times and not because of a profit motive. In more profitable periods, the co-operatives would dramatically improve the rewards for work. Furthermore, many people preferred to work in a co-operative because relations between labourers and superiors were exceptionally good and summary dismissals were only made for serious offences. However, the mass of the proletariat was disillusioned with the failures they had seen and experienced, especially those in the mining and heavy engineering industries. Trade unionism seemed to offer a better route to political power.

The Movement Today
Co-operatives today are still predominantly concerned with the morality of capitalist methods of production and the exploitation of labour. They are even more starved of capital than before, since firms in general have developed a greater need for external capital. Those attracted to this form of enterprise are again from limited sections of the middle and working class. The trade union movement remains interested but aloof. The biggest co-operative experiments – some in capital-intensive industries – have failed again, confirming the fears among the working class and other potential supporters that they are unworkable. But enthusiasm for less ambitious projects is still growing.

What then is different about this new wave of co-operatives? They have re-emerged at a time when state intervention in industry is widespread. Since 1966 governments have intervened to assist the process of rationalisation and restructuring by funding individual firms. With the establishment of the NEB in 1975/6, assistance to industry has been of a pump-priming nature. Without taking firms into state ownership with a majority shareholding, governments have achieved their objective of selective industrial regeneration by providing relatively small inputs of share and loan capital. These actions have been extended to the level of the local authority, where increasing unemployment has created social problems which councils are in a poor position to alleviate. Pump-priming capital has been given, albeit on a small scale, to small firms and co-operatives. This has helped to create jobs and rebuild the declining number of small firms. At the same time it has brought political *kudos* to councils as an imaginative, new idea.

A Crucial Weakness

Co-operatives have once again fired the enthusiasm of idealists. This time they are mainly young, middle class people on the fringes of the Labour Party but disillusioned by party politics and interested in alternative solutions to economic and social problems. But it is by no means automatic that people attracted to the idea will be socialists. Following the pattern set in the 1880s, co-operatives have again appealed in a period of economic crisis as a method of increasing productivity. It is easy for the co-operative idea to be embraced for capitalist ends. As commercial enterprises which, by themselves, do not attack the class nature of society, they can be paraded before the business world as an alternative form of company which should be supported. The clearest expression of this use of co-operation is demonstrated by JOL. So far, the socialist core of the sector has shown suspicion of JOL's motives but has been reluctant to express its fears publicly. For this would require defining a political perspective of its own.

There are, of course, advantages in creating a broad alliance which can encompass all political beliefs, particularly when the sector is increasingly dependent on the state for funds. The Italian movement has shown the benefits of this approach. All the main political parties have joined together for the purpose of negotiating with governments for better terms. However, if the dominant force of the workers' co-operative sector is not openly socialist, it is doubtful whether co-operatives can overcome their problems and form a genuine movement. The sector will remain a hotchpotch of ideas and ideals, full of internecine strife and moral judgements. It will be dominated by the 'small is beautiful' doctrine of the libertarians, and receive no more than a sidelong glance from trade unionists. For the sector to grow it must be taken seriously by the mass of the working class.

The small scale of the sector need not be hidden. It is more important that the idea has gripped the imagination of the Left. In a period of deepening economic crisis the Labour Party is searching for new ways of erasing the degrading conditions of the unemployed, and is grasping at any proposal to generate new firms. Labour Party MPs and councillors are increasingly mouthing their support for co-operatives. But co-operatives are still the victims of a sector which puts no restraint on propaganda. In the corridors of Whitehall and in council chambers, abundant myths about co-operatives' success are tossed around. There can be no doubt about the fact that the co-operative sector is tiny, weak, unbusinesslike and middle class, and is characterised by sweatshops. And for all the state assistance given to co-operatives so far, only some 900 jobs have been created or saved.

Living with Capitalism
Co-operatives are a product of capitalist society. They are rebel businesses because they have different objectives from private companies. They can benefit from forming a protective network among the various sectors of co-operation and among labour move-ment organisations, but they cannot avoid the capitalist market altogether. As the Italian movement demonstrates, they can never hide away completely in their own world. They are dependent on raw materials, markets and finance from outside their own sector. They must set wages and prices roughly in line with other firms, and offer attractive conditions of work. Co-operatives are not 'capitalist' in structure or aims. Nevertheless, they do contribute to capital accumulation.

Many British co-operatives have tried to ignore the world beyond their front door, or have dealt grudgingly with it, twisting and turning in an effort tó be true to a predetermined set of principles. But with this approach many opportunities for expansion have been missed. The strength of co-operatives in the building industry in both France and Italy has shown that the needs of capital and co-operative principles can be complementary. The recognition by co-operatives that they can contribute to the economy has, at the same time, helped them to strengthen their own sector. There is no truth in the fear among British co-operatives that selling to the state and private firms, and making profits, will destroy the idealism of the members.

It has to be said that co-operatives in France and Italy have faced many serious problems since the second World War. Some ventures

have become too large for the shop-floor workers who have felt
distant from decision making; and sometimes new recruits are less
committed to co-operative principles than the older members, and
are unwilling to contribute to the internal capital funds. Education
in the value of a co-operative sector has become an urgent need. But
in both countries the co-operative movements have accepted that
survival depends on the value of co-operatives to the economy. This
does not mean unlimited growth can be expected. Hostility from the
establishment will persist because co-operatives are a challenge to
capitalism. The *Scottish Daily News* witnessed the full extent of this
opposition. Even if it had been a better quality paper and had
attracted more start-up capital, it would not have survived because
it failed dismally to attract advertising.

The evidence from France and Italy shows that expansion is most
likely if co-operatives are providing a basic service to industry. Italian
co-operatives have succeeded in house building, road and rail building, all kinds of maintenance, and transport. These are industries
where the public sector in Britain has operated by itself through
municipal enterprise and nationalised industries. Few Labour Party
supporters would wish to see these institutions eroded but there may
be gaps in these services which would be better filled by co-operatives
than private firms. Housing co-operatives – by converting old
properties – have already shown that this can be achieved. The gap
in the market that they have exploited had opened up because other
methods had failed to cope with the housing problems of people
caught up in a declining economy.

Government Interest
Central government, regional authorities and local councils are
newcomers to co-operative development in Britain. In five years
their impact on the movement has been significant. Assistance in
various forms has swelled the number of new co-operatives and
enabled others to survive. While the sector is still very weak, with
few resources of its own to support co-operative ventures, the future
of the movement depends heavily on continued assistance from the
state. As well as good will, co-operatives require contributions
towards, for instance, funding, feasibility studies, formation costs
and management salaries.

The co-operative idea has appealed to the three main political
parties and, of course, it is the guiding principle of the Co-operative
Party. However, the degree of enthusiasm for this form of enterprise

varies, and the support of the political parties is based on different assumptions about what co-operatives can achieve. The ICO Act 1976 and the CDA Act 1978 both claimed all-party support, but most of the efforts to help individual co-operatives have come from Labour governments and Labour councils.

When the ideal is put to the test, co-operatives needing help have not presented themselves as politically neutral experiments in worker participation. Meriden, KME and the *Scottish Daily News* were all formed as defensive actions motivated by the political will of the workforce. As business ventures, they posed enormous problems and could only have attracted government assistance for political reasons. Many people have been quick to denounce them as untypical of co-operatives, and as giving the new movement a bad image. The claim made by others, that they were not given enough support to make them viable, has not been popularised in the media. In making this comment, no reflection is intended on the courageous efforts made by Tony Benn as a denigrated figure in a Labour cabinet hostile to his aims. In a different cabinet, full of people as determined as Benn to assist workers driven out of their jobs, the fate of co-operatives might have been very different.

At the local level many of the co-operatives funded by councils would have looked like non-starters to conventional funding bodies since they often lacked management skills, finance, a good product, or a solid market, and had no track record. There is no doubt that they were a high risk for anyone putting their money into them. Labour councils have committed themselves for several reasons. They like co-operatives because of their superior democracy over ordinary firms and because they are labour intensive, keeping people off the dole. Also, they believe the high risk can be reduced by providing advice as part of the councils' management of their loans. Discrimination in favour of co-operatives has not been half-hearted. Enough has been done to ensure that co-operatives provide permanent employment as successful firms. The future of co-operatives is very dependent on the return of a Labour Government and the continued interest of Labour councils.

Although much of the state's support for co-operatives has been based on a socialist ideology, in practice more weight has been put on their contribution to the state's interventionist policies in the economy. Co-operatives have been assisted as part of the small firms' sector. Their weaknesses have been recognised and they have received extra help, but in effect aid has been given within the broader context of industrial regeneration. Co-operatives have been helped along with other small firms to build up the local economy through the mechanism of pump-priming. This is particularly evident in the work of the MSC where little attention was paid to co-operative principles.

The Need for Commitment

There is another side to the co-operative coin. It has not been appreciated that co-operatives are essentially voluntary associations of labour. The roots of the movement are in the struggle for the emancipation of individual workers and are closely linked to those of the labour movement. The commitment of workers to their enterprise has come about because, in most cases, they have recognised that there is a scarcity of other jobs, or that other work available is meaningless. They are mostly formed out of frustration and despair. The idea of working in co-operatives as a way to reduce industrial conflict or increase productivity does not come from workers. The MSC and local councils are guilty of advertising co-operation, or setting up and assisting co-operatives among people without any ideological commitment. The idea has been imposed upon people because the establishment wants to further its own policy objectives. The collapse of some of the small, state-assisted co-operatives has often been attributed to financial or management deficiencies, or to a lack of skills. These weaknesses cannot be denied. But if commitment is lacking, co-operatives are very vulnerable. Similarly, the failure of state-backed campaigns to start co-operatives has been blamed on the community's poor appreciation of the value of collective working. But there is more to a co-operative than this.

Apart from the early rescue cases, there has been no concerted effort to form co-operatives out of collapsing companies, even though the fear of unemployment could be a spur for the workers to succeed. European experience has shown that viable co-operatives can be salvaged from the restructuring and rationalisation programmes of large companies. This does not mean offering redundant workers the chance to work in a semi-skilled capacity, making wooden toys. In Britain, time and again the opportunity to form co-operatives which produce a specialist product within a major industry has been missed.

Do Co-operatives have a Future?

There is value in helping small co-operatives, but if the Labour

Party is serious about building a co-operative movement, the resources of governments must be used more effectively. A large impact could be made if the fashionable contempt for the rescue cases were dropped, and if successful, large co-operatives were formed in the way described. Some of the important trade unions are alive to the possibilities of creating genuine workers' co-operatives. But they will not put their huge strength behind these projects unless they are convinced that they are firmly rooted in broad working class traditions. They will certainly treat with suspicion the perpetuation of workers battling to make ends meet in small, cramped factories.

Of course, the major fault does not lie with local and central government. Progress in this direction must come from the co-operative movement. A genuine workers' co-operative movement with a strategy for contributing to Britain's economic recovery and to socialism is a possible target. But it cannot be achieved if the co-operative sector continues to be dominated by the 'alternative movement', if it fails to distinguish between its socialist ideology and that of the Liberal Party, and if it does not recognise the opportunities it has within the economy.

The fundamental capital weakness of co-operatives must be recognised and sympathetic treatment sought both from the banks and the state. If better terms can be gained as a reward for efficiency, or for other features of co-operation, they can be regarded as a bonus. But they are not essential. Even at this early stage it is worth considering how the sector could begin to inter-trade and build trading links with other sectors of co-operation. The French movement is currently trying to learn from the Italian experiment with consortia which have significantly increased the efficiency of co-operatives, and at the same time has resolved the worrying questions surrounding growth.

However, integration between co-operative sectors can only be achieved with the help of a common perspective on the movement's aims. There can be no escape from the essentially political nature of co-operative activity. An open debate between the Labour, Liberal, Tory and other parties is needed to expose their views. Such an exposure would surely reveal that the true fate of co-operatives is linked indissolubly with the labour movement. But it would not be sufficient if that fact were grasped only by those who have taken part in the revival of workers' co-operatives in this country. To give the movement real shape and direction, a committed approach would be necessary from the Labour Party itself. This would not mean simply handing round the hat to individual co-operatives, but would involve an acceptance of this form of enterprise as part of a political programme and strategy. It would mean turning many shibboleths of the Labour Party on their heads, and rejecting the view formed long ago by the Webbs that industrial co-operation has little part to play in the economy.

Whether the Labour Party could take this course is open to question. But one of the arguments in favour of it – which is central to the Party's current thinking – is that workers need more say and control over their lives. Co-operation appears to be at home among the new ideas on industrial democracy. Whatever its defects, there can be no doubt that the co-operative way of life can do much to bring out the best social instincts in people. To succeed, co-operatives have to accept the rigours of democracy and stand up unflinchingly to capitalism. No-one can deny the courage of those taking part in this struggle in Britain today. With the power of a political will behind them, many of these people could be the pioneers of a new and exciting territory. Certainly, that territory would never be described as socialist, but at least it is a testing ground where men and women can say that they live with dignity and their lives have a purpose.

Appendix I
Co-operative Case Studies

Britain
1. Bardrec, Lanarkshire
2. Bradwell Signs, Milton Keynes
3. Brookhouse Ampersand, Denbigh, N. Wales
4. Calverts North Star Press, London
5. Chieftain Industries, Livingston, W. Lothian
6. Cinammon, Newcastle-upon-Tyne
7. Clogora, Skelmersdale, Lancs
8. Co-operative Build, Connah's Quay, N. Wales
9. Cotastone, Skelmersdale
10. Derby Printers, Derby
11. Doon Valley, Ayrshire
12. Dowlais Knitwear (Pandy Fashions), Merthyr Tydfil, S. Wales
13. Drym Fabricators, Seven Sisters, S. Wales
14. Equity Shoes, Leicester
15. Green City, Glasgow
16. Hawkesbury, Skelmersdale
17. Kennington Office Cleaners, London
18. KER Plant (Co-ownership Ltd), Northampton
19. Landsmans (Co-ownership), Buckden, Cambs.
20. Leeds Other Paper, Leeds
21. Leicester Printers, Leicester
22. Little Women, Sunderland
23. Marble Arch Intensive English Co-operative, London
24. Meriden Motorcycles Co-operative, Meriden (nr Coventry)
25. Michael Jones Jeweller, Northampton
26. Milkwood, Milton Keynes
27. Publications Distribution Co-operative, London
28. Queen Eleanor, Kettering, Northants
29. Recycles, Edinburgh

30. Scott Bader, Wollaston, Northants
31. Suma, Leeds
32. Sunderlandia, Sunderland
33. Telegraph Textiles, London
34. The Builders Collective, Leeds
35. Trylon, Wollaston, Northants
36. Tyneside Free Press, Newcastle-upon-Tyne
37. Walsall Locks, Walsall
38. Wandtronics, London
39. Warrington Industrial Trust, Warrington
40. Wirral Ceramics, Merseyside

France
1. L'Association des Ouvrières en Matériel Electrique (ACOME), Paris
2. L'Association des Ouvrières en Instruments de Précision (AOIP), Paris
3. Avel Nevez, Brittany
4. CERIA, Paris
5. Cootypographie, Paris
6. Manuest, Neuchâteau, Vosges
7. Scop Cogné, Le Mans

Italy, Bologna
1. Ceramice of Imola
2. Cooperative Imolese Reconstruzione
3. Edilfornacai
4. Graficoop
5. Manuten
6. Matisa

Appendix II
Definitions of Common Ownership and Co-operatives

The definition of a common ownership and co-operative enterprise under the Industrial and Common Ownership Act 1976 is as follows:

2-(1) For the purposes of this Act a common ownership enterprise is a body to which the registrar has given, and has not revoked, a certificate stating that he is satisfied:

(a) that the body is

(i) a company which has no share capital, is limited by guarantee and is a bona fide co-operative society; or

(ii) a society registered or deemed to be registered under the Industrial and Provident Society Acts 1965 to 1975; and

(b) that the memorandum or articles of association or rules of the body include provisions which secure:

(i) that only persons who are employed by, or by a subsidiary of, the body may be members of it, that (subject to any provision about qualifications for membership which is from time to time made by the members of the body by reference to age, length of service or other factors of any description which do not discriminate between persons by reference to politics or religion) all such persons may be members of the body and that members have equal voting rights at meetings of the body;

(ii) that the assets of the body are applied only for the purposes of objects of the body which do not include the making over of assets to any member of the body except for value and except in pursuance of arrangements for sharing the profits of the body among its members; and

(iii) that, if on the winding up or dissolution of the body any of its assets remain to be disposed of after its liabilities are satisfied, the assets are not distributed among its members but are transferred to such a common ownership enterprise or such a central fund maintained for the benefit of common ownership enterprises as may be determined by the members at or before the time of the winding up or dissolution or, in so far as the assets are not so transferred, are held for charitable purposes; and

(c) that the body is controlled by a majority of the people working for the body and of the people working for the subsidiaries, if any, of the body.

2-(2) For the purposes of this Act a co-operative enterprise is a body as to which the Secretary of State has given, and has not revoked, a certificate stating that he is satisfied that

(a) having regard to the provision which is made by the written constitution of the body as to the manner in which the income of the body is to be applied for the benefit of its members and all other relevant provisions of the constitution, the body is in substance a co-operative association; and

(b) the body is controlled by a majority of the people working for the body and of the people working for the subsidiaries, if any, of the body.

While the definition of a common ownership enterprise is precise, the definition of a co-operative enterprise has been left vague. There is no legal definition of a co-operative society. However, a reasonable guide can be obtained from the factors considered by the Registrar of Friendly Societies who is empowered to register co-operative societies under the Industrial and Provident Societies Acts 1965–75. In his Annual Report for 1973 the Registrar states that such a society 'must be able to show amongst other things that it will benefit persons other than its own members and that its business will be in the interests of the community'. The Registrar also considers whether the society is non-profit-making and that it is prohibited by its rules from distributing its assets among members. Also, interest must not be payable at an excessive rate, there should be no artificial restriction on membership, and the principle of 'one-person-one-vote' must be applied. Other principles may be followed, as recommended in 'model rules' such as those issued by the International Co-operative Alliance, e.g. membership must be voluntary, and educative services must be provided to propagate the principles of co-operation.

Appendix III
Criteria and Working Rules for Approval of Job Creation Programme Projects

The following criteria were laid down initially for funding JCP projects:

1. The project must be labour intensive and create new employment opportunities. It should not be used as a device for subverting normal labour costs.

2. The project must provide worthwhile work and make a contribution to the enhancement of the local environment or assist in the solution of a social or community problem.

3. The project should not duplicate existing services or facilities which are adequate to meet the needs of the community.

4. The project would not be viable without JCP funding.

5. The project must be financially viable as regards the costs not to be met by JCP funding.

6. If the project needs long-term financial support after the period of JCP grant, the funds for this expenditure should be guaranteed.

7. Any profit generated by revenue must be used either to defray JCP costs or be re-invested in the project.

8. The sponsor should have the resources and capability to undertake the project, to provide proper supervision and to keep the necessary statistical and financial records.

9. The project should not be purely for the personal gain of the sponsor.

10. All people employed in the project must be recruited through the Employment Services Agency (ESA) or the Careers Service.

11. The project should seek to provide a minimum of 30 man-months employment, but should be capable of termination within three months.

Appendix IV
Annual Accounts: Notes on
Methods and Assumptions

The text has made use of information taken from the Annual Accounts of ten firms: Derby Printers, Equity Shoes, Leicester Printers, Queen Eleanor, Walsall Locks, Landsmans, Michael Jones Jeweller, Scott Bader and Trylon. Where they were available, figures for six years were used, finishing with the most recent accounts. The CPF societies are registered under the Industrial and Provident Societies Act; the others are registered under the Companies Act. The following notes explain how the figures were used to calculate the gearing ratios and profitability or rate of return on capital.

Gearing

The controversial gearing ratio expresses the outside liabilities of a company's finance as a proportion of the shareholders' funds (i.e. the share capital, reserves and all internal finance). In the case of most of the CPF societies, however, this is not very appropriate since they are either totally, or almost totally, internally financed. Where there are external loans the conventional ratio has been used. Where there are none, or where they are very small, each of the constituent elements of the finance is expressed as a percentage of the total finance of the society; this gives an idea of the changing structure of the society's finances.

All 'other loans' have been considered as internal finance for the purposes of the conventional ratio since they consist of loans from members of the society or loans from internal funds of the society.

Profitability has been calculated on the following basis:

$$\text{Rate of return on capital } \% = 100 \times \frac{\text{Net profit before taxation} + \text{Interest payable on bank loans (and overdraft) and other loans}}{\text{Share capital} + \text{Bank loans and other loans} + \text{Reserves}}$$

where the net profit is for the year's trading. The fixed liabilities and the interest on them are for the beginning of that year (i.e. as expressed in the balance sheet for the end of the previous year).

For CPF Societies

Bank loans include overdrafts as well as any fixed-interest longer term loans. Although it is not usual, overdrafts have been included with loans in the calculations. This may cause some distortions. The average rate of interest paid on bank loans is calculated by dividing the net interest payable to banks into the loan capital received from banks in any one year.

The societies' accounts do not necessarily specify the terms of any loans nor do they present fixed-interest (long term) and overdraft (short term) loans separately.

'Other' loans in the accounts generally refers to loans from members of the society although on all accounts it does not specify that this is so. In other cases it seems that they have come from employees' funds within the Society, e.g. from a Provident fund or a small savings deposit. In all cases these loans have been considered, with the share capital and reserves, as internal finance of the society.

The rates of interest on these loans have been calculated on the same basis as those on the bank loans.

DERBY PRINTERS LTD

Activities: Printing
Registered on 21st December 1899
All accounts dated 31st December

Share Capital (withdrawable) Share Interest at 5%

On 31st December	No. of shareholding members	Total share capital £
1972	103	4,803
1973	100	4,571
1974	90	4,739
1975	85	4,339
1976	80	4,152
1977	77	4,072

Reserves

On 31st December	Education fund £	Tax equalization fund £	Development fund £	Investment grants £	Superannuation shares reserve £
1972	178	8,000	7,300	1,754	—
1973	—	8,000	8,800	1,754	—
1974	—	4,200	—	—	500
1975	—	5,850	—	—	—
1976	—	5,720	—	—	—
1977	—	5,400	—	—	—

Reserves (cont'd)

Interest guaranteed £	General reserve £	Unallocated surplus £	Total reserves £
2,500	14,500	2,665	36,897
2,500	14,500	4,409	39,963
—	34,604	4,722	44,026
—	40,604	995	47,449
—	42,604	1,313	49,637
—	45,604	2,049	53,053

Members' Loans

31st December	Members' loans £	Interest payable £	Rate of interest %
1972	971	37	3.8
1973	962	42	4.4
1974	1,232	47	3.7
1975	621	35	5.6
1976	624	26	4.2
1977	624	26	4.2

Profitability

For the year's trading	Net profit before taxation £	Rate of return on capital %
1972	2,366	—
1973	7,967	18.8
1974	12,823	28.2
1975	11,092	22.3
1976	5,909	11.3
1977	9,305	17.1

Gearing

All finance in the company is internal. The following table expresses the percentages of the parts of finance in the total finance.

On 31st December	Share capital %	Total reserves %	Members' loans %
1972	11.26	86.47	2.27
1973	10.05	87.84	2.11
1974	9.48	88.06	2.46
1975	8.28	90.54	1.18
1976	7.63	91.22	1.15
1977	7.05	91.87	1.08

Turnover

Year ending 31st December	Sales £
1972	77,857
1973	86,436
1974	103,805
1975	124,701
1976	124,447
1977	147,160

EQUITY SHOES LTD

Activities: Shoemaking
Registered on 11th January 1893
All accounts dated 30th November

Share Capital

30th November	No. of shareholding members	Transferable share capital £
1972	1,386	24,802
1973	1,358	24,714
1974	1,331	23,871
1975	1,313	23,322
1976	1,311	23,128
1977	1,300	22,952

Reserves

On 30th November	General reserve £	Social & welfare fund £	Interest guarantee fund £	Profit & loss account £	Total reserves £
1972	165,000	2,161	5,483	7,688	180,332
1973	215,000	2,547	5,483	9,971	233,001
1974	248,000	6,441	5,483	16,043	275,967
1975	289,000	7,953	5,483	16,352	318,788
1976	433,000	10,332	5,483	16,834	465,649
1977	643,000	12,148	5,483	6,474	667,105

Loan Capital

30th November	Members' loans	Interest payable £	Interest rate %
1972	41,662	1,224	2.9
1973	39,806	1,255	3.1
1974	40,450	1,197	3.0
1975	43,932	1,694	3.9
1976	41,061	—	—
1977	41,647	—	—

Profitability

Trading year	Net Profit before tax £	Rate of return on capital %
1972	57,262	—
1973	121,508	49.7
1974	104,671	35.6
1975	119,224	35.4
1976	193,538	50.6
1977	371,676	70.1

Gearing

31st November	% Share capital	% Reserves	% Members' loans
1972	10	73	17
1973	8	78	14
1974	7	81	12
1975	6	83	11
1976	4	88	8
1977	3	91	6

Turnover

Year ending 30th November	Sales %
1972	591,825
1973	852,245
1974	934,962
1975	1,053,439
1976	1,353,354
1977	1,912,996

LANDSMANS CO-OWNERSHIP LTD

Activities: The sale and hire of mobile caravan units
Certificate of Incorporation: 3rd September 1964
Accounts dated 31st December and 28th February for 1977–78:
No accounts for 1973

Share Capital

31st December	Share capital issued £
1972	42,290
1973	—
1974	65,768
1975	77,356
1976	75,545
28th February 1977	75,545
28th February 1978	75,545

Reserves

31st December	Capital reserve £	Revenue reserve £	Total reserves £
1972	2,205	—	2,205
1973	—	—	—
1974	4,796	—	4,796
1975	4,796	1,000	5,796
1976	—	—	15,579
28th February 1977	—	—	10,593
28th February 1978	—	—	2,935

Loan Capital

31st December	Debentures £	Mortgage loans £	Total £	Bank overdraft £
1972	9,150	14,064	23,214	18,502
1973	—	—	—	—
1974	6,950	11,568	18,518	20,240
1975	5,100	10,424	15,524	27,139
1976	1,900	9,280	11,180	25,652
28th February 1977	1,900	9,072	10,972	26,948
28th February 1978	1,900	—	1,900	3,284

Interest Payable

31st December	On debentures £	On mortgage loans £	Total £	Overdraft £
1972	986	1,265	2,251	1,849
1973	—	—	—	—
1974	904	2,435	3,339	2,403
1975	803	1,868	2,671	2,952
1976	929	1,639	5,239	3,053
28th February 1977	—	241	241	408
28th February 1978	227	1,448	1,675	3,140

Profitability

31st December	Net profit before tax £	Rate of return on capital £
1972	19,700	—
1973	—	—
1974	29,534	42.0 (estimating finance for '73)
1975	16,108	21.1
1976	13,133	18.6
28th February 1977	1,535	1.7
28th February 1978	2,844	4.6

Gearing

31st December	Loan capital (ex. overdraft) as proportion of shareholders' fund %
1972	52
1973	—
1974	26
1975	19
1976	12
28th February 1977	13
28th February 1978	2

Turnover £

to 31st December	
1972	164,631
1973	—
1974	47,411
1975	282,412
1976	293,848
28th February 1977	53,704
28th February 1978	297,728

LEICESTER PRINTERS LTD

Activities: Printing
Registered on 15th June 1892
All accounts dated 31st December

Share Capital 31st December	No. of shareholding members	Transferable share capital £
1972	380	44,513
1973	362	44,426
1974	340	44,076
1975	329	44,060
1976	321	43,834
1977	311	43,520

Reserves

31st December	General reserve £	Development fund £	Interest guarantee fund £	Taxation reserve £
1972	36,446	12,307	4,451	1,000
1973	36,581	12,621	4,451	1,000
1974	36,620	12,621	2,284	1,000
1975	36,650	12,621	95	1,000
1976	39,025	12,621	33	—
1977	39,832	15,021	2,433	—

Reserves (cont'd)

Graduated NI contributions to reserves	Profit & loss account £	Total reserves £
800	227	55,231
800	700	56,153
800	(9,444)	43,881
800	(3,887)	47,279
—	(16,973)	34,706
—	70	57,356

Bank Loans

31st December	Bank loans (incl. overdraft) £	Interest payable £	Average rate of interest %
1972	10,115	1,284	12.7
1973	30,177	1,788	5.9
1974	38,249	2,974	7.8
1975	42,448	3,327	7.8
1976	56,978	4,439	7.8
1977	49,822	4,004	8.0

Other loans, loan capital and small savings, provident and sickness benefit funds

31st December	Loans £	Interest payable £	Average rate of interest %
1972	60,868	3,310	5.4
1973	59,473	3,329	5.6
1974	103,925	3,916	3.8
1975	91,027	7,511	8.2
1976	83,036	7,499	9.0
1977	70,268	8,451	12.0

Profitability

Trading year	Net profit before tax £	Rate of return on capital %
1972	7,871	—
1973	3,646	7.3
1974	(9,684)	(2.4)
1975	6,168	5.7
1976	(12,504)	(5.6)
1977	24,480	11.2

Gearing

31st December	Outside liabilities (a) £	Internal liabilities (b) £	a/b %
1972	10,115	160,612	6
1973	30,177	160,052	19
1974	38,249	191,882	20
1975	42,448	182,366	23
1976	56,978	161,576	35
1977	49,822	171,144	29

Turnover

Year to 31st December	Sales (excluding VAT) £
1973	373,047
1974	478,772
1975	541,155
1976	590,752
1977	683,655

MICHAEL JONES JEWELLER LTD

Activities: Jewellers
Certificate of Incorporation: 9th January 1964
Accounts dated 31st January except the second report of 1977, at 30th September

Share Capital

31st January	Share capital £
1973	2,000
1974	2,000
1975	2,000
1976	2,000
1977	2,000
30th September 1977	2,000

Reserves

31st January	P & L appropriation account £
1973	26,399
1974	40,600
1975	59,222
1976	44,695
1977	66,656
30th September 1977	63,132

Loans

31st January	From related companies* £	Bank £	Total £	Overdraft £
1973	23,252	2,066	25,318	7,558
1974	19,303	1,730	21,033	59,753
1975	6,671	30,857	37,528	71,256
1976	8,156	39,125	47,281	83,959
1977	9,580	31,673	41,253	69,203
30th Sept. 1977	9,580	61,804	71,384	106,142

*Michael Jones Community Ltd, Claude S. Jones and Sons Ltd.

Profitability

31st January	Net profit before tax £	Rate of return on capital %
1973	30,627	—
1974	30,015	64
1975	36,097	74
1976	(10,587)	4
1977	(11,775)	10
30th Sept. 1977	(4,357)	9

Gearing

31st January	Loans as a proportion of shareholders' funds %	Interest payable £
1973	89	3,191
1974	49	4,550
1975	61	11,033
1976	101	14,695
1977	62	21,518
30th Sept. 1977	110	14,657

Turnover

Year to 31st January	Sales £
1973	270,003
1974	320,396
1975	448,088
1976	458,182
1977	441,753
30th Sept. 1977	298,766

QUEEN ELEANOR LTD

Activities: Clothing manufacture
Registered on 22nd November 1897
All accounts dated 31st October

Share Capital

On 31st October	No. of shareholding members	Withdrawable share capital £
1972	299	38,276
1973	291	38,353
1974	294	38,950
1975	284	39,219
1976	270	39,317
1977	224	39,195

Reserves

On 31st October	Education fund £	Development reserve £	Interest guarantee reserve £	Stock reserve £
1972	358	14,000	12,500	10,000
1973	278	14,000	12,500	10,000
1974	227	14,000	12,500	10,000
1975	200	14,000	12,500	10,000
1976	178	*Tax Reserve unallocated*		—
1977	169	7,983	566	—

Reserves (cont'd)

Provident fund £	General reserve £	Balance on appropriation account £	Total reserves £
1,100	68,500	394	106,862
884	69,500	174	107,336
814	83,000	142	120,683
661	83,000	132	120,493
601	79,600	82	80,461
521	133,935	—	143,174

Loan Capital

31st October	Bank loan & overdraft	Members' loans	Interest on members' loans	Rate of interest %
1972	22,133	27,172	1,303	4.8
1973	26,043	27,904	1,298	4.65
1974	32,196	29,555	1,390	4.7
1975	30,218	31,861	1,492	4.7
1976	46,130	34,530	1,640	4.75
1977	46,562	35,788	1,708	4.8

Profitability

Trading year	Net profit before taxation £	Rate of return on capital %
1972	14,121	
1973	8,517	5.0
1974	27,280	14.3
1975	10,245	5.3
1976	(39,924)	(17.3)
1977	18,458	10.0

Gearing

31st October	Outside liabilities (a)	Total shareholders' funds (b)	a/b %
1972	22,133	172,310	12.8
1973	26,043	173,593	15.0
1974	32,196	189,188	17.0
1975	30,218	191,573	15.8
1976	46,130	154,308	29.9
1977	46,562	218,157	21.3

Turnover

Ending 31st October	Sales £
1972	351,701
1973	386,814
1974	465,045
1975	505,550
1976	491,938
1977	485,058

SCOTT BADER COMPANY LTD

Activities: The manufacture and marketing of chemical intermediates and synthetic resins
Certificate of Incorporation: 10th April 1923
Accounts dated 30th June

Share Capital

30th June	Share capital £
1973	5,000
1974	5,000
1975	5,000
1976	5,000
1977	5,000
1978	5,000

Reserves

30th June	Reserves and retained profits £
1973	1,887,194
1974	2,060,892
1975	2,336,059
1976	2,842,639
1977	3,197,139
1978	3,396,979

Loan Capital

30th June	Loans from bank £
1973	424,570
1974	430,811
1975	583,659
1976	247,466
1977	188,793
1978	154,503

Profitability

Year to 30th June	Net profit before tax £	% Rate of return on capital
1973	249,835	—
1974	574,946	25
1975	919,242	37
1976	1,008,086	34
1977	935,474	30
1978	711,884	21

The figures for net profits before tax are calculated after the deduction of staff bonuses and the addition/deduction of the share of profits/losses of companies in which Scott Bader have a share interest.

Gearing

30th June	Bank loans as a proportion of shareholders' funds %
1973	22.4
1974	20.8
1975	24.9
1976	8.7
1977	5.9
1978	4.5

Turnover

30th June	Turnover £
1973	6,991,105
1974	9,492,282
1975	13,520,873
1976	16,297,640
1977	20,910,937
1978	22,747,498

TRYLON LTD

Activities: The production and marketing of resin products
Certificate of Incorporation: 4th April 1973
All Accounts dated 30th June

Share Capital (Authorised £11,000)

30th June	£1 Shares issued
1973	200
1974	200
1975	200
1976	200
1977	200
1978	200

Reserves

30th June	General reserve £	Founder's fund £	Retained profits £	Total reserves £
1973	5,000	6,000	18,171	29,171
1974	5,000	6,100	26,038	37,138
1975	5,000	6,200	27,637	38,837
1976	9,796	—	35,052	44,848
1977	9,796	—	44,331	54,127
1978	9,796	—	54,010	63,806

Loan Capital

30th June	Interest free loan* £
1973	5,000
1974	5,000
1975	5,000
1976	5,000
1977	5,000
1978	4,000

*Repayable in instalments commencing July 1985; £1,000 in fact, paid off early in 1978.

Profitability

Year to 30th June	Net profit before taxation £	Rate of return on capital %
1973	16,210	—
1974	14,996	44
1975	10,854	26
1976	8,858	20
1977	16,406	33
1978	7,742	13

Gearing

30th June	Loans as a proportion of shareholders' funds %
1973	17
1974	13
1975	13
1976	11
1977	9
1978	6

Turnover

30th June	Turnover £
1975	247,149
1976	261,603
1977	330,134
1978	352,262

WALSALL LOCKS AND CART GEAR LTD

Activities: Lock making
Registered in 1873
All Accounts dated 30th September

Share Capital

Beginning of year	No. of shareholding members	Total share capital £
1973	346	—
1974	348	77,607
1975	348	77,693
1976	360	79,751
1977	372	81,574
1978	378	83,392

Reserves

End of year	Earned income added during year £	Capital income added during year £	Reserves accumulated £
1973	8,840	None	(1,367)
1974	15,911	None	14,544
1975	30,732	None	45,276
1976	11,067	8,170	64,513
1977	1,567	7,296	73,373

Loans and overdraft

End of year	Bank loans and overdraft £	Members' loans £	Total £
1973	47,186	9,468	56,654
1974	52,024	8,604	60,628
1975	37,621	7,740	45,361
1976	52,924	7,623	60,547
1977	81,443	7,521	88,964

Gearing

Trading year end	Fixed interest capital as a proportion of shareholders' funds %
1973	55
1974	52
1975	28
1976	34
1977	50

Net profits/losses before tax

For year ending	Net profit/loss £	Rate of return on capital %
1973	9,064	
1974	29,253	27.18
1975	47,031	37.07
1976	46,394	32.85
1977	51,298	28.75

Turnover

Year ending 30th September	Sales £
1973	390,363
1974	455,712
1975	643,684
1976	722,366
1977	877,144

References and Notes

Introduction

1. Derek Jones, 'British Producer Co-operatives', in *The New Worker Co-operatives*, ed. Ken Coates, Spokesman Books, 1976.
2. For a full description of the legal structures available to co-operatives see Peter Cockerton, Tim Gilmour-White, John Pearce and Anna Whyatt, *Workers' Co-operatives: A Handbook*, Aberdeen People's Press, 1980.

1 Right Turn at Toad Lane

1. Raphael Samual, 'The Workshop of the World: Steam Power and Hand Technology in mid-Victorian Britain', *History Workshop Journal* No. 3, Spring 1977, p. 19.
2. Ibid., p. 10.
3. Ibid., p. 47.
4. Ibid., p. 8.
5. E. P. Thompson, *The Making of the English Working Class*, Penguin Books, 1978, p. 860.
6. Gordon Cherry, *The Evolution of British Town Planning*, Leonard Hill Books, 1974, pp. 17–23, 35.
7. E. J. Hobsbawm, *Industry and Empire*, Penguin, 1978, p. 124.
8. David Owen, *English Philanthropy 1660–1960*, The Belknap Press of Harvard University Press, 1964, p. 136.
9. A. L. Morton, *A People's History of England*, Lawrence and Wishart, 1976, p. 428.
10. J. Butt, 'Robert Owen as a Businessman', in *Robert Owen Prince of Cotton Spinners*, ed. J. Butt, David and Charles, 1971, p. 171.
11. Thompson, op. cit., p. 858.
12. A. J. Robertson, 'Robert Owen, Cotton Spinner: New Lanark, 1800–1825', in *Robert Owen Prophet of the Poor*, ed. S. Pollard and J. Salt, Macmillan, 1971, p. 149.
13. R. G. Garnet, 'Robert Owen and the Community Experiments', ibid., p. 40.
14. Morton, op. cit., pp. 883–884.
15. V. I. Lenin, *Selected Works*, Lawrence and Wishart, 1971, pp. 690–693.
16. Thompson, op. cit., pp. 820–837.
17. Morton, op. cit., pp. 432–434.
18. G. D. H. Cole, *A History of Co-operation*, Co-operative Union Ltd, 1944, pp. 62–63.
19. Ibid., p. 64.
20. Catherine Webb, *Industrial Co-operation, The Story of a Peaceful Revolution*, Co-operative Union Ltd, 1929, p. 85.

21. The Rochdale Pioneers made famous the 'dividend on purchase' rule – or the 'divi' as it became popularly known – whereby a proportion of the profits is paid to each member of the co-operative society in proportion to the amount spent at the store. See Arnold Bonner, *British Co-operation*, Co-operative Union Ltd, 1970, p. 47.
22. Cole, op. cit., pp. 97–113, and see P. N. Backstrom, *Christian Socialism and Co-operation in Victorian England*, Croom Helm, London, 1974.
23. Bonner, op. cit., pp. 60–67.
24. Cole, op. cit., pp. 110–111.
25. Ben Jones, *Co-operative Production*, Oxford Clarendon Press, 1894, p. 256.
26. Ibid., p. 334.
27. Ibid., p. 424. Wages and bonuses combined were rarely above the wage levels of competitors.
28. Ibid., p. 475.
29. John Foster, *Class Struggle and the Industrial Revolution*, Methuen and Co Ltd, 1974, p. 224.
30. Bonner, op. cit., pp. 81–03.
31. Cole, op. cit., p. 206.
32. Jones, op. cit., p. 792.
33. Bonner, op. cit., p. 114.
34. Beatrice Webb, *The Co-operative Movement in Great Britain*, Allen and Unwin, 1930, p. 149.
35. Bonner, op. cit., pp. 266–267.
36. Cole, op. cit., pp. 284–292.
37. Ibid.

2 New People, Old Ideals

1. *Job Ownership*, Job Ownership Ltd, November 1978, p. 2.
2. Royal Arsenal Co-operative Society Ltd, *Mondragon: The Basque Co-operatives*, 1979, pp. 3–4.
3. Alastair Campbell et al, *Worker-Owners: The Mondragon Achievement*, Anglo-German Foundation for the Study of Industrial Society, 1977.
4. JOL, op. cit., pp. 15–16.
5. Jennifer Wates, *Platform*, January 1980.
6. Ibid.
7. *Mutual Aid in a Selfish Society*, Paper No. 2, Mutual Aid Press, 1979.
8. Fred Boggis, 'Workers' Co-operatives', in *Participation in Industry*, ed. C. Balfour, pp. 25–26
9. Ibid.
10. J. H. Plumb, *Fifty Years of Equity Shoemaking*, c. 1937, p. 12.
11. *ICOM Newsletter*, August 1979.
12. This term was coined by the CDA to differentiate itself from the local groups. In practice, most are called agencies or associations.
13. Percy Redfern, *John T. W. Mitchell – Pioneer of Consumers' Co-operation*, Co-operative Union Ltd, 1923, p. 67.
14. Harold Campbell, *Wanting and Working*, Co-operative Union and Co-operative Party, 1947, p. 6.

15. Special powers and funds for assisting industry were given under this Act to partnership areas, programme authority areas and other named districts, all called 'designated districts'.

    Urban Aid money was first granted under the Urban Programme as defined by the Local Government Grants (Social Need) Act, 1969. Under this Act 75 per cent of additional expenditure incurred by local authorities in urban areas of special need was granted by the Secretary of State; 75 per cent was granted to certain local authorities and 100 per cent to some other bodies on the expenses of research. Since 1978 Urban Aid money has been increased under the Expanded Urban Programme. The Urban Programme and a number of other area-selective benefits and services were devised in response to growing unemployment and poverty. See J. Edwards and R. Batley, *The Politics of Positive Discrimination*, Tavistock Publications, 1978.
16. John Tilley, MP, *Co-operative News*, 3 October 1979.
17. SERA, *Local Co-ops Development News Letter*, No. 3, July 1979.
18. Peter Clarke, *Co-operative Development under Labour 1974–79*, Co-operative Party, 1979, p. 29.
19. The organisations represented were:
    Central Council for Agricultural and Horticultural Co-operation
    Co-operative Housing Agency
    Co-operative Party
    Co-operative Productive Federation
    Co-operative Union
    Co-operative Wholesale Society
    Credit Union League of Great Britain
    Fairhazel Housing Co-operative
    Federation of Agricultural Co-operatives (UK) Ltd
    Fisheries Organisation Society
    Industrial Common Ownership Movement
    National Federation of Credit Unions
    Union of Shop, Distributive and Allied Workers
20. The minority report was signed by ICOM, CHA, FHC and NFCU.
21. *CDA Annual Report and Accounts*, March 1979, Sections 50 and 51.
22. Roger Sawtell. *How to Convert a Company into an Industrial Co-operative*, Co-operative Development Agency, 1979.

3   Raising Money

1. David H. Wright, *Co-operatives and Community*, Bedford Square Press, 1979, pp. 65–87.
2. J. H. Plumb, *Fifty Years of Equity Shoemaking*, c. 1937.
3. Jenny Thornley, 'Hanging Separately', *Undercurrents*, No. 34, 1979.

4   Workers at the Helm

1. See Simon Watt, 'Dirty Work in Denbigh', *Undercurrents* No. 27, and Jenny Thornley, 'Hanging Separately', *Undercurrents* No. 34, 1979.
2. Tom Cunliffe, *Three Co-operatives Prove Success Can Span a Century*, CDA, 1979.
3. Robert Oakeshott, *The Case for Workers' Co-ops*, Routledge and Kegan Paul, 1978, pp. 93–101.
4. Ibid., p. 88.

5. Ibid., p. 95.
6. Ibid., p. 101.
7. *Criteria for Projects*, ARC, January 1978.
8. *Business Skills in Community Action*, ARC, November 1977.
9. Ibid.
10. It hoped to raise finance from the MSC, Scottish Development Agency, EEC Regional Development Fund, EEC Social Fund, Fife Regional Council, trusts, banks, and central government.

5 Producing for Capital

1. Boston Consulting Group Ltd, *Strategy Alternatives for the British Motorcycle Industry*, HMSO, 1975, p. 114.
2. 'Will Meriden come under the Tory Hammer?', *The Guardian*, 10 July 1979.
3. Lizzie Vann, 'Wholefoods Here . . .?', *Undercurrents*, No. 31.
4. CENA was the service co-operative of the Federation of Northern Wholefoods Collectives
5. Suma Wholefoods, Leeds, 'Food Co-ops', in *Ways and Means*, National Union of Students, 1978, pp. 45–46.
6. Anna Whyatt, 'Food: Towards a Collective Economy', *Peace News*, 3 July 1977.
7. Ibid.
8. P. Chedlow, *The Corporate Strategy of a Political Bean* (a history of Suma).

6 Living with the State

1. This information is based on a postal survey in 1979 of county and district councils in England and Wales, and of regional councils in Scotland, and on inquiries from promotional bodies. 42 out of 52 regional councils (81 per cent) and 130 out of 182 district councils (72 per cent) replied to the questionnaire.
2. Ibid.
3. Tony Benn, *Arguments for Socialism*, ed. Chris Mullin, Jonathan Cape, 1979, p. 67.
4. Ron McKay and Brian Barr, *The Story of the Scottish Daily News*, Canongate, 1976, p. 160.
5. Tony Benn, 'The Industrial Context', in *The New Worker Co-operatives*, ed. Ken Coates, Spokesman Books, Nottingham, 1976, p. 75.
6. Martin Leighton, 'Tale of Triumph', *The Sunday Times Magazine*, 4 June 1978.
7. Jock Bruce-Gardyne, *Meriden: Odyssey of a Lame Duck*, Centre for Policy Studies, 1978, p. 42.
8. John Elliott, 'Meriden Hope for Suzuki Rescue', *Financial Times*, 20 March 1980.
9. National Council of Social Service, *Enterprise Workshops under Threat*, NCSS, September 1979.
10. Manpower Services Commission, *Young People and Work*, HMSO, May 1977, p. 14.
11. Martin Loney, 'The Politics of Job Creation', in *Jobs and Community Action*, ed. G. Craig, M. Mayo and N. Sharman, Routledge and Kegan Paul, 1979, p. 229.
12. Social Services and Employment Sub-Committee of the House of Commons Expenditure Committee, *Joint Memorandum on the Job Creation Programme of the DoE and the MSC*, February 1977.
13. Richard Minns and Jennifer Thornley, *State Shareholding*, The Macmillan Press, 1978, p. 8.

14. R. Minns and J. Thornley, *Local Government Economic Planning and the Provision of Risk Capital for Small Firms*, CES Policy Series 6, Centre for Environmental Studies, 1978.
15. Ibid.
16. Ibid.

7   France – A Shield from the Establishment

1. Jenny Thornley, *Workers' Co-operatives in France*, CES Occasional Paper 6, December 1978.
2. Charles Fourier, writing from 1808, developed a 'meticulously exact Utopia' comprising associations of voluntary self-supporting communities. Only one such 'phalanstery' was formed in France, in 1832 at Conde-sur-Vesgre, but it quickly failed through lack of capital. From the 1830s Philippe Buchez experimented with his workers' productive societies; and Louis Blanc's similar ideas were taken up in 1848 by the state. See Leonardo Benevolo, *The Origins of Modern Town Planning*, Routledge and Kegan Paul, 1968.
3. S. Edwards, *The Paris Commune 1871*, Eyre and Spottiswood Ltd, 1971, p. 259, and A. Antoni, *La Co-opération Ouvrière de Production*, Confédération Générale des Sociétés Co-opératives Ouvrières de Production, 1970, pp. 7–13.
4. S. Edwards, op. cit., p. 10.
5. Ibid., p. 7.
6. Ibid., p. 4.
7. The Banque Coopérative des SCOP was formed as a fund for short term capital needs. See A. Antoni, op. cit., pp. 14–15.
8. Information about CERIA and all other co-operatives was obtained by interview.
9. Confédération Générale des SCOP, *Un peu d'histoire*, 1978.
10. A. Antoni, op. cit., pp. 29–32.
11. A. Antoni, *The Co-operative Way*, translated by Jim King, ICOM Pamphlet No. 8, 1979.
12. The regulations referred to here are discussed in A. Antoni, *La Co-opération Ouvrière de Production*, op. cit., pp. 25–38, and C. B. Burns, *Co-operative Laws*, Co-operative Union, 1977.
13. Co-operators must go through a probationary period before they can become members.
14. This information was obtained from the Caisse Centrale de Crédit Co-opératif, and from C. B. Burns, op. cit., p. 84.
15. An important source is the Crédit Agricole, which is usually approached before other sources because of its strong ideological links with the Caisse Centrale.
16. Between 1974 and 1978 some large building co-operatives went into liquidation after being supported for a long time with shares and loans from the Caisse Centrale and the Banque Coopérative (now the Banque Française de Crédit Co-opératif). The courts advised that the Caisse Centrale had not acted responsibly and ordered them to pay the liabilities due.
17. *Code des Marchés Publics*, 1976, Articles 62, 63.
18. Ibid., Articles 61, 65.
19. Robert Oakeshott, *The Case for Workers' Co-ops*, Routledge and Kegan Paul, 1978, p. 121.

8 Italy – A Political Strategy

1. Max Jaggi, Roger Müller and Sil Schmid, *Red Bologna*, Writers and Readers, 1977, p. 78.
2. *Credito e Finanziamenti, alla Co-operazione Credito Co-operativo*, Lega, 1977.
3. Article 2511 of the Civil Code establishes that firms which have a mutualistic aim can constitute themselves as co-operative societies with an unlimited or limited liability, according to how they are set up, and may specify the character of the co-operative society as distinct from other firms, social undertakings or societies.
4. 1st National Conference Papers, 1977.
5. Lega, op. cit., 1977.

9 The End of the Dream

1. E. J. Hobsbawm, *The Age of Capital 1848–1875*, Sphere Books Ltd, 1977, p. 250.

INDEX

Oakeshott, Robert, 56, 88–9
O'Brien, Bronterre, 18
O'Connor, Feargus, 18
Open University, 37, 117
Orbiston Community, 15
Ouseburn Engineering Works, 22
Outer Circle Policy Unit, 56
Owen, Robert, 17, 18, 21, 25, 30, 37, 131, 169
life and philosophy, 13–15
Owenite communities and experiments, and Owenism, 15–16, 18–19, 22, 31, 169

Paris Commune, 131
peace movement, 31
Pepper, Sidney, 84
Philips Medical Systems, 4, 124
Pilkington Brothers, 92
Pitt, Terry, 54
Port Sunlight, 13
Poste Télégraphe et Télécommunication (PTT), 146–7
profit-sharing, 12, 24, 26, 28
Publications Distribution Co-operative, 77, 84, 107, 179

Queen Eleanor, 78, 79, 85, 108, 179, 184, 196–7

Rahaline Community, 15
Raleigh, 101
Rank Xerox, 91, 98
rate provision
2p rate, 121, 123
Recycles, 76, 77, 101, 179
Reform Act (1867), 23
Reform Bill (1832), 17
Regional Planning Centres, 161
Registrar of Friendly Societies, viii, 4, 34, 39, 76, 86, 139, 182
Republican Party, 152
Robinson, Geoffrey, MP, 82
Rochdale Pioneers, 18–22
Rowntree Social Services Trust, 33
Rutherford, Dr, 22, 24

St Margaret's Trust, 75
Saltaire, 13

Sawtell, Roger, 88
SCOP, viii, 134–7, 139, 142, 144, 148, 149
see also Confédération Générale des Sociétés Co-opératives Ouvrières de Production
SCOP Cogné, 134, 180
Scott Bader, viii, 4, 5, 51, 66, 71, 74, 76, 88–9, 91, 103–4, 180, 184, 198–9
Commonwealth, 67
Development Fund, 74
Ernest Bader, 67, 88
Godric Bader, 88
Scottish Co-operatives Development Committee (SCDC), 49–50, 110, 128
Scottish Council for Social Service, 50
Scottish CWS, 28
Scottish Daily News, vi, 55, 57, 110–11, 134, 174, 175
Scottish Development Agency, 57, 66, 94, 110, 120
Scottish National Party, 69
Scottish Wholefood Collective, 66
Section 137, 121–2, 124, 128
Shell, 92
Smiles, Samuel, 17
Social Democratic Federation, 26, 37
Social Democratic Party, 152
Socialist Environment and Resources Association (SERA), 30, 47, 52–3
Socialist Party (PSI), 152, 164
'société anonyme', 138
Society for Co-operative Dwellings, 54
Society for Promoting Working Men's Associations, 21, 169
South Wales Anti-Poverty Action Centre, viii, 51
Special Temporary Employment Programme (STEP), 115–18
Spreckley, David, 41–2
Strand Glassfibre, 103–4
Strathclyde Regional Council, 128
Suma, 71, 75, 77, 105–7, 180